WOMEN
WHO
MADE
HISTORY

LUCREZIA BORGIA

A STUDY

BY
JOAN HASLIP

Preface by Nigel Balchin

Distributed by
HERON BOOKS

Published by arrangement with Peter Janson-Smith Ltd.

© *1953, Joan Haslip*

First published in 1953 by Cassel & Co. Ltd., London

© *Editor's Foreword, Preface and Appendix*
Edito-Service S.A., Geneva, 1968

CONTENTS

LIST OF ILLUSTRATIONS

EDITOR'S FOREWORD

Lucrezia Borgia. Just to say her name is to evoke the image of an adventurous woman living in a corrupt and venal age, a woman around whom swirled rumours of incest and murder, of wild orgies and of flagrant immorality. The Lucrezia Borgia which emerges from Miss Haslip's admirable study, however, is both something more and something less than this. Lucrezia was indeed a woman who lived with violence and sudden death; and yet she never lost the laughing gaiety, the irresistible charm for which she was so admired in her time. She was, it is true, very much a pawn in the hands of her ambitious family, but yet, as a woman of grace and intelligence, she was also very much a person in her own right. She was, in sum, one of the great women of the Italian Renaissance, and as such we have given her a place of honour in our series on WOMEN WHO MADE HISTORY.

The illegitimate daughter of Pope Alexander VI and sister to the ruthless Cesare, the model for Machiavelli's Prince, Lucrezia at the time of her family's rise to power was a golden-haired, high-spirited girl, her father's favourite and like him, both sensuous and gay. She grew up the centre of all eyes, accustomed to the pomp and luxury of the Papal court. We glimpse her, for instance, on the way to her wedding in Ferrara " surpassing herself in beauty in a magnificent black velvet gown, slashed and embroidered in gold, with the Este rubies round her neck, and on her head a coif of beaten gold ornamented with an enormous diamond. " Generally acquiescent, she allowed her marriages to be arranged by her father strictly in the Borgia interests, and reacted with resigned detachment to the murder of a husband and to the violence, intrigue and vice surrounding her. But she could also display considerable strength and ability. Undisputed mistress of the Vatican during her father's reign, she once even acted with competence as his regent.

Yet with all her strength and variety Lucrezia was no Catherine the Great, no Joan of Arc. These were makers and doers, women who played an active part in history. Although Lucrezia lived at the centre of an exciting and formative age, history rather played with her than she with it.

Then why has she become, so to speak, everyman's image of the Renaissance woman? There is good reason for it. She was a Borgia; and in the lawless anarchy of Renaissance Italy power was wielded above all by the great families: the Medici in Florence, the Sforza in Milan, the Este in Ferrara—and the Borgia, that exuberant, ruthless, upstart Spanish tribe which under the shield of the Papacy made a bold attempt to found a family dynasty and to carve out for itself a principality in central Italy. Thus Lucrezia's story is inseparable from that of the spectacular rise and fall of the Borgias—one of the most flamboyant and close-knit of families in a period noted for its famous families.

In his preface Nigel Balchin correctly points out that Miss Haslip's greatest achievement in this book is to " show us what Lucrezia was *not* " as well as " much of what she definitely *was*. " Lucrezia was first and foremost a Borgia; and as a Borgia she will always be remembered as one of the great women of the Renaissance.

Courtlandt Canby
Editor of the Series

PREFACE

Some years ago a popular London revue contained a scene in which two men and a woman in Renaissance clothes, presumably Rodrigo, Cesare and Lucrezia Borgia, sang a song of which the general theme was " The Borgias are having an orgy. There's a Borgia orgy tonight, " and explained to the audience, with ghastly glee, that all the food was poisoned.

That is, and has been ever since their own day, the common man's view of the whole Borgia family. They were a collection of deep-dyed villains who committed endless murders, usually by poison, and held unspeakable orgies.

Although decidedly limited, this view of Rodrigo and Cesare Borgia is, of course, to some extent justified. In their very different ways, both were highly able men of vast ambition who, even in an age of unscrupulousness, treachery and murder, carried all these qualities even further than most of their contemporaries. So much is clear from the contemporary records. The gossip of their enemies, and the statements of later Reformation writers, naturally carried this a lot further, so that all the best murders of the period tended to be ascribed to the Borgias, just as a few years ago all the best jokes were ascribed to Miss Dorothy Parker. (Thus, though there can be no doubt that Cesare was responsible for the murder of Lucrezia's second husband, Alfonso of Aragon, I doubt if any unbiased jury would convict him, on the evidence, of having murdered his own brother, the Duke of Gandia, with which public opinion has always charged him.)

It was inevitable that Lucrezia, merely by being the illegitimate daughter of Rodrigo Borgia, Pope Alexander VI, and the sister of Cesare, should be tarred with the general Borgia brush, and assumed to have been a sort of mixture of Clytemnestra and Messalina, with incest with her father and brother thrown in for good measure.

Miss Haslip's book does much to bring our view of Lucrezia into proportion by reminding us that at the beginning of the great days of the Borgias, Lucrezia was a child of twelve, and at the end of them, only just out of her teens; that she was utterly devoted to those two formidable characters, Cesare and her father, and always very much under their influence; that all her three marriages were arranged by them merely as moves in their complicated political chess games; that she seems genuinely to have loved her second husband, Alfonso of Aragon, and to have done all she could to prevent his murder; and that finally, despite great difficulties and the hatred and contempt of many of his relatives, she made a success of her third marriage to Alfonso d'Este, and as Duchess of Ferrara won both his affection and that of his subjects, and retained it long after the death of her father and the fall of Cesare.

As for her sexual morals, there is no doubt that she was present at some of the famous Borgia orgies. The curiously objective diaries of Burchard, the Papal Chamberlain, make this clear. She had no choice in the matter, and may even have enjoyed them. We do not know. But all the Borgias (and particularly the Pope himself) were extremely sensual by nature, and moreover had a passion for any sort of clowning and buffoonery, so that the teen-age Lucrezia may well have found the orgies amusing and exciting. According to Burchard's accounts they were usually little more than large and expensive versions of what may be seen any night in most of the great cities of the world in our own time.

It is equally certain that at various times Lucrezia had lovers. Even after her third marriage, when it was vital to make a success of life in Ferrara, she had an affair with the poet Bembo. Whether she had an illegitimate son by an earlier lover – that mysterious child who suddenly appeared, at the age of three, as some part of the Borgia family, is uncertain. The Pope added to the general uncertainty by first announcing that the child was Cesare's, by some unnamed woman, and then that it was his own by the same woman. It may or may not have been Lucrezia's by somebody or other.

But although Miss Haslip makes no effort to whitewash Lucrezia, she does remind us of the general level of sexual morality in the society in which she lived, and there is no evidence at all that she ever committed incest with her father or Cesare, as has been widely suggested. On the established facts, she seems to have been neither a nymphomaniac nor a pervert, and her morals seem to have been neither particularly better nor particularly worse than those of many of the great ladies of her day. Her sexual life seems, for example, to have been a good deal less lurid, (and certainly less of a public nuisance) than that of her one-time sister-in-law, Princess Sanchia of Naples.

Since her early life was so interwoven with, and determined by, the policies, successes and failures of the Pope and Cesare, any biography of Lucrezia Borgia must inevitably include a detailed discussion of these things, and indeed of political events in Italy, and a more or less complete picture of the times. This Miss Haslip does excellently, and here, of course, Lucrezia does not hold the centre of the stage. Hers is a supporting part to the two stars – the Pope and, particularly, Cesare.

To many of us, however, the great value of Miss Haslip's book is that whilst it correctly shows us what Lucrezia was *not*, it also shows us much of what she definitely *was*. Some historians have been content to dismiss her as a girl of no particular strength of character or interest, who was merely a pawn in the political games of her father and brother, and as such mainly an object of mild pity. A pawn in the game Lucrezia certainly was, and in much she is certainly to be pitied. But Miss Haslip shows us that there was a great deal more to her than that. She had, in fact, all the better characteristics which even their enemies could not deny the Borgia family – high intelligence, good looks, physical grace, irresistible charm of manner, and tremendous vitality and zest for life. Without these she could never have survived, and as Miss Haslip points out, in the Pope's frantic efforts to found a Borgia dynasty, Lucrezia, as the beloved Duchess of Ferrara, was in the end the only success.

Nigel Balchin

INTRODUCTION

SOUTHWARDS FROM Valencia, on the inland road to Alicante, lies Játiva, a pleasant unpretentious little town, which can have changed little since the days when Don Jaime of Aragon came down from the North to liberate Valencia from the Moors.

The flat-roofed houses retain their Moorish aspect, the crumbling patios are gay with the sound of running water. Surrounded by its orange groves and carob trees, protected by its ancient bastions, Játiva still evokes those summer days in the thirteenth century, when the celebrated 'Caballeros dela Conquista' descended into the Valencian plain and drove the infidel into the sea.

With these knights of Don Jaime came the Borjas, leaving their strongholds on the borders of Navarre to settle in Játiva, carving their escutcheon of the 'grazing Bull' over the delicate tracery of Moorish doorways, raising the Gothic Collegiato to the glory of their patron St. Philip. For two hundred years they lived as peaceful and prosperous citizens of Játiva, to the year 1440 when Alfonso II of Aragon laid claim to the throne of Naples, and his namesake, Alfonso Borja, canon of Lerida Cathedral, accompanied him to Italy as his private secretary.

The statue of the Borja who began life as a humble canon and died as supreme pontiff is still to be seen in Játiva's central square. But the stylized effigy of the seventy-five year old Calixtus III bears little resemblance to the young priest, who set out from Valencia in the middle of the fifteenth century to raise a family dynasty on the foundations of the Church.

The phenomenal rise of the Borja fortunes began in Italy, a country rent by rival factions still suffering from the effects of the great schism; a country which knew no other law than individual force and individual genius, where the Pope sat uneasily on his throne at the mercy of any successful

1

tyrant, while foreign princes from Anjou and Aràgon disputed the throne of Naples.

It was an age both of chaos and of evolution, of disruption and reconstruction, with the mysticism of the mediæval Church subjectèd to the searching light of the new learning. The doubts which filled men's minds were spreading to the body of the Church itself. During the long years of the schism the Italian states had been left without spiritual guidance. Personal ambition dictated the policy of the princes, and while grass sprouted in the streets of Rome and refuse littered the square of St. Peter's, Milan and Florence, and above all Venice, established their rival hegemonies. Venetian traders brought to Italy the luxuries and refinements of the Levant. And with the growth of commerce life became easier, material standards more assured, material values more important. The Popes had returned from Avignon to find that the old ideal on which the power of the Papacy was founded—that of a Christian commonwealth—had crumbled away.

Europe was sunk in a spiritual lethargy, and there was no longer any St. Louis or Richard Coeur de Lion to lead their people to a crusade. When in 1455 Alfonso Borja was raised to the Roman See under the name of Calixtus III, only two years had elapsed since the fall of Constantinople had shaken the foundations of Europe, but it was left for the Hungarian Hunjady to defend the honour of the Christian world, while the princes of Italy and Western Europe remained aloof, slaves to their 'sacro egoismo'.

The dominating ambition of Alfonso Borja's life was to lead a Christian army under the walls of the Holy Sepulchre, but he was already seventy-five years old when he became Pope and his Spanish fanaticism found no echo in the Italy of the Renaissance. The necessity of surrounding himself with people whom he could both trust and understand, was the main reason for the nepotism by which Calixtus III set a disastrous example to his successors. While still a cardinal, the Curia was infested by his relatives all hoping through his influence to become papal clerks and monsignori, chamberlains and captains of the Guard. And the most successful of all were his two nephews, Pedro Luis and Rodrigo Borja.

Legend has it that they were born in Játiva in the sad crumbling house which still stands to-day. Their father belonged to the local nobility and Rodrigo, who was the younger of the two, had a few years of military training before he followed in his uncle's footsteps by entering the priesthood. At the time of Alfonso Borja's accession to the Papacy he had already completed his studies of canon law at Bologna University and both he and his brother Pedro Luis were ready to assume the perilous roles of '*Principi Nipoti*'. They were young, handsome and brilliant, and to a lonely old man homesick for his native Valencia they represented the only people he could trust. Within a year of his becoming Pope, Calixtus III had raised the twenty-five-year-old Rodrigo to the position of Cardinal of Valencia and Vice-Chancellor of the Church, while Pedro Luis was made Gonfalonier of the papal forces and prefect of Rome.

Pedro Luis plays little part in the story of the Borjas. His career ended with his uncle's death, for Calixtus III had barely received the last sacraments when his proud and overbearing nephew was hounded out of the city to the cry of 'Down with the hated Catalan'. Safe in his sinecures at the Vatican, Rodrigo survived the storm, barricading himself inside his palace while hatred against the Spaniards vented itself in pillage and in riots. A man of lesser stature might have succumbed, but Rodrigo was not only brilliant and fascinating with that magnetic quality which draws both men and women, but he also possessed a chameleon-like quality of adapting himself to the necessity of the hour. All things to all men, he succeeded in acting as Vice-Chancellor to four successive Popes—men of such varied character as Pius II, Paul II, Sixtus IV and Innocent VIII. With the exception of Pius II, the Popes he served were men of little moral character and it is not surprising if in acting as their Vice-Chancellor he became ever more cynical and corrupt, ready to sell himself to the highest bidder in the conclave, helpful in the sale of indulgences, so long as a percentage of the sales remained in his pocket. In this he was no better and no worse than the majority of his colleagues. With his joyous sensual nature, his avid greed for life, he was a true child of his age. His shortcomings, which were manifest even at a time when cardinals, dressed as laymen, appeared in public with their mistresses, were tolerated and excused by pontiffs who made use of his talents and forgave his moral lapses. However assiduously he looked after his own interests, Rodrigo Borja never betrayed the interests of the Church. The disorders of his private life never interfered in his public duties, and he was one of the few to confront the problem as to what form the Papacy was to assume in the new political system which was slowly replacing that of the Middle Ages.

In Spain, in France and in England, the mediæval conception of politics was dead. Feudalism was crumbling with the various classes of the State centred round a strong and organized monarchy. The Papacy was still respected as a venerable and useful institution, but the Popes had gambled away their right to act as arbitrators of the Western world. And in the new spirit of nationalism which was being born beyond the Alps, the papal thunders no longer had the power to shake the foundations of a throne. No one realized this more clearly than the Franciscan friar who in 1471 succeeded to the triple crown under the name of Sixtus IV. Within a year Francesco della Rovere had exchanged the mendicant garb of the Franciscan for the militant trappings of an Italian prince, and though as a Franciscan he can have had little in common with the wealthy and ostentatious Cardinal Borja, as Pope he was quick to appreciate his accommodating Vice-Chancellor, who by temperament and natural ability was eminently suited to second him in consolidating his temporal power.

At the time of della Rovere's accession to the Papacy Rodrigo was barely forty, but he had already had fifteen years of experience in the Sacred College and had seen the old ideals of the Papacy die at Pius II's deathbed at Ancona, where only the Pope's death had prevented the last attempt at a crusade from ending in a dismal failure. In Italy as elsewhere popular liberty had disappeared. Francesco Sforza, Cosimo de' Medici and Alfonso of Aragon had established dynasties strong enough to assert the rights of dictatorship. In Milan the assassination of the sadistic Duke Galeazzo Maria had resulted in the power passing into the hands of his brother Ludovico Sforza, who as regent to his sickly nephew gave free rein to his own

4

ambitions. In Florence the failure of the Pazzi conspiracy had increased the power of the Medicis. Lorenzo was now the undisputed ruler of his town, but a ruler without expansionist ambitions, content to be the principal citizen of the 'Athens of the Renaissance'. In Naples, Ferrante of Aragon, Alfonso's natural son, had asserted his legitimacy by a combination of force and guile, suppressing the revolt of his barons with such sanguinary ferocity that the last supporters of the House of Anjou had fled to the court of France.

The methods of the greater princes were emulated by the lesser ones. There were those who like the Montefeltros of Urbino, the Estes of Ferrara and the Gonzagas of Mantua, vied with the Medicis as patrons of art and science, others who like the Baglionis of Perugia and the Malatestas of Rimini imitated and even surpassed the Sforzas and the Aragons in their deeds of vicious cruelty. But the most characteristic feature of this age of individualism run riot was that there was no tyrant so depraved that he was not capable of appreciating the teachings of humanism, no ruler so enlightened as to hesitate in resorting to violence in ridding himself of an unwanted neighbour. Every action could be excused by the one guiding principle of 'the end justifies the means', and Sixtus IV was the first Pope who so openly acted according to these principles.

Pitted against three of the astutest men of the age, Ferrante of Aragon, Lorenzo de' Medici and Ludovico Sforza, Sixtus IV entered the political arena, not as a successor to a great tradition, the upholder of a sacred institution, but as a fighter with drawn sword, bent on establishing the Papacy as the principal temporal power in Italy, with himself as the dictator of Italian politics. The advancement of family interests as practised by Calixtus III was converted by Sixtus into a political system. He needed men whom he could trust and he deliberately chose his nephews as the instruments with which to carry out his new policy. To achieve his ends he plunged the whole country into war; going so far as to connive at assassination in order to bring about the overthrow of the Medicis in Florence; leaving Venice to fight alone against the Turks while he concentrated his energies on seizing states and benefices for his family. In setting himself up as an Italian prince, Sixtus IV destroyed the very foundations on which the Papacy had rested. Maybe the foundations were insecure but they had succeeded in withstanding the onslaught of barbarism throughout the centuries. The new cardinals he created were all political appointments, and before long the moral tone of the Curia had degenerated to a level where cardinals' bastards, parading as their nephews, aspired to patrician rights, and no one found it strange for Rodrigo Borja to maintain his illegitimate family in the very shadow of the Vice-Chancellor's palace.

Throughout these years Rodrigo had expended his diplomatic talents in healing the wounds inflicted by the bellicose Pope. Dissimulating his natural arrogance, he had suffered the pretentions of the upstart della Rovere nephews, hoping at Sixtus's death to secure for himself the triple crown. But owing to the rival ambitions of his colleagues he saw it pass into the hands of Cardinal Cibo, the weak and indeterminate Innocent VIII, who within a few years had not only lost all the material advantages gained by his predecessor but had also sacrificed the last vestige of papal dignity. The scandal of a Pope publicly acknowledging his children and presiding at their wedding feasts re-echoed through the courts of Europe; sowing in Germany the first seeds of the Reformation, fanning in Spain the flames of the Inquisition.

As leader of the Spanish party in the Vatican, Cardinal Borja maintained a neutral attitude in Italian affairs. Forty years had gone by since he had left Valencia to follow in his uncle's footsteps. Though Borja had long since been Italianized into Borgia, he still remained uncompromisingly Spanish, surrounding himself with Spanish counsellors and servants, many of them from his own native town of Játiva; dictating his correspondance in the Valencian dialect; deliberately educating his bastard children to be Spaniards rather than Italians. 'Down with the hated Catalan' had re-echoed through St. Peter's Square when Calixtus III lay dying, but over half a century was to pass before Italy saw the last of the Borjas. Even when Rodrigo's son was brought as a prisoner back to Spain, to wake from his dream of a nuited Italy in the grim fortress of

Medina del Campo, the Spanish influence lingered on at Ferrara, where surrounded by her Spanish Court, Rodrigo's daughter still sang Valencian love songs. And some of the songs which the women of Játiva sing to-day as they draw their water from the wells are to be found among the parchment files of the Este archives at Modena, transcribed in the fine slanting script of Lucrezia Borgia, Duchess of Ferrara.

I

IN THE HEART of the Sabine mountains, almost sixty miles east of Rome lies Subiaco, dominated by the castle and the monastery founded by St. Benedict. To-day an atmosphere of sanctity hangs heavy over Subiaco, the pilgrims toil up the stony path to the 'sacred cave'. But few climb the road to the gutted castle, where only the faint tracings of an armorial bearing depicting a grazing bull recalls the day when Subiaco was the favourite residence of Rodrigo Borgia, Cardinal of Valencia, Bishop of Oporto, Abbot of Subiaco and Vice-Chancellor of the Church.

The Borgia legend plays little part in Subiaco, their spirits have long since been exorcised by the monks. But during his life time the Cardinal Rodrigo appears to have had so great a predilection for his mountain palace as to have forced his pregnant mistress to accompany him to Subiaco at a time when the snow was still lying on the heights and the winds from the Apennines whistled round the castle. For here in the month of April 1480 was born the little girl whom history was to know under the name of Lucrezia Borgia.

No portraits survive of Vanozza dei Catanei, the woman who succeeded in holding Cardinal Borgia's volatile affections for over fifteen years and whose legendary beauty was inherited by her children. The popular tradition describing her as a dark full-bodied woman of the people fails to convince us, for Vanozza's charms must have been of a far subtler kind to fascinate a man who, in the words of a contemporary chronicler, 'attracted women as a magnet draws iron'. Even physically she must have been of another type, for where else did her children get their gold and auburn hair, their slim supple bodies so different from their father's massive strength? We know little about her, except that her family came from the north of Italy, where the name of Catteneo or Cattanei is still common in Mantua and in Venice, and that she can never have

8

been a courtesan, for even the most libellous of chroniclers describes her as an 'honest woman'.

At the time of Lucrezia's birth Vanozza was already thirty-eight, and as she travelled across the Campagna, exhausted and heavy with child, she envisaged a future when the lover who now absorbed her life and thoughts would be no more than a powerful patron. Her dazzling beauty was on the wane and she could no longer hope to rouse passion in a man whose insatiable appetite for life was still that of an eighteen-year-old boy. All his contemporaries agree as to Rodrigo Borgia's extraordinary fascination, though neither the fleshy features in the Pinturicchio fresco in the Vatican, nor the heavy jowl in the bust in the Berlin Museum show any trace 'of his heroic beauty and joyous presence'. And we have to rely on the written word to evoke the physical attraction of this soft-voiced Spaniard, in whom the hardy mountain blood of Aragon mingled with the suppleness of the Valencian 'the most lascivious and amorous people in all Spain', and in whom the conflicting strains of Visigoth and Arab, and maybe even of Jewish, blood resulted in a being inordinately sensual, of super-abundant vitality, difficult to hold and almost impossible to satisfy.

To have succeeded in remaining Rodrigo Borgia's mistress for over fifteen years must have required an infinite tolerance and understanding, an infinite tact and patience. And even from the scanty records Vanozza emerges as warm, lovable, intensely human, and what to a man of Cardinal Borgia's temperament must have been the most endearing of all traits, endowed with a limitless capacity to forgive. She had five children by Cardinal Borgia, and though from the very first she knew she could play no part in their lives, she was content to accept as a tribute of his love, that though he had had numerous children by other women, hers were the only ones whom he looked upon as his legitimate heirs. And the eldest, Pedro Luis, was but a few years old when the protection of his so-called uncle obtained for him the inheritance of the Spanish dukedom of Gandia.

Sent to be educated at Queen Isabella's court, Pedro Luis was no more than a name to his younger brothers, who in

1480, the year of Lucrezia's birth, were still living with their mother. There was Cesare aged five, and Juan aged four, handsome, overbearing little boys who already gave themselves the airs of princes, and for whose future the Cardinal was making plans, over which Vanozza was not even consulted. Being a sensible woman she realized the only solution for her problems lay in a respectable marriage, and her arguments must have been of a nature to appeal to Rodrigo's practical realism, for before Lucrezia was six months old the Borgia children were provided with a stepfather.

A handsome house, a vineyard in the 'Suburra' and a large dowry succeeded in obtaining for Vanozza the hand of the Venetian scholar Giorgio di Croce, apostolic clerk to Pope Sixtus IV. Their marriage, far from being a convenient makeshift, appears to have been very happy, for within two years Vanozza had presented both her lover and her husband with sons. And it speaks for the charm of the apostolic clerk that in later years Pope Alexander VI was apt to question the parentage of his youngest son. The doubt cast on Joffré's origin marked the end of Rodrigo's amatory relations with Vanozza, but he always remained a devoted friend and patron, and up to the time of her husband's death in 1486 she continued to live with her children in a house which adjoined the Borgia palace. This palace, re-faced and modernized, still stands at the end of the Corso Vittorio Emanuele, not a stone's throw from the St. Angelo Bridge, but no trace survives of Vanozza's house, with the loggia from which her children would watch entranced the comings and goings across the way, the cardinals arriving on their white mules bridled in silver, the masked ladies stepping out of curtained litters.

They were born into the turbulent Rome of Sixtus IV. They grew up to the sounds of battle. Their home was in the most crowded part of the city, in the heart of the Ponte quarter dominated by the Orsini faction who at the slightest sign of trouble would come sweeping down from their fortress on Montegiordano to protect their territory from the depredations of the Colonnas. Lucrezia was only four when the death of Pope Sixtus IV caused a general uprising in the city, with shots resounding across the Tiber where, from the bastions of

St. Angelo, Caterina Sforza Riario, the amazon wife of the old Pope's nephew, held out against the cardinals. With the election of a new Pope the people hoped for peace, but influenced by his predecessor's nephew, the bellicose Cardinal della Rovere, Innocent VIII provoked a profitless war with Naples. For months Rome was in chaos with the Orsinis as allies to the Neapolitans reducing the town to a state of siege, while the Colonnas retaliated by setting fire to the enemy stronghold.

Barricaded in their home, the Borgia children were witness to the horrors of internecine strife. They saw the flames of Montegiordano lighting the whole sky by night, heard the great piles of masonry come crashing down the hill, smelt the sweet acrid scent of burning wood, the sicklier smell of burning flesh, till gradually they became immune to violence, and the sight of pillaged houses, of corpses left rotting in the gutter, of women violated in broad daylight were as familiar to them, as much part of their daily life as the pilgrims who came to pray at the graves of the Apostles.

But so long as they lived under their mother's roof, Vanozza appears to have given them a feeling of protection and security. And with her kind, complaisant husband, she made life very pleasant for these strange Spanish changelings she called her own. Cesare was his mother's favourite, but from the very beginning Juan had succeeded in ingratiating himself with the Cardinal. And Rodrigo Borgia's obvious preference for this spoilt beautiful boy who reminded him of the beloved brother who had died in exile at Civita Vecchia, sowed the first seeds of dissension between Cesare and Juan. Another cause for quarrel was their relations with their sister, whom both attempted to dominate in turn. Four years younger than Juan, of a gay and happy nature, Lucrezia was ready to be her brothers' willing slave, till she became aware of her power to disrupt their relations. It was dangerous knowledge for a little girl and instinctively she used it as a weapon with which to defend herself against their egotism.

We can picture Lucrezia as a child, for even as a woman she still retained that curious look of immaturity. It was a face pretty, rather than beautiful, of which the most distinctive

11

features were the eyes, the famous '*occhi bianchi*' sung by poets, pale and transparent with long dark lashes. Critics might decry the nose as too long and pointed, the mouth too large, the throat too full and sensual, but the general effect was enchanting. It was not a face from which one would expect a strict moral standpoint or an irrevocable decision. With her everything was soft and pliable, her very nature was fluid, flowing with the tide, accepting with a smile whatever life had to offer, interpreting her brothers' jealousy as a tribute to her charm.

Of the two Juan was the easier to understand, being garrulous and boastful, but withal good-humoured, quick to forgive and to forget, so centred in himself, so lost in admiration of his own image that he lived in a world of mirrors. Lucrezia and Juan had the same vanity, the same passion for finery and jewels, but it was Cesare and never Juan who gave her the pretty trinkets she loved so much, Cesare who with his careless generosity would hand her whatever she asked for, even to his golden collar and jewelled crucifix.

Juan was the easier to understand, but it was Cesare who enthralled her, a figure calculated to stir the imagination of any child, let alone an adoring sister. As a boy Cesare must have been even more fascinating than as a man. Frustrated ambitions had not yet warped his character and the chroniclers describe him as 'gay and high spirited, of modest aspect and princely bearing', which combined with a tall supple figure, glowing colouring and auburn hair made of him the most striking, if not the most beautiful of all the Borgias. Juan might possess the classical perfection of a young narcissus, but he had none of Cesare's strength and virility, none of those qualities which already in the boy betrayed the leader, and it is strange that someone so astute as Rodrigo Borgia should have committed the mistake of making Cesare into a priest and Juan into a soldier.

Juan was barely ten when, in the spring of 1486, he was sent to join their eldest brother at the Spanish Court, while Cesare remained in Italy to study canon law at the universities of Perugia and Pisa, before he became eligible for a Spanish Bishopric. For after all the years of exile, Rodrigo Borgia's ambitions for his children were still centred in Spain, and it was inevitable that Vanozza should be sacrificed to these ambitions. The year of Juan's departure coincided with the death of Giorgio di Croce. And while the benevolent cardinal busied himself in making new matrimonial plans for his former mistress, he availed himself of the opportunity of removing his children to what he considered to be more suitable surroundings. Vanozza appears to have accepted his decision with her usual admirable common sense. And there is no greater proof of her fascination than that at the age of forty-four she should have been able to inspire devotion in the Mantuan humanist, Carlo Canale, the friend of Poliziano and protégé of the Gonzagas.

Both to Cesare and to Lucrezia her remarriage spelt the end of their childhood. From the warmth and security of her presence they were transported to cold and alien surroundings, where they had only one another to rely on for sympathy and understanding. From a worldly point of view Cardinal Borgia could have made no better choice than in entrusting his children to the care of his Spanish kinswoman Adriana Mila. The daughter of one of his numerous cousins who had migrated to Italy in the reign of Calixtus III, Adriana had succeeded by virtue of her beauty and her talents in marrying into the great feudal house of the Orsinis. Left a widow at an early age, she lived with her son in the family stronghold on Montegiordano, presenting to the world a dignified spectacle of Spanish widowhood, hiding her beauty behind thick mourning veils, eating off earthenware as prescribed by the customs of her country, and what to her kinsman represented her greatest asset, being prouder of her Valencian origin than of being married to an Orsini. Without love or loyalty for her husband's country, she lived as a foreigner in the heart of Rome. Under her tutelage the young Borgias were to grow up as Spaniards fit to take their place in the hierarchy of Spain, but this foreign bias to their education was to have a deplorable effect on both Cesare and Lucrezia, accentuating their natural arrogance and self-sufficiency, so that from the time they came to live in the Orsini palace they regarded themselves as aliens, and while conforming to the rules of a feudal community they made no attempt either to like or to understand the people among whom they lived.

Used to the freedom and gaiety of their mother's house, life in the Orsini palace must have seemed as cheerless as a prison. With its crenellated walls and massive towers it had made no concession to the florescence of the Renaissance, but was still a frowning mediæval fortress keeping guard over the Tiber. And though for the moment the truce with Naples and the Pope's alliance with Florence had brought a brief spell of peace to Montegiordano, it did little to alleviate the gloom of those rust-coloured walls, which shut out alike the teeming life of the Roman streets and the sunlit ruins on the surrounding hills. Gone were the simple pleasures they had enjoyed while living with their mother; the excursions on the Tiber, the al-fresco meals in her vineyard in the 'Suburra'; the entrancing visits to the Campo di Fiore, where among the broken columns of Pompey's theatre, the migrating population of a former Empire peddled their wares, and shepherds from the Apen-nines rubbed shoulders with pilgrims from the Levant. But neither the cries of the Roman market, nor the laughter of the Roman streets could penetrate behind the fortified walls of Montegiordano. Here were only the hammers of the stone-masons restoring the towers destroyed in the recent fire and the shiver of steel against steel of the pages practising fencing in the outer court-yards.

It was an armed camp rather than a palace under the com-mand of the head of the family, Virginio Orsini, who sub-jected every man and boy in his household to a rigorous mili-tary discipline. And before long Cesare Borgia, a cardinal's nephew destined for the Church, was distinguishing himself as the ablest of his pupils. But Cesare only spent a year in Montegiordano before he was sent, at the age of twelve, to study theology at Perugia University; a year during which he and Lucrezia developed a relationship far closer than they had ever had before. Leading their curiously isolated existence in the midst of the Orsini clan, Lucrezia had grown to look upon Cesare as the only stable figure in her life. And though she was no more than seven when they in turn were separated, he had already laid claim not only to dominate but to absorb her life, so that later when strange obsessions intruded into the ties of brotherly affection, she was to accept them as

14

unquestioningly as she now accepted the lessons she learnt from Adriana Orsini.

For though there were months of loneliness after Cesare's departure, she gradually acclimatized herself to life in the Orsini palace, regarding Adriana half as a governess, half as a foster-mother. Apart from the fact that she was always dressed in the Spanish fashion and waited on by Spanish maids, her education was that of any well-brought-up young woman of the Renaissance. A smattering of Greek, a knowledge of Latin, a taste for poetry and the ability to construe in verse both in Spanish and Italian, the art of embroidery and of playing the lute, all formed part of her curriculum. Her religious instruction was entrusted to the nuns of St. Sixtus, Dominican Sisters famed for their piety and learning. But though the good nuns could teach her the dogma of the Christian Church and inspire her with the spirit of charity and obedience, they could hardly hope to set the moral standards of a child whose very existence gave the lie to their teachings. It was not for them to criticize the circumstances of her birth nor the world in which she lived, not for them to question the favours which the all-powerful Vice-Chancellor bestowed upon their Order. All they could do was to teach her a doctrine contrary to everything she witnessed in the Orsini palace.

Whatever may have been Adriana's worldly advantages, she was hardly a suitable governess for a precocious little girl. Though she lived surrounded by priests and dour-faced duennas, and was pious to the point of fanaticism, her heavy mourning veils masked a nature utterly amoral and corrupt, in which hypocrisy was carried to a fine art and a calculated cynicism dictated every action. Under her tuition Lucrezia developed certain already latent characteristics, a natural talent for dissimulation, the habit of subordinating her personal feelings to the exigencies of the hour, and the knowledge that with men, particularly her uncle the Cardinal, smiling acquiescence was more profitable than scenes or tears. By the age of ten she was sufficiently experienced to accept unquestioningly the situation which arose when Julia Farnese, the fifteen-year-old bride of Adriana's one-eyed son, came to live in the Orsini palace.

II

THE GIRL whose legendary beauty laid the foundations of the Farnese fortunes was little more than a child when an ambitious brother first brought her to the notice of the fifty-seven-year-old Cardinal Borgia. Built on a heroic scale, radiant with the first glow of youth, a classical goddess sprung from the earth of her native Etruria, where the Farneses had their origins in the lands round Lake Bolsena, Julia's looks were of a kind most likely to appeal to a man who was already past his prime. There is no record as to when she first became Cardinal Borgia's mistress, or whether her marriage to the young Orsino Orsini in the spring of 1490 was the direct outcome of this relationship. But the fact that her wedding took place in the Borgia palace, with the Cardinal acting as principal witness, shows that they must already have been on intimate terms at the time and that Julia's mother-in-law must have been fully aware of the connection.

The only victim appears to have been the seventeen-year-old bridegroom whose sickly physique still further impaired by the loss of an eye was not calculated to inspire affection in a girl who had fallen under the spell of the most accomplished libertine in Rome. At fifty-seven, Rodrigo Borgia was still accounted to be one of the handsomest men of his age, and added to his physical attractions there was the persuasive charm of his manner, the soft voice with the slight lisp which betrayed his Spanish origin, the technique which made it difficult for any woman to resist him, let alone an inexperienced girl. But most likely Julia Farnese never attempted to resist, for as a dutiful sister she was probably only too willing to further her brother's career. And within a month of her marriage, the protonotary, Alexander Farnese, had already been made a bishop.

The close friendship between Adriana Orsini and her daughter-in-law leaves little doubt that she must have been partly responsible either in arranging the marriage or in acting as a screen to Julia's amatory relations with the Cardinal. For though in the past Adriana had shared in her kinsman's transitory favours, ambition and astuteness had long since led her to exchange the temporary rôle of mistress for the more permanent one of confidante. And now she was ready to welcome Julia as the rising star who would bring into her orbit all those who were anxious to curry favour with the great Vice-Chancellor. The worldly Spanish woman saw that the moment had come for her to cast off her widow's weeds and to make her re-entry into Roman society as Julia's mother-in-law and Lucrezia's guardian.

No one welcomed the advent of Julia Farnese more warmly than Lucrezia, for Julia's natural exuberance and gaiety succeeded in breaking down the restrictions of her hitherto cloistered existence. Her visits to her uncle's palace were once more as frequent as in the days of her early childhood, and Julia invariably accompanied her on these visits, the inseparable friend and companion, whom she was only too ready to admire and to imitate. It was not long before she became aware that the Cardinal she called her uncle was in reality her father, and that her father was Julia's lover. But it was a knowledge which can hardly have shocked her, for on her occasional visits to the Vatican she saw the beautiful Teodorina Cibo openly recognized as Pope Innocent's daughter. In company of Julia and of Adriana she assisted at the wedding festivities of Franceschetto Cibo and Lorenzo de' Medici's daughter, when bonfires blazed on the seven hills and the fountains ran with wine and for the first time in history the head of the Christian Church, seated among his female guests, assisted at the wedding of one whom he openly recognized to be his son.

Other sights even more scandalous were witnessed in the reign of the Cibo Pope, for never did Christian chivalry sink to a lower level than when the whole of Rome turned out into the streets to see Prince Djem arrive as hostage to the Pope. The younger son of Sultan Mahomet II, Djem had risen in revolt against his elder brother Bajazet, and after being defeated at Broussa had sought refuge with the Knights of Rhodes, only to find that instead of being treated as a friend he was looked upon as a hostage in coming to terms with Bajazet. For the price of a cardinal's hat, the grand master, Pierre d'Aubusson, then handed his valuable prisoner in custody to the Pope, who sank to the level of acting as a Sultan's jailor, by accepting from Bajazet a yearly salary of forty thousand ducats to pay for his brother's maintenance.

The corruption of Rome was such that everything was accepted, everything was tolerated, and despite the cold austerity of the Orsini palace, the outward decorum of Adriana's household, Lucrezia cannot fail to have been influenced by the all-invading corruption. In appearance she was still a child, but her pale transparent eyes already distracted the thoughts of her professors of Greek and Latin, and her father's colleagues in the Sacred College paid visits to the Orsini palace for no other reason than to see her perform the Valencian dances she learnt from her Spanish maids. As her governess, Adriana deliberately encouraged her to receive these princes of the Church, regardless of many of them being handsome, virile young men, who had been promoted to the purple through family connections rather than on account of their religious ardour.

Lucrezia was ten years old when the death of her brother Pedro Luis brought Cesare back to Rome, full of high hopes that his father would now release him from the priesthood in order to inherit his brother's dukedom. Having taken no other than the first vows, his laicization would have been comparatively simple, but Rodrigo Borgia had already made his plans and Cesare had been summoned to Rome to be invested by Pope Innocent with the Spanish Bishopric of Pampaluna, leaving his younger brother Juan to inherit not only the dukedom of Gandia, but the royal bride, to whom Pedro Luis had been betrothed shortly before his death.

Embittered and disappointed, Cesare returned to Perugia, and by the following year Lucrezia was already betrothed to a Spanish nobleman, a certain Don Cherubino de Centelles, lord of the Val d'Ajora in the province of Valencia. Little is known of this first suitor, other than that he was educated with Pedro Luis at the Spanish Court, and that the marriage contract is still in existence; which stipulates that a portion of Lucrezia's dowry, payable in Valencian timeres, was to come from her deceased brother's estate. The prospective bridegroom appears to have had as little interest as the bride in what must have been purely a family alliance, for he made no attempt to assert his rights when, after a few months, the engagement was broken off for no other reason than that Cardinal Borgia had made other and more ambitious plans for Lucrezia's future. His second choice was also a Spaniard, but Don Gasparo di Procida, Count of Aversa, was not only a grandee of Spain, he was also connected by marriage with the Neapolitan branch of the royal house of Aragon, and Lucrezia's future appeared to be definitely settled when Pope Innocent's death at the end of July, 1492, threw her fate once more into the balance.

Never had the succession to the Papacy been more bitterly disputed. The old Pope was not yet dead before the quarrels of rival cardinals intruded into his sickroom, with Giuliano della Rovere and Rodrigo Borgia insulting one another at his bedside. Breathing his last in the arms of his son—an exemplary death for a family man, but hardly a suitable end for a Pope—Innocent VIII left behind him the inheritance of the Roman See fallen into such disrepute that the princes of Europe no longer acknowledged its spiritual suzerainty. Intimidated by the pretensions of his cardinals, frightened of his barons, Innocent had grown to rely implicitly on the counsels of his ally, Lorenzo de' Medici. And it was largely thanks to the efforts of Lorenzo that Italy had known peace for the past four years. But the great Florentine, who had won the name of 'La Bilancia d'Italia', had preceded Pope Innocent into the grave, and Italy now remained at the mercy of those two rival opportunists, Ferrante of Aragon, King of Naples, and Ludovico Sforza, Regent of Milan.

Ostensibly their quarrel centred round the person of Ludovico's nephew, Gian Galeazzo, the rightful Duke of Milan, whom his uncle held a virtual prisoner at Pavia. Son of the murdered duke Galeazzo Maria, and the princess Bona of Savoy, whose follies as regent had resulted in the usurpation of her powers by her brother-in-law Ludovico, Gian Galeazzo, had been affianced, when still a child, to Isabella of Aragon, a granddaughter of King Ferrante. Ten years later Ludovico had allowed this marriage to take place, but after being crowned as Duke and Duchess of Milan, Gian Galeazzo and his bride were confined to the castle of Pavia, and even after Isabella had given birth to a son, Ludovico still retained his power as regent. To justify his action he maintained that his nephew was unfit to rule—a statement which was partly true for both the young Duke's mind and body were weakened by a debauchery in which he was said to have been deliberately initiated by his uncle But what he lacked in energy was supplied by his wife, a beautiful and ambitious Neapolitan princess who bitterly resented seeing her rights usurped by her cousin, Beatrice d'Este, who as Ludovico's wife reigned in the castle of Milan, surrounded by the most brilliant court in Italy.

In despair Isabella appealed to her grandfather, and moved by political considerations rather than by family feelings, King Ferrante espoused her cause. But though the succession of Gian Galeazzo provided the motive, the quarrel between the King of Naples and the Regent of Milan was a struggle for Mediterranean hegemony. The Neapolitan 'Regno' was still the largest and richest of the Italian states, but internal disaffection and the fear of foreign intervention were robbing it of its strength. The last revolt of the supporters of the House of Anjou had been suppressed, but the claims of the Angevin princes were still kept alive by Neapolitan exiles who during the past year had come flocking to the French court, inciting a young and ambitious king to assert his right to the Italian inheritance of the dukes of Anjou. Frightened of the future intentions of Charles VIII, Ferrante of Aragon provoked a quarrel with Milan, gambling on the restoration of Gian Galeazzo and his Aragonese duchess, which would turn Milan into a Neapolitan bulwark in the north.

Also Ludovico was no friend of France, fearing lest one day King Charles's cousin, the Duke of Orleans, might through his grandmother Valentina Visconti lay claim to the duchy of Milan. But when Ferrante of Aragon chose to espouse the cause of Gian Galeazzo his immediate response was to despatch an embassy to the court of France. Ostensibly this embassy had no other purpose than to congratulate the young king on his marriage to Anne of Brittany, but in a personal letter written in his nephew's name, Ludovico assured his majesty 'that should the moment come when France had need of allies, then the Duke of Milan would be ready to assist him with all the means at his disposal'.

Ludovico may have had no intention of fulfilling his pledge, but it was sufficient to fan the waxing ambitions of the Valois. And among the dissensions which raged round the Pope's deathbed and invaded the Sacred College, France now asserted her right to interfere in Italian affairs.

Her candidate was Giuliano della Rovere and it was rumoured that 200,000 ducats had been paid into a Roman bank in order to secure his election. But the wars of Sixtus IV were still fresh in people's minds, and there was too much of his bellicose uncle about della Rovere to recommend him to the peace-loving prelates in the Curia while opposed to him were the two most powerful cardinals in the College, Ascanio Sforza, brother to the Regent of Milan, and the Vice-Chancellor, Rodrigo Borgia.

As Cardinal of Valencia, Rodrigo had remained aloof from Italian politics. Spain was rapidly rising to a predominant position in Europe and the news of the conquest of Granada had resounded through the Christian world; news which was celebrated by Cardinal Borgia in traditional Spanish fashion by staging a gigantic bullfight in the Square of St. Mark's. As a Spaniard and a neutral he now asserted his right to the Papacy. And while political rivalries and personal quarrels embittered the relations between his fellow cardinals, he alone appeared to be filled with benevolence towards his colleagues. The benefices he had received from four successive Popes were at the disposal of his friends and even the hated della Rovere was included in his generous offers of future awards. The chronicler Infessura writes of 'how every evening during the days which elapsed between Pope Innocent's death and the opening of the conclave, mules laden with gold were seen leaving the Borgia palace under an armed guard'.

In the torrid heat of a Roman August the cardinals entered into conclave, each in his separate cell, waited on by his own trusted attendants. Yet rumours succeeded in penetrating through locked doors, whispered from mouth to mouth; secret messengers hurried to and fro between the Vatican and the strongholds of the Roman barons. And the French ambassador was already proclaiming his triumph, when at the first scrutiny it was found that Cardinal Borgia had secured only seven votes as against the eleven cast in favour of della Rovere. Rodrigo's enemies were still powerful; many a good man was questioning his conscience as to whether he could vote in favour of a Pope whose private life was a scandal to the Church; others remembered with apprehension the nepotism of Calixtus III and dreaded a second Spanish invasion of the Curia. But this was the moment when Ascanio Sforza, seeing that he had no chance of the Papacy, consoled himself with the promise of the Vice-Chancellorship and the rich bishopric of Nepi. And by the time of the second scrutiny the whole of the Milanese party had given its support to Borgia. Never had simony been more flagrant, but Rodrigo was only following his predecessor's example on a wider and more generous scale. By the night of August 10th news of his election was already circulating round the town. The last waverers now rallied to cast their votes, disappointed candidates attempted to salvage some lucrative benefice from the wreckage of defeat. And at the eleventh hour even Giuliano della Rovere sank so low as to accept the legation of Avignon from one whom he called 'that Spanish Jew'.

In the early dawn of August 11th, 1492, the crowds who held vigil in St. Peter's Square heard the silver mallet strike against the walled-up window and a stentorian voice announce that Rodrigo Borgia, Cardinal of Valencia and Vice-Chancellor of the Church, Bishop of Oporto and Abbot of Subiaco, had been unanimously elected Pope and had taken the name of Alexander VI. Jubilant and triumphant, the new Pope stepped out onto the balcony. For thirty-four years he had waited for this day, and now in spontaneous joy he cried out: 'I am Pope and Vicar of Christ on earth'. The first recorded act of the new reign is to be found in the diary of the German master of ceremonies, Johann Burchard, who in his grave and Teutonic fashion deplored 'the indecent haste with which the new Pope had donned his pontifical robes'.

III

O N AUGUST 26TH, 1492, Rodrigo Borgia wa.
crowned as Pope. All Rome had taken a holiday
to celebrate the event, and despite the intense heat
the crowds lined the streets to watch the procession from St. Peter's to St. John Lateran.

From far and near they had come; princes and prelates,
beggars and hucksters, village priests and mendicant friars,
travelling by foot and horse, by mule and litter along the old
Roman ways; camping on the heights above the town, among
the broken columns of the Palatine, the ilex woods of the Pin-
cio; sleeping in the shadow of the Colosseum and under the
arch of Constantine. Mediæval Rome was enclosed within so
small a space, that only the great ones of the earth, the prelates
and ambassadors, could find lodging in her overcrowded inns
or in the palaces of the feudal barons. The pilgrims had to sleep
under the summer sky; in boats on the Tiber, or seek hospitality of the Jews. But what matter when the whole town was
in holiday mood, and in the Square of St. Mark's a gigantic
golden bull, the emblem of the Borgias, poured wine from its
gilded horns. The richest and most liberal cardinal in Rome
had been elected Pope and the populace were ready to share in
his triumph. Every balcony and roof displayed the Borgia
arms; hawkers sold sugared sweetmeats in the shape of bulls,
while triumphal arches bearing epigrams to the glory of the
Borgias decorated the streets. No wonder the people cheered,
for coming out of St. Peter's into the blazing light of the midday sun Alexander VI was of a beauty and magnificence rarely
encountered in a Vicar of Christ. In panegyric terms the
ambassadors paid tribute to 'the admirable composure of his
mien and the nobility of his countenance', while in fulsome
admiration the poets and chroniclers waxed lyrical over 'the
heroic beauty of his body, given him by nature so that he

might adorn the seat of the apostles with his divine form in place of God'.

Forgotten for the moment were the plots and disturbances of the past weeks, the lawless bands who had invaded the city, pillaging and murdering in their wake. To-day peace reigned over Rome. Colonnas and Orsinis rode together in the procession; the ambassadors of Naples and Milan were seen in friendly converse. And immediately behind the Pope's golden baldaquin at the head of a procession of seven hundred cardinals and priests, rode Ascanio Sforza and Giuliano della Rovere.

'Never has one seen such a beautiful Pope or witnessed a more brilliant ceremony', wrote the Florentine ambassador. For with his love of pageantry and pomp Rodrigo Borgia had staged a coronation more magnificent than any of his predecessors. The uniforms of his guards outvied those of the princes. Twelve pages dressed in cloth of silver led by their golden bridles the twelve riderless white horses—tribute of the papal fiefs. As hostage of the Vatican, Prince Djem had his place in the procession, dressed in the full regalia of a Turkish sultan, while five Knights of Rhodes escorting a group of captured Janissaries, made an exotic contrast to the barefooted friars who followed in their wake. Every cardinal and ambassador had his own retinue, so that it took over two hours for the procession to proceed from St. Peter's to St. John Lateran—two hours in a blinding midday sun, during which the sixty-year-old Pope sat erect on his white horse, blessing the multitudes.

'Rome raised Caesar to greatness—and now Alexander, but the one was a man, the other is God' chanted a group of boys who with garlands of flowers greeted the Pope on the St. Angelo bridge. And to the pilgrims who had trudged the sun-baked roads of Lazio, or landed in fever-ridden galleys at Ostia, Alexander VI seemed the very incarnation of Christ on earth. Only for a moment did he weaken, when overcome with heat at the end of the two hours' ride, he fainted in the Lateran church before reaching the papal throne. Then the gigantic Cardinal San Severino picked him up in his arms and with his immense bulk hid him from public view. But no sooner had he recovered than he went on with the ceremony, and against the advice of his cardinals he insisted on riding back to the Vatican.

Watching the celebrations outside St. Peter's from the balcony of a cardinal's palace, was a little girl whose resemblance to the new Pope was so striking as to arrest the attention of every passer-by. She had the same full red mouth and soft receding chin, the same wide nostrils and laughing eyes, and above all the same look of an exuberant and joyous vitality. The secret of Lucrezia's origin was common knowledge, and despite the fact that she was officially affianced, Milanese and Neapolitan interests were already in conflict as to whether some relative of the upstart Sforzas or some bastard of the House of Aragon would succeed in marrying the daughter of the Vicar of Christ.

But all unconscious of these schemes and speculations for her future, Lucrezia watched entranced the pageant of her father's triumph, taking for granted the strange happenings of the past week; the new obsequiousness in Adriana's manner; the fact that from now on she was to have a court with ladies-in-waiting and pages and buffoons, like those she used to play with in the Borgia palace; accepting it all with her radiant smile, her candid look. Why should she question, when the good nuns of St. Sixtus had wept with joy at Cardinal Borgia's elevation to the Papacy, and all the bells of Rome were ringing in his honour, and the crowds were kneeling in adoration. She was too young to know that the mantle of Teodorina Cibo had already fallen on her shoulders, that from now on she was to be the cynosure of a thousand eyes, the object of fear, suspicion and envy. Already as a cardinal Rodrigo Borgia's nepotism had given rise to criticism: and within the first week of his accession, the Ferrarese ambassador was writing to Duke Ercole d'Este: 'His Holiness has promised to make many reforms, to dismiss dishonest secretaries and corrupt officials, and above all to keep his sons away from Rome'. But those who had witnessed the abuses of the Cibos and had knowledge of Rodrigo's character were inclined to be sceptical, and the presence of the little girl on the balcony of Cardinal Zeno's palace augured ill for the future.

Nevertheless for the moment the new Pope seemed willing

to abide by his promises. When the young bishop of Pampaluna arrived in Rome to congratulate his father on his accession, he was not only refused a private audience, but publicly admonished from the papal throne. In his beautiful voice, which made every word sound heartfelt and sincere, Alexander VI gave warning to his son that it would be better if he realized at once that

> We are pontiff for the glory of God, not merely for the glory of our family, that we are Vicar of Christ to procure the salvation of souls and not merely in order to further personal ambitions.

But when Cesare returned to Pisa to continue his studies of canon law, the Pope let only a few weeks elapse before he created him archbishop of Valencia with a revenue of sixteen thousand ducats a year—a revenue he expended 'not for the glory of God', but to form while he was still at university the nucleus of a court.

With Cesare at Pisa, Juan in Spain and Joffré still in the schoolroom, Lucrezia was the only one of the Pope's children to share in the triumphs of the first months. Deprived of the company of his sons, Alexander VI lavished his paternal affection on the little girl, who despite her youth was already so sympathetic and understanding, so tactful in her ready acceptance of his wishes. Julia was always at Lucrezia's side, to all outward appearances her dearest and closest friend. And despite her obvious pregnancy, a pregnancy which before long had earned her the name of 'the bride of Christ', the Pope's mistress continued to appear at every public function, with ambassadors and cardinals vying with one another in flattery and attentions.

The first public scandal of the new reign was when, as the result of a transaction between the Pope and his old friend, Cardinal Zeno, the palace of Santa Maria in Portico was leased to Lucrezia Borgia. And the twelve-year-old girl, accompanied by the ladies of the Orsini family, moved into a palace which was not only adjacent to, but actually communicated with, the Church of St. Peter's.

Even a more rigid nature than Lucrezia's might have been undermined by the conflicting influences in her new life.

From now on her days were punctuated by the bells of St. Peter's; the scent of incense drifted through her windows. In a sense her whole existence was enacted in the Square, with her father the central figure of a gigantic pageant, compromising between the majesty of his sacred office and his all too human failings. It is not surprising if she came to regard as normal the abnormalities and inconsistencies of her daily life, deeming it wiser to ignore the happenings in her immediate vicinity, the circumstances of Julia's pregnancy; the muffled steps she heard at night hurrying along the secret passage, which led from her palace direct into the sacristy of St. Peter's, and from St. Peter's to the Vatican and the Pope's private apartments. It was so much easier to maintain the attitude of smiling acquiescence, which delighted the Pope, set Adriana's mind at rest and earned the gratitude of Julia. Meanwhile the gifts and adulation of the papal courtiers encouraged her natural vanity and greed. Furs from distant Sweden, silver-bridled jennets from the famous Gonzaga stables, brocades from Venice, sparkling wines from Capua—the gifts poured into the palace of Santa Maria in Portico where the Pope's mistress and the Pope's daughter held court under the tolerant eye of that impeccable duenna, Adriana Orsini. And gradually the envoys and place-seekers began to discover that for all her Spanish pride, Madame Adriana was ready to receive both gold and jewels in return for her pupil's favours. When the Mantuan agent confided to her that Francesco Gonzaga had set his heart on obtaining a cardinal's hat for his brother Sigismondo, he was discreetly informed that 'Madonna Lucrezia was excessively fond of pearls'.

Behind all the flattery and presents, diplomats were staking their rival claims. Naples and Milan were in the forefront of the field, and the illuminations which lighted Milan on the night of the papal coronation reflected the hopes and ambitions of Ludovico Sforza, whose brother's votes had helped to put the new Pope on the throne. But though Alexander VI kept to his promises and Ascanio Sforza received as his reward both the office of Vice-Chancellor and the gift of the Borgia palace, it soon became apparent that the Spanish Pope made his own decisions and settled his own policy. Within a month of his

27

accession the Curia was already invaded by his Spanish relatives, and the first cardinal to be nominated was one of his nephews.

The energy and enthusiasm with which Alexander VI set out to restore order in his capital won him the admiration of the ordinary citizen. Both physically and mentally he was still a young man and 'his flourishing health and resistance to every form of fatigue surpassed imagination'. During the first months it really seemed as if he had no other concern than to raise the position of the Papacy. The wave of crime, which during the past weeks had been paralysing the city, was stamped out with a vigorous justice; murderers who were caught were publicly hanged and their homes razed to the ground. The Pope himself received in audience any citizen who had a legitimate grievance, while a special commission was appointed to inquire into the cases of prisoners who had been unjustly detained.

In striking contrast to his predecessor, the new Pope was economical in his household expenses and his table rarely consisted of more than a single dish, though that dish had to be a rich one. Unlike the majority of his fellow cardinals, he had always been a strict observer of fast days, and now when Isabella d'Este asked the Mantuan agent to intercede in procuring her a dispensation from fasting during Lent, she was informed that 'His Holiness was averse to granting dispensations of this kind'. This rigid adherence to every form of religious discipline was one of the most curious anomalies of the Borgia character. The Pope, who publicly flaunted his pregnant mistress and openly acknowledged his daughter, was nevertheless so jealous of the privileges of the Church that when the diffusion of printing threatened to spread heresy among the masses, he introduced what remains to this day one of the most powerful—and according to its opponents, one of the most corroding weapons of the Catholic Church—the literary index.

But it was primarily as a politician that Alexander VI displayed 'the subtlety and knowledge of mankind' which enabled him to cope with the thorny problems which beset the Papacy in the early days of his reign. The follies and weaknesses of his predecessors had left Rome at the mercy of the feudal barons, and her frontiers exposed to the encroachments of ambitious neighbours. In his shameless nepotism Innocent VIII had bequeathed to his son property which by right belonged to the Church. And no sooner was his father dead than Cibo made haste to sell it. Before the new Pope had time to lodge a protest, the two fortresses of Cervetri and of Anguillara, strategic strong points on the main road between Rome and the port of Civita Vecchia, had passed into the hands of Virginio Orsini, captain general of the Neapolitan forces and head of a family who, though momentarily at peace with the Papacy, had throughout the centuries menaced the security of the Vatican. Piero de' Medici, brother-in-law to both Cibo and Orsini, had negotiated the sale, but more alarming than any family alliance was the fact that the forty thousand ducats paid to Cibo were supplied by King Ferrante of Naples, and that this flagrant spoliation of Church property was condoned in full consistory by no less a person than Giuliano della Rovere, who, dominated by his antagonism to Rodrigo Borgia and Ascanio Sforza, openly espoused the cause of Naples.

At a time when Italy was in need of a guiding hand to steer her free of the quarrels of rival princes, and the new Pope was sincere in his desire to act as a mediator of peace, the acquisitive greed of the King of Naples and the personal rancour of Cardinal della Rovere forced him to concentrate on the defence of his temporal possessions. It was not so much out of gratitude to Ascanio Sforza, as out of anger at the equivocal conduct of the King of Naples, that in the autumn of 1492, Alexander VI condescended to receive the visit of Cardinal Ascanio's young cousin, Giovanni Sforza, lord of Pesaro and Count of Cotignola—a visit which coincided with the news that the betrothal between Lucrezia Borgia and Don Gasparo di Procida was officially dissolved.

IV

LETTER FROM THE Ferrarese envoy to Duke Ercole d'Este, dated November, 1492, tells of the inopportune arrival from Spain of Don Gasparo di Procida, Lucrezia's rejected suitor. No sooner had he heard that Cardina Borgia had been elected Pope, than Don Gasparo had set sail for Italy, fired with ambition at the prospect of becoming a Pope's son-in-law. And according to the Ferrarese envoy he was now 'making a great show of bravado in the Castillian fashion, angrily asserting his rights and declaring that he would put his case before all the Princes of Christendom'. But, as the ambassador added, 'In the end he will have to resign himself in good grace', for it needed more than an impetuous young man to disturb the equanimity of Rodrigo Borgia. Within a week Don Gasparo's pride had been mollified by the gift of three thousand ducats and another suitor passed out of Lucrezia's life—one of those phantom figures whom her father conjured up at will and dismissed within a few months.

Don Gasparo's visit to Rome coincided with that of two other young men—one of them Giovanni Sforza, the other Alfonso d'Este, who as heir to the Duke of Ferrara had come to pay homage to the new Pope. Sforza's visit was incognito and Lucrezia was probably never even aware of his presence in the city, but she must have been constantly meeting Alfonso d'Este at her father's court.

Blunt in his manner, taciturn in his speech, a soldier rather than a courtier, the young Este prince must have struck an alien note among the smooth-tongued prelates and subtle diplomats of the papal entourage. Nor were his rugged features and thick-set body likely to appeal to a spoilt sophisticated child who set her standards by the beauty of her brothers. Ten tragic years had to elapse before Lucrezia finally found a haven as Alfonso d'Este's wife. For the moment the Estes regarded the Borgias as no more than Spanish upstarts, and despite his overweening ambition, Alexander VI had still to content himself with a bastard Sforza as a prospective son-in-law.

Belonging to a collateral branch of the Sforzas of Milan, Giovanni was the natural son of Costanzo, Lord of Cotignolo and tyrant of Pesaro. Living in an age when bastardy held no stigma, he had not only inherited his father's state, but had been considered a suitable husband for a Gonzaga. And it was as brother-in-law to the Marquis of Mantua and to the Duchess of Urbino, that he had developed a certain humanistic bent, which placed him above the level of the ordinary petty tyrant. Now, when at twenty-six he found himself a widower with an impoverished exchequer, he used these elegant manners and superficial talents to attract another and more powerful alliance. But beneath his courtly exterior he was as small-minded and rapacious as any of his neighbours in the Romagna. He was servile with his superiors and harsh with his dependants, cowardly and cruel at the same time. And dominating all was the ambition which tempted him to accept the invidious position of a Pope's son-in-law.

To Alexander VI, Giovanni Sforza represented a strategical manoeuvre rather than a man of flesh and blood. So long as the fortresses of Cervetri and of Anguillara remained under Neapolitan control, he had no other choice than to ally himself with the Sforzas. The Lord of Pesaro was their cousin, and his domain, though seemingly insignificant on the map, lay in the very heart of the papal states, on the shores of the Adriatic, which at the beginning of the century had been little more than a Venetian lagoon, but which during the past decade had witnessed both the raids of Turkish galleys, and what was even more disturbing to the Pope—the expansionist policy of the House of Aragon. Pesaro itself might consist of little more than a small port and the surrounding hills, but with a son-in-law entrenched on the Adriatic and his allies the Sforzas in possession of Genoa, Alexander hoped to secure the papal states from east to west. And so it came about that the young man, who was secretly introduced into the Vatican in the late autumn of 1492, was by the New Year rumoured to be Lucrezia's prospective bridegroom.

Only Lucrezia remained impervious to these rumours, for during the past year she had come to regard her various suitors as fugitive, elusive figures, none of whom ever succeeded in crossing the threshold of her palace. And she was probably far more excited by the news that Cesare was returning to Rome than that Giovanni Sforza had paid a secret visit to the Vatican.

The return of Cesare Borgia as Archbishop of Valencia was the first public proof of papal nepotism. For not only did the young Archbishop make no attempt to live up to his calling, but his aversion to the priesthood was as pronounced as ever. His tutors at Perugia and at Pisa had not confined themselves to the teaching of canon law, and in the company of humanists such as Paolo Pompilio he had imbibed all the conflicting ideas by which men in the fifteenth century were groping for truth. It was probably owing to Cesare that one of the first acts of the new Pope was to revoke the charge of heresy brought by his predecessor against the young philosopher, Pico della Mirandola. And though we know little of Cesare's life in Tuscany, a letter addressed to Piero de' Medici, asking a favour for one of his Spanish entourage, would lead us to believe that he was on friendly terms with the Medicis, and that in the last year of Lorenzo's life he had attended those alfresco suppers in the gardens of Fiesole and Careggi, where Poliziano recited his latest odes and Pico della Mirandola expounded the mystical doctrines of the Cabala.

Under whatever influences Cesare may have fallen during his two years in Tuscany, they were not conducive towards helping him in a career for which he felt no vocation. The Ferrarese ambassador describes meeting him in the Borgo, shortly after his return to Rome.

> I met Cesare yesterday [he writes]. He was just on his way to the chase, dressed in a costume altogether worldly—that is all in silk and armed, and with only a little tonsure like a simple priest. I conversed with him for a while as we rode along. He possesses marked genius and a charming personality. He bears himself like a great prince, and is lively, merry and fond of society. It is evident he has never had any inclination for the priesthood.

1. Lucrezia Borgia as a young girl. It has long been presumed that she was the model for this St. Catherine, painted by Pinturicchio in the Borgia Apartments at the Vatican.

2. Ceiling of the Borgia Apartments at the Vatican with frescoes by Pinturicchio. One panel, depicting the adoration of the sacred bull, is an allusion to the Borgia bulls, heraldic symbol of the family.

3. Pope Alexander VI, Rodrigo Borgia, is shown in a detail from a fresco by Pinturicchio in the Borgia Apartments at the Vatican. The frescoes were painted in the years after 1492.

From this account it appears as if Cesare made no attempt to hide his indifference to the ecclesiastical honours conferred on him by the Pope. At eighteen he already acted as a law unto himself, fascinating men and women alike by the beauty of his supple body, the magnetism of his smile. But underlying the charm was a corroding scepticism, a perverse streak. Those who were unhappy enough to love him became no more than his possessions with no right to a life or loyalties of their own.

It was as a dangerous and disturbing influence that he now came back into Lucrezia's life, haunting her with common memories of their childhood, filling in her adolescent dreams a part he had no right to play. Six weeks after Giovanni Sforza's visit to the Vatican, when behind closed doors the Borgia family notary was already preparing the preliminary draft of Lucrezia's marriage contract, Cesare Borgia took up residence in the Borgo, within a stone's throw of his sister's palace.

Surrounded by the corruption of the papal court it was inevitable that the young Archbishop who ignored the obligations of his calling and the lonely little girl should find in one another the answer to their problems. There were times when Cesare's restless energy and unexploited talents led him to exhaust himself in dissipation. Then in the loneliness and frustration resulting from these orgies, he would turn to his young sister, who with her gaiety and sweetness helped him to overcome the morbid strain in his nature. Pliable and feminine, Lucrezia needed to be dominated, and her tragedy was that so long as she remained in the Vatican, no one dared to attempt that domination; no one except the brother who from her devotion exacted a love which some have ventured to call passion, a loyalty which became an obsession. How else explain that limitless capacity to forgive, for it was not fear alone which led her to submit to a jealousy that was half insane, a possessiveness bordering on the sadistic.

Meanwhile there were rumours of Cesare Borgia being released from his vows in order to marry a princess of Aragon. With characteristic cynicism, the King of Naples had put forward this proposal in the hopes of checkmating the ambitions of the Sforzas. But though the Pope encouraged the rumour and welcomed the Neapolitan envoy with every semblance of good will, he was already taking military precautions in order to guarantee his frontiers against any possible incursions by either Naples, Florence or the Orsinis. And while Cesare remained an Archbishop, wasting his days in idle discontent, Juan Borgia was summoned back from Spain by a father who cherished the illusion that education at the Spanish court had fitted him for the rôle of a military leader.

Coinciding with the Duke of Gandia's arrival in Italy, came the news of the official betrothal by proxy of the twelve-year-old Lucrezia Borgia to Giovanni Sforza, Count of Cotignola and Lord of Pesaro. The Pope's nepotism was no longer a secret. It was clear that from now on his family interests were identified with those of the Church and though for the moment the Sforzas were in the ascendant, even Ludovico could be under no illusion as to a cynicism which outmatched his own. The mutual distrust which characterized the relations between Pope and Duke was apparent in the haggling which went on over the marriage contract, when the Pope forced the unwilling Ludovico to appoint his cousin to a highly salaried condotta in the Milanese forces, at the same time as reserving to himself the right of withholding Lucrezia's dowry of thirty-one thousand ducats till after the consummation of the marriage, while in the event of her dying childless, the money was to revert to her brother, the Duke of Gandia.

The news of the Sforza-Borgia alliance placed Rome on a military footing. The papal guards levied fresh recruits, and the defences of St. Angelo were strengthened against all eventualities. Alarmed at the turn of events, Cardinal della Rovere fled the city, while in bitterness and disappointment at the success of his enemies, Ferrante of Aragon wrote to his cousin, the King of Spain:

> The new Pope leads a life which is a public scandal, without any regard for the position which he occupies. He cares for nothing but to advance the fortunes of his children by fair means or foul. Rome over-runs with soldiers. They are more numerous than priests. As for the Cardinals, they are either terrorized into silence or driven like della Rovere out of Rome.

Barely three months after King Ferrante had dictated this letter, he was once more negotiating a matrimonial alliance with the Borgias. But in the meantime Lucrezia had served as a pawn to the political exigencies of the hour. And on the 8th of June, 1493, the banners of the Sforza lion and the Borgia bull fluttered over the Roman roof-tops to celebrate Giovanni Sforza's entry into the capital.

A royal welcome had been prepared for the Pope's son-in-law. To the sound of bugles and of trumpets and the acclamation of the crowds, he rode through the Porta del Popolo. The cardinals had sent members of their households to meet him at the gates; the ambassadors of Milan and Venice had come in person, the one to remind him of his cousin's everlasting friendship, the other to assure him of the goodwill of the neighbouring Republic. And outshining every other figure in the procession both by their manly bearing and the richness of their apparel, were his two future brothers-in-law, the Archbishop of Valencia and the Duke of Gandia. This must have been the hour when Giovanni Sforza had most reason to be grateful for the generosity of the Gonzagas, who by presenting him with one of their famous Barbary horses, and lending him one of those golden necklaces of exquisite workmanship without which no nobleman of the Renaissance considered himself adequately dressed, enabled him to hold his own with those magnificent Spaniards, who escorted him in triumph down the Via Lata.

Neither Francesco Gonzaga, nor the eminently practical Isabella d'Este, would have been so ready to oblige their former brother-in-law had they not been hoping through his influence to secure the coveted cardinal's hat for the Marquis's brother. Their agents had already informed them that the Pope could refuse nothing to his children, least of all to the little girl, whom 'he loved in such a superlative degree, that Giovanni Sforza would be a great man, so long as His Holiness ruled'. It was equally characteristic of Ludovico Sforza that for all his promises, he had not yet presented his cousin with so much as a roll of brocade or a suit of armour. The Regent of Milan did not trust the Pope sufficiently to make any unnecessary expenditure before the marriage had taken place.

Therefore the whole cost of Giovanni Sforza's retinue down to the satin for the pages' doublets, the silver trappings for the horses, and the golden bonnet for the court jester, had to be defrayed from the scanty resources of Pesaro's already impoverished exchequer. But the cheers of the Roman public, the flattering attentions of the ambassadors and the warm welcome of the Borgias were sufficient guarantee of future prosperity. In the exhilaration of the moment Giovanni Sforza could forget the fears and doubts of the past weeks, the nervous trepidations of a timid nature which ambition had forced into the centre of the stage.

Proudly the cavalcade swept through the Campo di Fiore, and across the St. Angelo Bridge into the Borgo, coming to a halt outside the palace of Santa Maria in Portico, where in the glittering summer sunlight, Lucrezia stood waiting on her loggia. It was the first time she had seen her bridegroom face to face and the impression was a pleasing one. For there was a certain elegance about Giovanni Sforza's appearance, which is apparent in the medals stamped with his effigy. Lucrezia was neither old enough, nor critical enough, to notice his shortcomings—the shifty eyes, the weak mouth and frigid smile. She only observed the gallantry of his manners, the graceful way in which he bent low over his horse to salute her—admiring the brilliancy of his retinue and sharing the delight of the crowds, when the standard-bearers tossed their multi-coloured banners in the air and the officers of his guards unsheathed their swords and swore allegiance to their future countess.

In her dress of crimson satin, oversewn with pearls and rubies, her oval face framed by her golden hair, Lucrezia's fragile prettiness had blossomed into beauty, waking a responsive look in frigid eyes, inspiring the loyalty of her future subjects. Since dawn she had been waiting for Sforza's arrival with Adriana at her side, profuse in her advice, instructing her in every word and gesture. But though Adriana was thorough in her schooling, it is doubtful whether she had anything to say on the sacredness of marriage ties or a wife's duties towards her husband. Lucrezia's marriage was purely a political alliance, from which every possible advantage must be gained. If she were so foolish as to fall in love with her husband, it would only prove an embarrassment should the Pope fall out with the Sforzas. For as his Holiness's friend and confidante, Adriana was well aware that for all his apparent pleasure at the marriage, the Pope was watching with an ever-growing distrust Ludovico's machinations with France.

But none of these doubts transpired in the Pope's effusive welcome to his son-in-law, nor found an echo in his daughter's smiles. That night Giovanni Sforza wrote to his cousin that 'he was well satisfied with his future bride and that His Holiness had been in his most charming and most condescending mood'.

V

THE ASTROLOGERS having decreed the stars to be favourable, Lucrezia Borgia's wedding was celebrated on the 12th of June, 1493, and, on that day 'Forty noble ladies of the city, together with certain high officials, senators and envoys attached to the papal court were invited to the Pope's palace beside St. Peter's to assist at his daughter's wedding'.

One can picture the turmoil and excitement reigning in Lucrezia's home, with Adriana in conference with the papal master of ceremonies and the ante-chambers crowded with tailors, goldsmiths and hairdressers, all waiting to dress the bride; the comings and goings of Lucrezia's chaplain, the last visits of the nuns of St. Sixtus. And in the midst of all the bustle and confusion, the thirteen-year-old bride, dazed and bewildered, but too much of a Borgia not to delight in the splendour of her wedding chests, the pomp and pageantry of a political alliance.

In the blazing heat of June they dressed her in her golden wedding gown, worth fifteen thousand ducats, half of her entire dowry. But the very sophistication of her clothes only served to accentuate her immaturity. Julia and Adriana adorned her with all their experienced art. The pale cheeks were painted, the eyebrows plucked according to the fashion of the day, the long fair hair confined in a jewelled net, and as the very refinement of elegance, a little negress wearing an exact replica of her dress acted as her train-bearer. The papal favourites gathered round, women famous for their beauty and their charm, exposing their magnificent bosoms, their superb shoulders; women whose voluptuousness made her seem even more of a child. The last injunction was whispered in her ears, the last jewel adjusted on her gown, and she was ready for her brother, the Duke of Gandia, to escort her across the square.

The tall elegant figure glittering with a hundred thousand ducats' worth of jewels, bore little resemblance to the Juan she remembered as a child. The handsome arrogant face was now framed in an adolescent beard, the soft mouth had grown dissolute and cruel, and the grey eyes, pale and transparent like her own, were hard and empty. Yet his smile had all his father's fascination, and beside him even her good-looking bridegroom seemed colourless and insignificant.

Heralded by trumpeters and preceded by pages carrying garlands of flowers, brother and sister rode across the square. But neither their youthful beauty nor the enthusiasm of the crowds won a word of praise from the German master of ceremonies, who was waiting to receive them at the entrance to the Vatican.

As usual Burchard was obsessed by questions of discipline and of orders of precedence. A Pope assisting at his daughter's wedding was sufficiently scandalous, but it was even more deplorable when, owing to lack of space, important ambassadors and senators were kept waiting in the ante-chamber till the hour of the wedding-feast, while behind locked doors the Pope, eleven of his cardinals and a host of bishops and Curia officials in company 'of the forty Roman ladies' assisted at the nuptial mass. And Burchard's worst fears were confirmed when in their eagerness to secure the best places, the younger and more frivolous of these ladies so far forgot themselves as to omit their genuflections in front of the Pope. And in his festive mood, His Holiness did not even seem to notice this deplorable breach of etiquette.

The wedding took place in the Pope's new apartments where Pinturicchio had only just begun the frescoes which to-day immortalize Rodrigo Borgia and his court. Kneeling before the Resurrected Christ we see the Pope, sensual, thick-lipped and heavy jowled—a man of the earth, earthy and yet endowed with an immense dignity—the very portrait of Alexander VI as he must have appeared on the morning of June 12th, 1493, robed in his white and gold vestments, seated on the papal throne, facing the altar, where Pinturicchio's St. Catherine recalls the memory of his thirteen-year-old daughter, when shy, hesitant and half afraid, she appeared as a bride before the curious eyes of the papal court.

In those small and overcrowded rooms, where the smell of incense and of dripping wax, of jewelled pomanders and of scented oils, mingled with the sweat of overheated bodies, and cardinals in their red and purple robes rubbed shoulders with the loveliest women of Rome, Lucrezia appeared as a rather pathetic little figure, kneeling beside the stranger whom from to-day she would have to call her husband, and whose cold smile she may now have noticed for the first time.

The ceremony was long and tedious and the Pope and his guests began to grow restive before the Bishop of Concordia had finished his address—a fact which Burchard noted with displeasure. It was time for the festivities—those interminable festivities which lasted far into the night, starting off by the wedding banquet which, according to Burchard, was on so extravagant a scale that a hundred pounds of the finest sweetmeats were thrown out of the windows to the crowd below. 'It was a night of merrymaking, and whether it was good or bad I leave your Highness to judge', wrote the Ferrarese envoy to Duke Ercole d'Este. The 'merrymaking' started early in the day, for the excessive heat and rich food and wine combined to loosen tongues and free restraint. The first to cast off every semblance of restraint was the Pope himself, and the unfortunate Burchard was powerless to intervene when in rollicking mood, his Holiness seized one of the silver goblets full of confetti and deliberately threw it at his female guests, aiming so that the confetti fell not into their laps, but into their widely-exposed bosoms. The Pope's behaviour set the tone. From now on the masques and comedies became ever more obscene, cardinals whispered lascivious proposals to their neighbours, laughter became more intimate, gestures more daring. And later in the evening at the private supper party given by the Pope, to which only three cardinals and four ambassadors had been invited, his Holiness presided as host with Julia Farnese at his side.

The supper guests reflected the political orientations of the Vatican. The ambassadors of France, Milan, Venice and Ferrara, the cardinals Borgia, Sforza and Colonna, each of whom, by the richness of his gift, paid tribute to the Spanish Pope. First and foremost were the Sforzas, who now that the wedding had taken place outvied with one another in the magnificence of their presents, and the ruby rings and rolls of rare brocades presented by the Regent of Milan, the superb golden dinner service given by the Cardinal Ascanio were such as to impress even the venal-minded Borgias.

Cesare appears to have been the only Borgia absent from the Pope's supper party. The brother who till now had dominated Lucrezia's life had no part to play at her wedding, and we only hear of his making a brief appearance during the nuptial mass. Otherwise he seems to have deliberately kept away, as if he preferred to avoid the sight of his sister in her wedding robes.

And what of Lucrezia herself, who for sixteen hours had played a part carefully rehearsed by Adriana, performing her set gestures, smiling a mechanical smile? Was she as much of a puppet as the little negress, who carried her golden train? Or was there a time when the barriers broke down and infected by the general atmosphere she came to life, afire with the wild blood of the Borgias? All she had seen and heard in those sixteen hours, the lewd comedy which had delighted her father, but which she only half understood, the obscene songs which brought a blush to her husband's cheek; the sly glances, the laughing innuendoes—all must have contributed to make her pulse beat faster, her transparent eyes grow brighter, till she forgot all Adriana's instructions, forgot the stiff young man sitting at her side, and left her bridal throne to dance with Juan the Spanish dances of their childhood; dancing with her long hair falling about her shoulders, her childish figure swaying to the music, while the Pope's guests applauded her lissom grace, and Sforza watched with his shifty nervous eyes and his Holiness beamed his fond, paternal smile.

But at dawn when the party ended the little bride retired to her virginal bed, leaving her husband to wander out into the streets to still his doubts in the brothels of the town. This wedding night was characteristic of many nights to come, and it was not long before Giovanni Sforza realized that the clause in the marriage contract stipulating that 'owing to Madonna Lucrezia not yet being ready for marriage, she was only to accompany her husband to Pesaro in a year's time' meant that for the time being he was no more than a stranger in her palace. Nevertheless, there were compensations. Two days after his wedding he made his first public appearance as the Pope's son-in-law, when in company with the Duke of Gandia, he escorted the new Spanish ambassador into Rome. And on this occasion a chronicler records that 'both the provincial lordling and the Pope's bastard gave themselves the airs of kings'.

The arrival of the Spanish ambassador heralded the greatest event of the century—an event so far-reaching in its consequences, so incalculable in its result, that as yet it was impossible to grasp. While in Italy rival princes were absorbed in their petty intrigues, Christopher Columbus had arrived in Barcelona bringing to the Spanish court the news of the discovery of a continent. The Spanish flag now floated over the new world, seas as yet uncharted had become the Spanish Main. To the men of the Renaissance athirst for the unknown, the vision of Hispaniola with its rivers running gold opened out fresh fields to conquer, new aims for a crusade. The Tables of Ptolemy, the calculations of the Nuremberg philosophers, the suppositions of Marco Polo were all equally obsolete now that the barriers of the world had broken down and the horizon stretched limitless to the west. But in the first reports which circulated round the courts of Europe, there was as yet no real understanding of the tremendous implications. There was always the same recurring sentence, 'this country abounds in gold'; the gold with which the Spanish sovereigns replenished their coffers emptied by the costly wars against the Moors; the gold to decorate the madonnas and gild the cathedral reyas and raise the proud white spires of mission churches into the clear skies of the new world; the gold to recruit the infantry and man the ships, by which for nearly a hundred years Spain asserted her hegemony in the Western world; the gold which by way of Valencia and of Saragossa found its way into the coffers of the Vatican, and which is still to be seen in a tangible form on the ceiling of Santa Maria Maggiore, where the heraldic Bull of the Spanish Pope recalls the day when Alexander Borgia dedicated to the Basilica the first gold received from the New World.

As a Spaniard the Borgia Pope shared in his country's triumph, recognizing the divine hand of providence in the coincidence by which an Italian navigator in the service of Spain made the greatest discovery of the century in the year when a Spanish Pope was elected to the Roman See. And in addressing themselves to the Holy Father, who as Vicar of Christ on earth had authority to dispose of all lands inhabited by the heathen, the Spanish sovereigns were fortunate in dealing both with a diplomat and a fellow countryman. However much Queen Isabella may have resented the Pope's deliberate refusal to identify himself with the fanaticism of the Inquisition, and his tolerance in regard to the Spanish Jews who were flocking into Italy; however shocked she may have been by the reported disorders of his private life, the scandals which 'were exposing the Christian religion to peril', she was ready to overlook the gravest of these scandals for the sake of the concessions with which the Borgia Pope rewarded the holy zeal of Spain.

The Pope had need of all his diplomatic skill, for with her flag flying over the Azores, Portugal was ready to dispute the Spanish claim to the New World. In two successive Bulls His Holiness now defined the respective rights of the rival powers. By drawing an imaginary line from the North to the South Poles, at the distance of a hundred leagues west of the Azores and Cape Verde Islands, he decreed that all territory discovered, or still to be discovered west of this line, was to pass into the hereditary possession of the Spanish kings. Curiously enough this arbitrary method of disposing of an as-yet-uncharted hemisphere appears to have satisfied both Spain and Portugal. And in all due gratitude the Spanish sovereigns now sent an ambassador to Rome bringing as tribute to the Vatican the first gold of the New World.

But the pretensions of Ferdinand and Isabella had grown in proportion to their power. Spain had not been a united country for ten years before they were interfering in Italian affairs. The protests of Ferrante of Aragon against the Borgia policy had fallen on sympathetic ears, for though the Spanish sovereigns had little love for their cousin of Naples, they had every interest in preventing the French influence from extending to

Southern Italy, where it could menace the life-line between
Sicily and the Spanish ports. The alliance between the Vatican,
Venice and Milan was viewed with suspicion by Spain—a fact
of which the ambassador was bidden to inform his Holiness,
in the hopes that he might influence, and, if necessary, coerce
him into changing his policy.

But there was no need for coercion, for no visit could have
been better timed. The Borgia Pope had barely risen from his
daughter's wedding feast, than he was already regarding the
Sforzas with a jaundiced eye. The French ambassador had been
an honoured guest at the wedding, but his correspondence with
the Sforzas was intercepted by papal spies, and the eleven Neapolitan galleys, at anchor off Ostia, under the shadow of Della
Rovere's fortress castle, made the Pope in a receptive mood to
listen to the dictates of Spain.

Little did Giovanni Sforza suspect, when full of pride and
self-importance he escorted the Spanish ambassador into the
city, that as a direct result of this visit his position would be
imperilled, before he had even so much as enjoyed his wife's
company in bed.

Meanwhile the Spanish ambassador was received in Rome as
the representative of the greatest power in Europe and a fellow
countryman of the Pope, and barely a month after he had
referred to Alexander VI as a 'menace to Christendom', Ferrante of Aragon was signing a family contract with the Borgias, offering one of his granddaughters in marriage to the
eleven-year-old Joffré, of whose parentage his own father stood
in doubt.

Protected by the Spanish ambassador, a Neapolitan embassy
arrived in Rome, together with Cardinal della Rovere and
Virginio Orsini, who by gracious permission of the Pope was
allowed to retain possession of his fortresses on the condition
that the sum of forty thousand ducats, already paid out to Cibo,
should be handed over to the papal treasury. Diplomatically,
His Holiness had triumphed, and a Milanese agent wrote to
Ludovico Sforza:

> Many people assert that since his election the Pope has lost
> his head, but in my opinion it is just the contrary. He has been

clever enough to marry his daughter to a Sforza, for whom he has secured a revenue from the dukedom of Milan. He has managed to humiliate Virginio Orsini and made him pay heavily for his friendship. Now he has got King Ferrante to contract an alliance between their two families. Are these the acts of a man who has lost his head? At present all he wants to do is to enjoy his power in peace.

VI

LUCREZIA WAS now a married woman, but as yet she had only the trappings and none of the obligations. Giovanni Sforza was no more than a figurehead in the palace, where the Pope's mistress held her court of papal sycophants and the Pope's daughter entertained her brothers at all hours of the day and night. The chronicles of the time give occasional glimpses of Lucrezia presiding at a joust in the Campo di Fiore; sitting enthralled at a bull fight, while the Archbishop of Valencia performed the rôle of matador in front of an admiring crowd; riding with her brothers up the slopes of the Monte Mario, and watching the falcon trials with as eager an interest as their own. Her palace was the favourite setting for their balls and masquerades and neither Julia nor Adriana ventured to question their influence or to remind her of a wife's duties towards her husband. Indifferent to Giovanni Sforza's presence, they reconstructed the closed intimate world of their childhood, joking with their Spanish clowns, talking among themselves in their quick Valencian dialect, the brothers rivalling for the sister's favours, the sister finding more pleasure in their rivalries than in the timid advances of her legal husband.

Giovanni Sforza was rarely admitted to those family gatherings at which Lucrezia practised the dance steps Juan had learnt in Spain, or at Cesare's bidding tuned her lute to the songs of their court poet, Serafino of Aquila. Their violent quarrels, their passionate reconciliations, their abnormal jealousies of one another, were emotions for which Giovanni had neither sympathy nor understanding. Judged by the standards of the Gonzagas and the Montefeltros, his new relatives seemed coarse and primitive in their amusements. In his eyes it was unsuitable for a Countess of Pesaro to assist at bull fights and perform lascivious Spanish dances in front of the Pope and his cardinals.

But though he was officially master of his wife's household, no one asked either his opinion or advice.

Barely two months after the wedding from which he had hoped to obtain so much profit and glory, Giovanni was forced to attend the ceremony which marked the signing of the Neapolitan alliance, when the eleven-year-old Joffré Borgia was betrothed to the sixteen-year-old Sanchia of Aragon, a natural daughter of Alfonso of Calabria. Even the betrothal was turned into a comedy, when the Prince of Altamura who stood proxy for his niece performed such a skilful imitation of a timid virgin that the Pope and his intimates were convulsed in laughter. The laughter was all the louder when the Neapolitans informed their hosts that the beautiful Sanchia, far from being a timid virgin, was said to be already versed in all the arts of love.

While her husband appeared as a silent spectator at these feasts, Lucrezia joined in the merrymaking. Under her brothers' tuition she was rapidly growing up, and the tact and understanding she had inherited from her mother now stood her in good stead, for since Juan's return the atmosphere in the palace of Santa Maria in Portico was complicated not only by Cesare's hatred and jealousy of his brother, but by their mutual loathing of the Farnese influence, and their determination to drive both Julia and Adriana from her palace.

Julia was still at the height of her power. In his doting passion His Holiness had even promised to make Alexander Farnese into a cardinal. Nevertheless, it was almost impossible for any one woman, however young and ardent, to satisfy a Borgia, and since their return the Pope's sons were deliberately pandering to their father's excessive sensuality, encouraging him in the erotic pastimes over which even Burchard preferred to draw a veil. There were rumours of young girls, disguised as pages, being introduced by night into the Vatican, and of the Duke of Gandia having brought from Spain both a Valencian nun and a Moorish slave, whose favours he shared with the Pope. Even as adolescents, the sons were more vicious than the father, who, however insatiable in his sexual appetites, was fundamentally normal in his tastes and instincts. Whatever his enemies may have said to the contrary, there is no proof of Rodrigo Borgia ever having indulged in any of the perverse practices so common among the princes of the Renaissance. However great his excesses the hardy mountain blood of Aragon dominated the Arab strain of his Valencian forbears, whereas in his hybrid sons the Italian seems to have assimilated more easily with the Moorish than with the Spanish blood. There was a certain decadence about them—an innate perversity which led them in quest of new sensations, and before long the stories which circulated regarding Juan's friendship with Prince Djem, the Turkish hostage of the Vatican, were such as to scandalize even the pleasure-loving Romans. Pilgrims to St. Peter's would see the Pope's son, in company with the Sultan's brother, riding out of the Vatican, both dressed in oriental costume complete with turban and embroidered 'abah'. And even the most indulgent of fathers was beginning to grow anxious lest rumours of oriental debaucheries in the precincts of the Vatican might reach the ears of the Spanish sovereigns before Juan's marriage had taken place.

This marriage was vital to Borgia interests. And in the middle of August the young Duke of Gandia was forced to tear himself away from the delights of Rome, to claim the royal bride he had inherited together with his Spanish dukedom. All Italy was rifled to provide the velvets and brocades with which Juan Borgia was to outvie the richest grandees of Spain. Roman goldsmiths were kept working day and night in setting the gems the Pope bestowed upon the son who was said to be 'the very apple of his eye'.

Writing to his Gonzaga patrons, Juan's stepfather describes the Duke of Gandia's triumphal reception at Barcelona, where he was met

> by the highest officials in the city, and escorted by the Infante of Cordoba and the Duke of Granada, proceeded to the royal palace, where the King and Queen welcomed him as a member of their family and presented him in person to the bride.

This letter, dated from Caprarola, while Canale was on a hunting expedition with Cesare, shows that both Vanozza and her husband were on intimate terms with the Borgias. And in his correspondence with the Gonzagas, Canale is constantly boasting of his good relations with his 'illustrious stepsons'.

What the stepfather relates with pride must have given intense pleasure to the Pope, but at the same time he continued to be somewhat apprehensive as to his son's future behaviour. And his letters to Juan are full of admonitions and advice. At one moment he is a loving father, at the next a diplomat anxious to retain the goodwill of Spain, reminding the Duke

> not to offend against Spanish customs and decorum, not to touch the revenues of his dukedom without the advice of his ministers, and above all to be a good husband and keep his wife company at night.

But neither his father's advice, nor the warnings of his chaplain, could prevent Juan Borgia from falling into evil ways. Within two months of his arrival in Barcelona the Pope received the unpleasant tidings that his son had already dissipated a fortune of over two thousand ducats and had not only been involved in several drunken brawls, but had 'taken such an aversion to his long-faced Spanish bride, that the marriage was not even consummated'.

However loving a father and however much in sympathy with a temperament so akin to his own, Alexander VI demanded implicit obedience from his sons. Loud and clear sounded the papal thunders, loud enough to intimidate Juan into performing his conjugal duties. And by the New Year His Holiness heard with satisfaction that an heir was expected to the dukedom of Gandia and the Borgia dynasty was secure.

With Lucrezia married to a Sforza, Juan established in his Spanish dukedom and Joffré assured of a Neapolitan principality, there remained only Cesare to be promoted to the purple. The promotion was difficult in view of the fact that Cesare made no effort to abet his father's schemes. While the Borgia party in the Sacred College were canvassing their colleagues to secure his election, he was to be seen riding through the streets dressed as a layman, accompanied either by his sister or Fiametta, the red-haired Florentine courtesan, whom he had established in her own palace in the Borgo. It was not surprising if the Spanish sovereigns, however politically indebted to the Borgia Pope, objected to the cardinalcy of Valencia being given to an eighteen-year-old boy, who appeared to dedicate his life to the pleasures of the chase and made no attempt to hide his contempt for the priesthood.

But despite the opposition of cardinals and kings, Alexander VI was determined his son should succeed to the richest See in Spain. First it was necessary to prove his legitimacy. And to this effect a special commission of cardinals, chosen from among the Pope's most intimate friends, was appointed to inquire and to report into the circumstances of Cesare Borgia's birth. From information laid before them, this highly respectable commission was led to assert that Cesare had been born in wedlock, the son of Vanozza dei Catanei by a certain Domenico D'Arignano. At the same time the Pope made no attempt to deny his other illegitimate children, even going so far as to declare that out of affection for Vanozza and their son Juan, born after the death of Arignano, he had adopted Cesare as a member of his family and given him the right to the Borgia arms. But though a small group of his supporters were willing to commit perjury on the Pope's behalf, and the Spanish monarchs withdrew their opposition, bribed by the promise of a cardinal's hat for Queen Isabella's favourite confessor, there was still a certain faction in the Sacred College, headed by Cardinal della Rovere, who remained bitterly opposed to the nomination of the Pope's bastard.

Anticipating trouble, His Holiness summoned a consistory at a time when the excessive heat and the threat of the plague had sent the majority of the cardinals flying for safety to their country villas. Less than half of the members were present when, on September 20th, the College of Cardinals was asked to approve the nomination of twelve new members. Apart from Cesare Borgia and Alexander Farnese, the list gave proof of the Pope's diplomatic skill, for it included representatives of the leading European powers and the principal Italian states. Nevertheless the flagrant manner in which Alexander VI forced the Sacred College to accept both his illegitimate son and his mistress's brother was enough to arouse the anger of even the most spineless of his cardinals. Led by della Rovere, there was a storm of threats and protests, and for the first time since his accession the Borgia Pope found himself menaced by the possibility of a schism. Defied by his cardinals, he revealed himself in his true light. Rising from his throne, a huge menacing figure, his usually smiling face now dark and scowling, his usually melodious voice grown hoarse with anger, he shouted:

You may not be in favour of our nominations, but to spite you we will create double the number, and then you will see what kind of man is a Borgia Pope.

These ominous words re-echoed throughout Italy. The Pope's refusal to commit himself to any definite policy, the cynicism in which he used political alliances as a means of enriching his family, caused apprehension to both enemies and allies. Once more Giuliano della Rovere deemed it wiser to flee the city and to put himself under the protection of the Colonnas, while his former rival, Ascanio Sforza, stayed on at the Vatican, a hostage to the strained relations between Milan and the Papacy.

Seeing his cousin, the great Vice-Chancellor, suddenly so reduced in power, Giovanni Sforza began to have sleepless nights as to his own future. Placed between the Borgias and his kinsmen of Milan, in the throes of divided loyalties, he made no secret of his fears, writing to Ludovico Sforza, 'My Lord, had I foreseen the position in which I would be placed, I would rather have eaten the straw under my body, than have entered into such an alliance'. His fears were not unjustified, for despite the Pope's profession of neutrality, Rome provided no healthy sojourn for a Sforza. If he remained in the Vatican, he was continually spied upon by silent-footed Spaniards, if he ventured across the St. Angelo Bridge, he risked falling into the hands of the Orsinis, the allies of Naples, who would have little scruple in effecting the disappearance of the Pope's son-in-law. It was not surprising that by the autumn he was hankering for the fresh breezes of his Adriatic home, though the fear of the plague, which the summer heat had brought to the city, was hardly a chivalrous excuse for absenting himself from his young wife.

Till now Lucrezia had barely noticed the husband whose only duty was to appear at her side at public functions, and her instinctive reaction was to hope that the Pope would now dissolve her marriage as easily as he had broken off her previous engagements. But to her surprise she found that Giovanni Sforza's departure caused concern and anger both to her father and his entourage. Blandishments, bribes and even threats were used to induce a recalcitrant bridegroom to return. Doctors were summoned to the palace, curious questions were asked, and before Lucrezia had opened her eyes to the depressing reality of her marriage, the Pope was writing urging his son-in-law to return without delay, '*Pro totale consumatione matrimoniae*'.

VII

THROUGHOUT THE autumn Giovanni Sforza remained in Pesaro, turning a deaf ear to papal briefs, and it was only in the New Year that he finally consented to return to Rome—a decision probably made under pressure of his cousins of Milan, who in common with the Pope had no wish to advertise an open breach with the Vatican. Ludovico Sforza was already regretting his overtures to King Charles VIII, but his jealousy of Naples was still stronger than his fear of France. Meanwhile, seeing that the Pope was making no effort to strengthen the Neapolitan alliance by a military pact, Cardinal Ascanio stayed on in the Vatican, despite the King of Naples, who was for ever pressing for his removal.

'I would not turn a dog out of my house, still less a member of the Sacred College', was Rodrigo Borgia's proud rebuff to an ally who was beginning to feel that he had obtained very little in return for the alliance by which the Pope had secured for the youngest and most doubtful of his sons an Aragonese princess and the principality of Squillace, together with a revenue of seventy thousand ducats. The old King's bitterness at the Pope's refusal to break off relations with the Sforzas is reflected in his letters to Ferdinand of Spain, when he writes: 'What have we done to be so martyrized, for though the Pope is a native of our own country, it is impossible to come to terms with him'.

Pope Alexander was playing for time, but time was against him. All his attempts to temporize and to preserve the balance of power in Italy were powerless to prevent an invasion the Italian princes had encouraged through their internal quarrels and dissensions. Too late they discovered that the condottieri serving in their armies, the feudal barons who had promised their support, were ready to betray them as readily as they had betrayed each other in the past. Charles VIII of France was such an unimpressive figure that at first his ambitions appeared to be

53

ridiculous. But though the beauty-loving Italians might mock at the 'cod-eyed, bow-legged little King, with his hanging lips and heavy stutter', behind him lay the concentrated force of a united country and the strength of a 'standing army'.

With peace and prosperity at home, Charles of Valois could afford to indulge in dreams of foreign conquest, and unlike his forebears, his ambitions centred neither on the Rhine nor on the channel ports, but on Italy and more particularly on Naples, that realm of myth and legend, where only a century had passed since the dukes of Anjou reigned in the shadow of Vesuvius. In a country where the art of living had acquired a refinement undreamt of in the northern courts, but where patriotism was still an uncoined word, Charles of Valois planned to revive the Mediterranean empire of the Hohen-staufens.

In politics the French king was as astute as his opponents. Before launching out on his expedition, he assured the security of his frontiers. He made peace with England and ceded to the Emperor Maximilian part of the Burgundian heritage. The neutrality of Spain was obtained at the price of the disputed frontier provinces of Cerdagne and Roussillon, so that by the time the French armies crossed the Alps, the King of Naples found himself deserted by his Aragonese cousins. But it was not so much the neutrality of the foreign powers as the attitude of the Italians themselves which guaranteed the success of King Charles's Neapolitan adventure. In those last months of freedom before the foreign invader set foot on Italian soil, the selfishness of the princes left their country defenceless, their people without leadership. And in the midst of a divided Italy lay the Papacy, with its treasury exhausted by the follies and extravagances of the previous reign, the Sacred College divided by the dissensions of rival cardinals.

By January, 1494, France was openly asserting her right to the Neapolitan throne, and a French mission arrived in Rome to claim the investiture of Naples for King Charles VIII and his heirs. But though the Borgia Pope welcomed this mission with all the arts and blandishments at his command, King Charles received nothing more concrete in answer to his demands than the coveted order of the 'Golden Rose'. Meanwhile French intrigues had succeeded in uniting those two former enemies, Cardinals della Rovere and Sforza, and rumours circulated round the town that in the event of the Pope being deposed, della Rovere would succeed to St. Peter's chair. With little to rely on but his own diplomatic skill, Alexander VI continued to juggle with the rival powers, till the death of King Ferrante of Naples and the succession of his son Alfonso forced him to show his hand. Ferrante and he had had too many differences in the past to be any other than suspicious allies, but the new king was ready to pay a high price for the friendship of the Borgia Pope, and while the French envoys backed their master's claims with vaguely-worded threats of exposing the simony of the last papal election, Alfonso of Aragon offered ducats for the papal treasury and lands and benefices for the Pope's sons, with the result that by the early spring the Papacy was definitely committed to uphold the claims of the House of Aragon.

Such was the political situation when Giovanni Sforza was finally induced to return to what the Pope definitely stated to be 'a nuptial couch'. It was hardly a propitious moment to resume relations with a family who no longer made any secret of their Aragonese sympathies. Joffré Borgia, a pretty effeminate boy of twelve, was already on his way to Naples to become the husband of a princess, who was over five years older than himself, and accompanying him as Papal legate was his cousin, the Cardinal of Monreale, bearing the anointed sword with which to invest Alfonso of Aragon as legitimate successor to the Neapolitan throne. It was typical of the situation that Giovanni Sforza's first official duty on his return to Rome was to escort the Neapolitan ambassadors on their state entry into the city. And when he timidly asked his father-in-law to define his position, he was told that 'his only duty lay towards the state which paid him a regular salary'—a somewhat unpleasant reminder that, whereas his salary as a captain of the Church was always paid up to date, the money due from his Milanese 'condotta' was constantly in arrears. Yet still he continued to place his trust in his Sforza cousins, begging Ludovico 'to help him in preserving the little nest which his ancestors had left him, thanks to the clemency of Milan'. But entangled in his own intrigues, Ludovico had little time to spare for his cousin's tribulations. And Giovanni had to derive what comfort he could from the knowledge that as long as the Pope's daughter remained Countess of Pesaro, the independence of his Adriatic township was assured.

Outwardly he was treated with every mark of deference, and though Lucrezia may have viewed his return with indifference, she was sufficiently obedient to papal orders to play the rôle of a loving wife. Three years later both she and her father were to deny the very existence of this barren marriage, but in the first weeks of their belated honeymoon there appear to have been moments when Lucrezia touched some responsive chord in her husband's frigid nature. And the fact that Giovanni Sforza now received the full payment of his wife's dowry is proof that, whatever the Pope and his daughter may later have said to the contrary, at the time His Holiness appears to have been fully convinced of his son-in-law's virility.

Summer came early to Rome in this year of 1494, and with the dust and the flies came a return of the plague carts, and the flight of the rich to their country villas. But there was no question of 'villegiatura' for the papal court. Fearless of contagion, the Pope remained in Rome, inspecting the fortifications of St. Angelo, discussing matters of military strategy with the Neapolitan captains, while one after the other the opposition cardinals fled the city; della Rovere to France, to assist in the invasion of his native country; Ascanio Sforza, more cautious and more subtle, venturing no further than the Colonna stronghold at Marino, from where he could keep a watchful eye on the turn of events. Rome was honeycombed with spies. Both the Colonnas and the Savellis had been won over to the cause of France, and the whole quarter of the city stretching from the Capitol to the Aventine re-echoed to the cries of 'Francia' and 'Colonna'. War was now inevitable, and in the circumstances even the most loving of fathers, the most ardent of lovers, was forced to realize that a city in the grip of the plague and teeming with soldiers was no place for women. To part from both mistress and daughter was a cruel sacrifice for someone of Pope Alexander's disposition, but fear for their safety and the necessity of making some concession to public opinion at a time when his enemies were spreading reports regarding the

56

scandals of his private life, finally decided the Pope that the moment had come for Lucrezia accompanied by Julia to visit her husband's state.

Curiously enough, the news was welcomed, not only by Giovanni Sforza, but by Lucrezia who was beginning to be bored, living barricaded in her palace, not daring to venture out for fear of contagion. The threat of war was bringing ever more factious elements into the city, and recently there had been one or two occasions when she and Julia had gone out on the loggia to take the evening air, and an ugly crowd in the pay of the Colonnas had gathered outside the palace, hurling insults and abuse. Even her intimates were no longer so irresponsible and gay. Julia lived in constant dread of infection, Adriana spent her days praying in her chapel, while Cesare sulked in his palace, humiliated at being unable to take a military command in the Neapolitan armies. But while Lucrezia welcomed the prospect of a journey, she never envisaged Pesaro as her future home. The Alban hills were the boundary of her horizon, the Tiber spanned her world, and only Giovanni Sforza seems to have deluded himself in the belief that his Borgia bride would settle down in his Adriatic home.

The chroniclers describe the pride with which the Lord of Pesaro took his place at the head of the magnificent cavalcade, which on the 31st of May, 1494, assembled in St. Peter's Square before setting out on the long journey across the Apennines. So delighted was Giovanni at the thought of leaving the oppressive atmosphere of Rome, that he raised no objection to his wife's enormous retinue of secretaries and waiting-women, priests and clowns, not to mention the numerous ladies including both Adriana and Julia, all of whom would be living at his expense. Small wonder he was proud, as town after town greeted him and Lucrezia with fanfares and triumphal processions. The finest tapestries were hung out in their honour and even great dukes like the Anontefeltros of Urbino, rode out to welcome them at the city gates. And Giovanni, who till now had been no more than a poor relation of the Anontefeltros, basked in the reflected glory of the Triple Crown.

The arrival in Pesaro was singularly inauspicious, for a sudden squall blowing from the Adriatic had ruined the elaborate decorations prepared by the townspeople. The triumphal arches had fallen in the mud, flowers and banners were soaked by the rain, and the local poets delivered their laudatory addresses huddled under the eaves of the palace court-yard. The new Countess, so eagerly awaited by her subjects, presented but a sorry spectacle as, wrapped in a heavy cape, she hurried through the streets with no thought except to dry her clothes and retire to a warm bed.

But next morning when the sun came out, reflecting on sea and mountain, and the rain-washed streets shone under a summer sky, the little Countess of Pesaro, who had never travelled from Rome as far as Ostia, regained her buoyant spirits. From the windows of the Sforza palace Pesaro had a gay, holiday aspect, masques and tight-rope dancers, jugglers and buffoons, brought to the narrow streets the riot of carnival, while the harbour was ablaze with orange sails of boats which had come in from all along the coast bearing their loads of curious sightseers. And in all truth Julia Farnese was able to write to the Pope:

> Your Lucrezia is well satisfied and is in excellent health. This is an extremely civilized town and the people are devoted to Sforza. There are continual festivities with dancing and singing and masques.

So long as the dancing and the singing lasted Lucrezia was happy, performing her duties with such disarming modesty that all who met her fell under her spell, seeing in her slightest smile the reflection of Papal favour.

The clouds of war receded behind the Apennines and in the gaiety of those first weeks Lucrezia gave little thought to either father or brother, while proud in the possession of his girl wife Giovanni Sforza forgot the onerous obligations of a Pope's son-in-law.

VIII

P RESERVED IN THE parchment files of the Vatican archives are a group of letters dating from the year 1494, letters which show the Borgia Pope in his closest, most intimate relationships as a doting but tyrannical father, a passionate but capricious lover. Studying these letters against the background of time and circumstances, we gain fresh insight into Pope Alexander's curiously dual personality, for here is a man who as a statesman and a politician steered the Papacy successfully through one of the most critical years of its history, and who when all Italy was falling apart, remained firm in his resistance to French demands, but who at the same time was so obsessed by what Burchard calls his excessive 'carnality' that his daughter and mistress had barely been gone a month before he was pressing for their return.

Every detail of Lucrezia's life was of absorbing interest to him, and she had only to retire to bed with a fever for him to imagine her to be dying. In an anguished letter he implores her to reassure him:

> Think of what we have suffered on account of the immense love we bear you. Greater love have we for no one on this earth. Therefore, let us receive a letter, written in your own hand, even if badly written and showing that you are still weak. Nevertheless it will set our mind at rest. Thank God and our Lady that at least you are out of danger, though we will not be really satisfied till we see you with our own eyes.

But only a few weeks later this same adoring father was writing to his daughter in a fit of hysterical rage for no other reason than that Julia had been summoned to her eldest brother's death bed and had dared to leave Pesaro without waiting for his permission. For this Lucrezia was held responsible.

It is bad enough [he writes] that a daughter should be so lacking in filial love that she shows no wish to return to her father, but that she should choose to disobey and betray him passes all understanding.

In her letters to her father Lucrezia emerges for the first time as an adult woman. Signing herself 'Your unworthy slave', she humours him in his moods, submits to his orders, reasons with him over his grievances, while all the time maintaining an intrinsic dignity, the dignity both he and his mistress lack when it is the question of either their passions or their interests. Even in absence Julia Farnese continued to foster, in her sexagenarian lover, what he himself called 'the demon of his sensuality'. While describing the gaiety of the first weeks in Pesaro she writes

being absent from your Holiness, on whom I depend for my happiness and my whole existence, prevents me from taking any pleasure in my surroundings. My heart has remained behind with the one who is the treasure of my life.

And the brilliant, cynical Borgia appears to have been so dotingly in love as to accept such fulsome adoration.

It was soon made evident that this adoration was interested rather than sincere. For after attending Angelo Farnese's funeral, Julia and Adriana, disregarding the Pope's orders to return to Rome, stayed on at Capodimonte, while a long-neglected husband suddenly asserted his marital rights, and Cardinal Farnese, who owed his whole career to his sister's relationship with the Pope, supported his brother-in-law's claims. Even more curious was the attitude of Madama Adriana who after assisting for years at the cuckolding of her son, now declared in an access of conscience that 'she would more readily disobey the Pope than violate a husband's rights'. Meanwhile, Julia remained a willing prisoner in her family home, from which it would seem that she was beginning to tire of the age-ing lover whom a few weeks previously she had referred to as 'the treasure of her life'. Other less creditable motives may also have played a part. The Farneses were known for their pru-dence, and Julia may have judged it wiser to identify herself as an Orsini, rather than as the Pope's favourite at a time when the French armies were descending into Italy, and there were rumours of a council to depose Alexander VI.

All the Pope's jealousy and rage over Julia's 'perfidious behaviour' was vented on his fourteen-year-old daughter, who had sufficient troubles of her own, without having to sympathize with her father's grievances. Giovanni Sforza was only in Pesaro for a few weeks before the Pope ordered him to take up a command in the Neapolitan army. And from his letters to his daughter, it is clear that Alexander VI had neither sympathy nor understanding for the problems which beset his son-in-law. While referring to him as 'our beloved son', he inveighs against his pusillanimity and weakness, interpreting his reluctance to fight as cowardice, rather than as loyalty to his Sforza cousins. Unfortunately Giovanni's later behaviour proved his father-in-law to be right in his judgment. For the only part he played in the war was that of a spy in the interests of Milan. He had barely been in the Neapolitan camp for a week before he was intriguing with Ludovico Sforza, though all the time in fear lest his Holiness had any knowledge of his dealings, 'in which case his very life would be in danger'.

If Lucrezia suspected her husband of treachery, no word of it transpires in her letters to her father. She is always the Countess of Pesaro, guarding Giovanni's honour, helping in his absence to administer his state, and despite her youth, already displaying the natural tact and common sense which served her in lieu of statecraft. For a short time Pesaro had been a gay and happy place, her husband had had no other thought than to arrange masques and banquets for her entertainment—but when he left on her father's orders, life became very dull for a girl used to the brilliance of the papal court. And though she did her best to adapt herself to her new rôle in encouraging local talent and protecting the arts, she was too much her father's daughter to content herself with intellectual pursuits. Dancing and adulation were necessary to her very existence, and when Julia and Adriana left for Capodimonte, she had only her Spanish waiting-women to alleviate the monotony of her days. Bored and restless, she toured her husband's summer villas, moving from the slopes of the Monte Accio to the Castle of Gradara, where the rust-coloured bastions overlooked the road running northwards to Rimini, and the frescoed walls evoked memories of the Malatestas, from whom the Sforzas had won the castle not many years before. But though a Paolo and Francesca had found a fitting trysting place on the parapets of Gradara, there was little to attract a spoilt and sophisticated girl, homesick for the sounds and smells of Rome. As she whiled away the hours in embroidering banners and devices for her husband's soldiers, many were the times when Lucrezia wondered why her father had been so anxious to marry her to a Sforza, for viewed against the dramatic events which were being enacted on the other side of the Apennines, Pesaro seemed but an insignificant domain and its lord an even more insignificant figure.

On September 3rd, 1494, the French armies crossed the Alps, and the Italians, used to the bloodless wars of the Condottieri, first experienced the horrors of invasion.

While Ludovico Sforza paid homage to a foreign king, Gascon and Swiss mercenaries looted the homesteads of Piedmont and of Lombardy, and a naval battle won by Louis d'Orleans over the Neapolitan fleet at Rapallo laid waste the Ligurian coast. Never had the intrinsic baseness of the Italian princes, the apathy of the masses, been so evident as now, when in the space of a few weeks the white banners of the Valois, bearing the proud inscription, 'Voluntas Deo', swept from the Alps to the Apennines. Small wonder if Philippe de Commines wrote in his journal, 'Our advance is little short of miraculous'.

From north to south the French advance was marked by treachery and guile. When Charles VIII made his triumphal entrance into Pavia, he visited the unfortunate Gian Galeazzo and was sufficiently young and impressionable to be moved by the tears of the lovely Isabella of Aragon. From Ludovico's viewpoint such sympathy was dangerous, and the French king had barely reached Piacenza before he received the news that Gian Galeazzo Sforza had succumbed to a sudden fever. People spoke openly of murder, but in an assembly packed by his supporters Ludovico was unanimously elected as Duke of Milan.

From Piacenza the French armies crossed the Cisa pass to the Mediterranean. And to Charles's camp in the Carrara mountains came Piero de' Medici, deserting his Neapolitan allies, offering to the foreign conqueror the keys of the Tuscan fortresses. But this time treachery did not help to preserve a throne. From the pulpit of St. Mark's the Dominican, Savonarola, incited the Florentines to revolt, and when Charles VIII rode into Florence, Piero de' Medici was already an exile.

Most dastardly of all was the defection of the Captain General of the Neapolitan army, Virginio Orsini, who at the eleventh hour instructed his sons to surrender their castles to the enemy. The treachery of the Orsini was never forgiven by the Borgia Pope, who when he received the news exclaimed in contempt,

> the only weapons the French have need of with which to conquer Italy are pieces of chalk with which to mark their billets.

All Italy was crumbling, but at the core there was still the Papacy with Alexander VI refusing to treat with King Charles VIII except on his own terms. Though French galleys were already at the mouth of the Tiber and the defection of the Orsini laid open the road to Rome, His Holiness declared that 'he would lose his mitre, his lands and his life, rather than fail King Alfonso in his need'. All the warlike blood of his Spanish ancestors spoke out when he harangued the crowds outside the Vatican.

> We know that no one with Roman blood will be able to stand the pretensions and arrogance of the French, that like us they will prefer to die and be cut to pieces rather than yield.

Well might his daughter take pride in his resistance, anxiously awaiting the letters which trusted emissaries still brought across the Apennines. Protected by its mountains, Pesaro remained immune from the devastations of war, but its repercussions were already disrupting Lucrezia's life. Any feeling of affection she may have had for her husband withered in their conflicting loyalties. As Spanish as her father, she looked down on

> those despicable Italians, indifferent both to their own and to their women's honour, those worthless soldiers who were good for nothing but parade.

But how could even the most admiring of daughters reconcile the defiant tone of the Pope's public utterances with the hysterical ravings of his private letters.

Julia was still at Capodimonte, and consumed by his desire for his absent mistress, Alexander VI lost all semblance of dignity and decency. Julia, her mother-in-law, husband and brother, were all in turn threatened with the perils of excommunication. Swayed by his hysterical jealousy of the one-eyed Orsino Orsini, the Pope degenerated into a coarse lecherous old man. And in a letter preserved in the Vatican archives, we read:

> Perfidious and ungrateful Julia, in telling us your intention is not to return to Rome without your husband's permission. Though knowing now both the wickedness of your nature and of those who advise you, we can only suppose that you wish to go to Bassanello in order to resume relations with that stallion of a husband.

This deplorable letter appears to have been written in a language Julia could understand, for on receiving it she set out on her return journey to Rome, both she and the Pope ignoring the fact that the French king was already at Siena and that the roads were no longer safe for travel.

As usual, it was Isabella d'Este who was the first to hear of an event which 'was a great insult to the Pope', but which all the gossipmongers related with relish and delight. In a letter dated November 29th, an agent informs the Marchioness of Mantua that

> the day before yesterday Madonna Julia, accompanied by 'Madama' Adriana, set out from the castle of Capodimonte bound for Viterbo. But when about a mile from that place,

4. A Papal procession approaches the Castle of St. Angelo at Rome. From the Legend of St. Ursula, painted by Carpaccio at the end of the fifteenth century.

5. Portrait of a courtesan, by Carpaccio. In Renaissance Italy such women often held positions of much power and influence.

6. Portrait of Machiavelli, by an unidentified artist. As statesman and political philosopher, Machiavelli was interested above all in the uses of political and military power.

7.   A French political caricature, dating from the end of the fifteenth century, which pokes fun at the complexities of Papal politics. Shown are such leading figures of the time as Pope Alexander VI, Lucrezia's father (No. 4), the Emperor Maximilian (No. 5), Louis XII of France (No. 1), and the Duke of Venice (No. 3).

they met a troop of French cavalry, by whom they were taken prisoner and led to Montefiascone.

One can picture the hilarity with which this news was received in all the courts of Italy, the delight it aroused in Milan, particularly when it became known that in his anxiety for the fate of his beloved Julia the Pope had dispatched a chamberlain to the Colonna stronghold at Marino, begging Cardinal Sforza in the name of their old friendship to help in securing her release. And the alacrity with which the accommodating Vice-Chancellor hastened to carry out his wishes gives the first clue of the double treachery being contemplated by the Sforzas.

The only person who appears to have behaved with dignity on this occasion was the King of France. Though he might well have followed the advice of Cardinal della Rovere and held Julia as a hostage, to force the Pope into accepting his terms, he not only released her for the comparatively small ransom of three thousand ducats, but ordered her to be treated with every courtesy during her stay in the French camp. As a tribute to her importance no less than four hundred French cavalry escorted the Pope's mistress to the gates of Rome, where she was met by the papal chamberlain and, according to one ambassador, 'straight away lodged in the Vatican'. Yet another report goes so far as to say that when

> the lady Julia arrived in Rome, His Holiness rode out to meet her arrayed in a black velvet doublet bordered in gold brocade and girt with a beautiful belt in the Spanish fashion, complete with sword and dagger and wearing Spanish boots and a velvet beret in a right gallant manner.

But it is difficult to believe that the Borgia Pope would have exposed himself to public ridicule by riding out to meet his mistress in the costume of a Spanish grandee. And this was probably merely another of those fantastic stories circulated by his enemies.

It was sufficient that Julia was back in Rome, a chastened, submissive Julia, who from the honours accorded her in the French camp realized that Charles VIII had not so much the intention of deposing Alexander VI as of securing him as an ally. The Spanish Pope was still firm on his throne and though the Cardinal della Rovere had his hour of glory in riding through Italy on the right hand of the King of France, it was not bringing him appreciably nearer to the triple crown. Strengthened by Julia's presence, the Pope's dual personality reverted to that of an astute, far-seeing politician. Ascanio Sforza stayed on in Rome, ostensibly as a prisoner. But while Ludovico officially protested against his brother's forcible detention, he was secretly instructing the Cardinal to sound the Pope as to his views on the forming of a league to drive the foreigner out of Italy. 'The French are a bad race. Let us defend ourselves from having them as neighbours', wrote the man who, but a year before, had beguiled the young King to his adventure across the Alps. And by the middle of December, when Charles VIII was publicly announcing his intention of spending Christmas in the Vatican, all unsuspecting of the treachery in his rear, Ludovico Sforza was informing both the Pope and the Signory of Venice, 'The King has shown himself so insolent and cruel in his behaviour that I have only one wish, to be rid of him.' Burchard records that on the day when the French armies stormed Civita Vecchia, His Holiness and the Cardinal Ascanio were 'so busy talking all during mass, that they paid but slight attention to the elevation to the Host.' And only two days later the Cardinal was officially released to negotiate King Charles's entry into the city.

No sooner were the French soldiers camped on the slopes of Monte Mario than the Pope retired to St. Angelo, and in the late hours of January 1st, 1495, the King of France staged his triumphal entry into the city. By the light of a thousand torches the astonished Romans beheld the gigantic Swiss and German mercenaries, the serried ranks of Gascon archers, D'Aubigny and his Scotsmen, marching to the skirling of their pipes, the thirty-six bronze cannon of the finest artillery of Europe. And in the midst of this concourse of cardinals and nobles, this great and victorious army, a pathetic stunted little king weighed down by his golden armour, presenting an aspect so physically repulsive that the beauty-loving Italians turned away in disgust.

Barricaded in his fortress on the Tiber, the Pope heard the cries of 'Francia, Rovere and Colonna' re-echoing through the winter night, but they were not of a nature to intimidate a man who had survived so many political storms. The moment of resistance was over. It was now the time to negotiate, and the hour of the Pope's surrender marked the overture of his diplomatic triumphs.

IX

ISOLATED IN her Adriatic stronghold, Lucrezia saw her neighbours in the Romagna profiting by the French successes to throw off the papal yoke. In her very presence people spoke of a council to depose the Pope, and at heart she knew that only fear and his financial dependence prevented her husband from following his neighbours' example. Giovanni's intrigues with his Sforza cousins were no longer a secret, and the Neapolitan army had no sooner left the Romagna than he returned to Pesaro. He was home by the middle of November, when her father was addressing her an impassioned appeal,

> begging her to come to Rome, while there was still time, and to leave her husband to guard his dominions against the French who were arriving in great numbers by land and sea.

But by the time Lucrezia received his letter, she was no longer in a position to obey her father's orders, for the French had already crossed the Cisa pass, the Apennine fortresses were garrisoned by their troops, and she had no other alternative than to winter in the provinces, in the company of a husband to whom she felt ever more alien and remote.

Every messenger from Rome brought graver news. The French had penetrated into the city and her father was virtually a prisoner in St. Angelo. As the price of his homage, King Charles dictated his terms, claiming as hostage both Prince Djem and the Cardinal of Valencia, demanding the right of free passage through the papal states. For a fortnight the Pope succeeded in evading these demands, till a chance shot from a French cannon caused a rift in the seemingly impregnable walls of St. Angelo. And the following day, all Italy resounded to the news that His Holiness, Pope Alexander VI, and his Christian majesty, King Charles VIII, had come to terms.

At first Lucrezia may have had doubts and apprehensions, particularly as to what lay in store for her brother when he accompanied the King to Naples in the rôle of legate cum hostage, but it was not long before her father's letters reassured her that Cesare had lost neither position nor prestige. The young king was flattered and caressed, gifts and indulgences rained on his entourage, even to the bestowal of a cardinal's hat on his favourite, the Bishop of St. Malo. But spiritually the Pope had triumphed, for whatever passing sacrifice he had made of his temporal powers, his position as the head of Christendom remained unimpaired. Men no longer spoke of a future council, when in full consistory before the assembled cardinals and ambassadors, the King of France made humble obeisance before the Borgia Pope, and by the time King Charles set out for Naples, he had not yet succeeded in persuading Alexander VI into granting him the investiture of his new Kingdom. Even after fear had turned Alfonso of Naples into a gibbering religious maniac, the Pope, so litttle trusting and so little trusted, remained loyal to the House of Aragon.

Riding out of the Lateran gate at the head of a victorious army, with the Pope's son as a hostage in his hands, the French King was ready to forgive what he regarded as an 'old man's obstinacy'. Had he possessed a greater knowledge of the Borgia character, King Charles would have known that it was not in the Pope's nature to be obstinate, nor was loyalty one of his dominant characteristics, unless he wanted the echoes of that loyalty to be heard on the other side of the Mediterranean where, during the past months, the Spanish monarchs had been viewing with a jealous eye the uninterrupted successes of France.

Nothing could have been more friendly than the Pope's goodbyes, and no one could have been a more delightful companion than Cesare Borgia, as they rode down the Appian Way. The hardy Frenchmen who had mocked at the seventeen velvet-covered wagons, which contained the young Cardinal's travelling equipment, changed their tune when on the first evening Cesare discarded his scarlet robes and, naked to the waist, joined in their wrestling bouts and downed their own champions. But on the second night at Velletri, the last of the hill towns before the road descends into the desolate swamps of the Pontine Marshes, King Charles was woken before dawn with the news of the Cardinal's disappearance. Disguised as a muleteer, Cesare had escaped from the camp, crossed the town on foot, and made his way to a small tavern outside the walls, where a servant was waiting with a horse. By the following night he was back in Rome, where he remained in hiding so as to enable his father to deny all knowledge of his flight.

The King of France now realized he had been the dupe of the Spanish Pope. Every detail of Cesare's flight had been carefully planned and the crowning bitterness was when, on sequestrating the Cardinal's baggage, it was found that all of the seventeen wagons were empty. Protestations were of no avail, for when the King made representations to the Pope against the infringement of their pact, threatening reprisals unless Cesare returned, His Holiness professed to be in complete ignorance of his son's whereabouts.

But if the Pope deliberately closed his eyes to Cesare's presence in the city, not many days elapsed before a mendicant friar, travelling across the Apennines, brought Lucrezia news of her brother's escape. Then for the first time in many weeks, the Sforza palace re-echoed to her laughter, for there was nothing the Borgias enjoyed so much as deliberate trickery. Whatever her father might write in his official letters intended for the prying eyes of French spies, she now knew that Spanish pride allied to Spanish guile had succeeded in evading the traps set by their enemies. And she was probably never so sweetly loving to the husband she despised, than when she told him of Cesare's escape.

Meanwhile the French armies advanced into the Regno, and apart from a few isolated pockets of resistance their progress was as swift and triumphant as in the north. Within a month of their leaving Rome, the first French outriders were already encamped in the gardens of Baia. Reacting against the tyranny of their Aragonese princes, the Neapolitans hailed them as their liberators and amidst scenes of general rejoicing Charles of Valois reclaimed the throne of his Angevin ancestors.

Nevertheless, Cesare Borgia's flight from Velletri was the

first of a series of French setbacks. The second hostage, the melancholy and corpulent Prince Djem, whose life was valued at so high a sum, was taken ill soon after his departure from Rome. Nothing was more natural than that a debauched and pampered oriental, used to a sedentary existence, should have succumbed to a chill when suddenly exposed to the rigours of winter travel. And when the news of his death reached Rome, neither envoys nor chroniclers thought of ascribing it to any other but normal causes. It was only later when the number of Borgia victims became incorporated into legend that certain historians, such as the Florentine Guicciardini, asserted that Prince Djem had died of a slow-working Borgia poison administered in the form of sweetmeats. But, unlike some of his Italian contemporaries, Alexander VI was not a poisoner by instinct. No crime graver than that of simony was ascribed to him either as a cardinal or in his first years as Pope. And it was only later, when he fell under the influence of his half-Italian son, that the use of the famous 'Cantarella' came into evidence.

Far graver to the King of France than the loss of his two hostages, was the effect of the Italian climate upon himself and his army. The dissolute morals of the Italian nobles and the facile charms of their wives were corrupting both King and entourage. The lovely and licentious princesses of Aragon had fled from Naples, but the companions of their revels remained behind; warm-voiced Neapolitans with clinging hands who, like the sirens of old, beguiled the young King from his duties, making him blind to the treachery and disaffection in his rear. While beyond the orange groves of Baia, in the teeming streets and infected brothels of a port rampant with all the diseases of the East, the finest army in Europe was gradually disintegrating from debauchery and illness.

While King Charles succumbed to the delights of Naples, 'an old man's obstinacy' was re-establishing the balance of power in Italy, or rather the balance of power in Europe; for the mediæval conception of politics was dead, and both Spain and the Empire now gave their adherence to a league in which Milan, Venice and the Papacy pledged themselves to unite against future aggression. On the eve of his coronation as King of Naples, Charles VIII woke to the imminence of his danger, and acting for once on the advice of his ministers, he decided to return to France before his former allies had cut off his line of retreat. But first he declared that on his way through Rome he would force the treacherous Pope to grant him the investiture of Naples. Alexander however had no intention of waiting on a guest who was no longer in a mood to solicit, and when the French armies passed through Rome at the end of May 1495, they found the doors of the Vatican open to them, but the Pope himself had fled. At Orvieto, the Umbrian city of which Cesare was now governor, His Holiness waited on the turn of events.

Meanwhile in Pesaro the reconciliation between the Pope and the Sforzas helped to improve the relations between Lucrezia and her husband, although Giovanni's behaviour as a condottiero had scarcely been conducive towards increasing her respect. While Lucrezia was only dreaming of the day when she could return to Rome, Giovanni was already bargaining for his future position, begging His Holiness to use his influence in procuring him a highly-salaried condotta in the armies of the league. The Pope seems to have been under no illusion as to his son-in-law's capacity or trustworthiness, and with the utmost frankness he warned him that if

> he wanted to become a captain, he had better try and give the impression that he was ready to serve the interests of his allies, and to look after the welfare of his men, instead of being only concerned with his own personal advantage.

In the future, he advised him

> to conduct himself as a good and loyal soldier and to spend his salary in raising efficient troops rather than in frittering away the money either on himself or on unnecessary fripperies.

From these words it would seem that the Pope was fully aware of his son-in-law's underhand practices, but reports from Pesaro told him that Lucrezia was unhappy and longing for her family. And the only way of ridding her of her husband was to procure Giovanni some suitable appointment. The rich

Republic of Venice was now allied to the Papacy, therefore, in the eyes of the Pope, it was incumbent on the Venetians to employ even the most incompetent of his relatives. But at first the signory refused to be blackmailed into giving condottas to inefficient condottieri, and it was only after months of bargaining, during which His Holiness even went to the lengths of presenting the Doge with the order of the 'Golden Rose', that both the Lord of Pesaro and the Duke of Gandia, who was still absent in Spain, were enrolled as captains of the Republic.

But even now Giovanni was not satisfied, for the difference between the thirty-one-thousand ducats paid to his Borgia brother-in-law and his own paltry four thousand ducats was an insult both to his avarice and pride. And his bored young wife had to listen to his interminable grievances, though she can have had little sympathy with a husband who had come skulking home rather than fight, and who now claimed a reward for what had been nothing less than treachery.

Restless and disillusioned, sexually awakened and unsatisfied, indifferent to, if not actually repelled by, a man whose frigidity and shyness made their married life a duty to be endured rather than a pleasure to be enjoyed, it was only Lucrezia's facile disposition which enabled her to play the rôle of an affectionate wife. Like many timid and uncertain natures, Giovanni was possessive, dependent on her vitality and warmth. Above all he was jealous of her both as a possession and as a wife. And his instinctive reaction was to refuse, when at the end of May a papal brief ordered him to accompany Lucrezia to Orvieto. The state of the roads with one army in retreat and another on the march, gave him ample justification not to expose his wife to a journey across the Apennines. But as usual His Holiness was utterly indifferent to every other consideration but his own wishes. Impervious to danger, he dismissed his son-in-law's reasonable excuses as an attempt to thwart his will. When the approach of the French armies forced him to leave Orvieto for Perugia, he found time within an hour of his arrival to dictate a second papal brief threatening the Lord of Pesaro with the perils of excommunication if he failed to bring his wife to Perugia.

So, on the 13th of June, 1495, Lucrezia, escorted by her husband and a troop of eighty cavalry, set out from the town where she had ruled for little more than a year. But during this one year she had grown from a child into a woman—a woman to whom Pesaro had brought neither interest nor affection. Everything she loved and clung to belonged to the past, the past to which she was returning with nostalgic longing and from which in the future she would never be able to escape.

X

THE PAST WAS waiting for Lucrezia in Perugia, waiting for her in the form of an adoring but imperious father, a dominating brother, a servile court. In this first family reunion the unwanted husband was relegated to the background. And when he left after four days, neither wife nor father-in-law pressed him to prolong his stay. There was no place for Giovanni Sforza in this Borgia family reunion. His sympathies with the enemy were too pronounced. Loyal to his Milanese cousins, he was unable to appreciate the tales of Spanish guile by which the Pope, abetted by Cesare, had succeeded in tricking Ascanio Sforza and in outwitting the French King. If Giovanni really cared for his wife, and in his reserved and frigid way he seems to have done so, he must have resented the rapt entrancement with which she listened to Cesare's account of his flight from Velletri, and still more must he have resented the possessive manner in which father and brother claimed her entire attention. 'The Pope loves his daughter in a superlative degree', wrote the Ferrarese ambassador when Lucrezia was still a child. But never had this love been so evident as now, when in all the radiance of her fifteen years she returned to take her place as mistress of the Vatican and of her father's heart.

In the past Lucrezia had had her relations with her father overshadowed by Julia's presence and complicated by Adriana's instructions. For the first time she saw him with an unbiased and adult eye. Never was a father so fascinating or so lovable, so brilliant or so inconsistent, such an extraordinary mixture of faith and cynicism, of ruthlessness and tolerance. There was no one with whom she could laugh so heartily, or with whom she felt more in tune, for in their irrepressible gaiety and buoyant optimism lay their real affinity. There was never any question of joking with her husband. He was one of those people who were born old, perpetually offended and on his dignity, continually complaining of his own misfortunes. What a contrast to her father, who at sixty-five, with his court in exile and the threat of the French invasion an ever-present reality, still managed to preserve his outward serenity.

Neither Julia nor Adriana formed part of the exiled court of Perugia. No sooner had the French armies entered Rome than they had taken refuge in the Orsini palace, rather than share the Pope's captivity in St. Angelo. But now it seemed as if it were his daughter, rather than his mistress, who was indispensable to the Pope's happiness, as if his passion had spent itself in those hysterical scenes of jealousy and reconciliation of the past year. Julia's excessive prudence may also have helped to cool his ardour, and though his admiration for the beautiful Farnese survived their separation she no longer formed part of the intimate family circle.

From the bishop's palace of an Umbrian hill town, Alexander VI was directing a policy designed to transform what was primarily a defensive pact into a concerted offensive to cut off the French armies in their retreat. The whole of the Roman Curia was on the road, and at any hour of the day could be seen riding up the hillside, through the olive orchards, some red-robed cardinal on his white mule, or some ambassador of the league surrounded by an armed escort. But after dismissing the ambassadors, the Pope would summon a groom and, dressed as a simple monk, ride out to the convent of the most holy of all nuns, Sister Columbia of Rieti, where he would spend the rest of the day in prayer and meditation. It was characteristic of his dual nature that he seemed equally at home in the cell of the miracle-working nun as at the supper table of Gian-paolo Baglioni.

As a fief of the Church under the rule of the Baglioni, Perugia feasted the Pope and his daughter, and no host could be more fascinating than Gian-paolo Baglioni. His fascination was such that men were ready to forget that he had risen to power over the bodies of his murdered kinsmen, and was living in open incest with his lovely sister. The dungeons of Perugia re-echoed to the cries of his victims, yet nobody questioned his right to act as host to the head of Christendom, least of all the Pope himself, who delighting in the charm and beauty of his hosts, made no attempt to condemn their moral failings. What matter if in company of this brother and sister the fifteen-year-old Lucrezia witnessed certain scenes which later led her to question her own complicated relationships?

After the restricted monotony of Pesaro, Lucrezia revelled in the freedom of the exiled court. But however eagerly she embraced the past, there were certain changes she could not help but notice. Though her father was still as young and light-hearted as ever, Cesare was very different from the brother she had left a year ago. The high spirits were no longer so spontaneous, the moods of melancholy more frequent, and the indifference with which he wore his scarlet robes so obvious as to be almost contemptuous. During the past months he had played an active part in public affairs, and the King of France had recognized his importance in claiming him as a hostage. But Cesare had no wish to confine his energies to the intrigues of the Roman Curia, when all Italy was uniting in a brief burst of patriotism under the command of Francesco Gonzaga, Marquis of Mantua, Captain General of the League. Even the despised Giovanni Sforza had succeeded in obtaining a condotta from Venice. And Cesare no longer attempted to hide his bitterness, a bitterness which inspired fear. Lucrezia had a new aspect of her brother's character when she saw cardinals turn pale at his sudden rages, rages which were all the more frightening because they were so quickly got under control. It was rumoured that he had been responsible for the massacring of the Swiss soldiers who had looted their mother's house in Rome, and though the Spanish mercenaries who had conducted the massacre had succeeded in escaping, and no one had given evidence, Lucrezia had not the slightest doubt of the rumour being true. Even as a child Cesare had been unable to bear an insult, and the pride which dominated them all now seemed to have become an obsession with him. There was so much she could not begin to understand, and still she loved him, even to the length of excusing what she could not deny, continuing to give him as a woman the unquestioning adoration of a child.

Meanwhile the days of papal exile were drawing to a close. Charles VIII had renounced all hope of procuring an interview with the Borgia Pope, and the threatening attitude of his former allies was forcing him to hurry northwards by forced marches. Hostilities opened when the Duke of Milan attacked the French garrison at Asti. But owing to differences among members of the league and the slowness with which the condottieri mustered their men, the main forces did not come into contact till the beginning of July, by which time the French armies had crossed the Apennines and reached the banks of the Taro on the borders of the Lombard plain.

At Fornovo the Italians regained their self-respect. At the end of a hard-fought battle the armies of the league forced King Charles VIII to flee the field, leaving behind him both his booty and prestige. But after performing miracles of valour, Francesco Gonzaga made the mistake of accepting a truce when victory was within his grasp, and while his undisciplined mercenaries delivered themselves to an orgy of looting, the French King, profiting by the general confusion, escaped through the enemy lines.

'*Passa il re de Francia, Italia al tuo dispetto*', was the verdict of posterity. But at the time Fornovo was called a great victory and the Marquis of Mantua was hailed as the saviour of his country. The only satisfaction left to Charles VIII before leaving Italy was to disrupt the unity of the league. By concluding a separate peace with Ludovico Sforza, he brought upon Milan the enmity of Venice and the contempt of the Spanish Pope. Five years later, when his successor, Louis XII, laid claim to the Milanese inheritance of his grandmother, Valentina Visconti, the Sforzas had occasion to regret their game of double treachery.

Charles VIII recrossed the Alps and Alexander VI made a triumphant return to the Vatican. By the following spring the last of the French garrisons left in Southern Italy had surrendered, and the Neapolitans welcomed back their Aragonese princes with the same enthusiasm with which they had cheered the French King. But however ephemeral had been their conquest, the armies of Charles VIII had served as pathfinders to those legions of Austria and of Spain who were to trample and desecrate Italian soil for the next four hundred years. The French King had returned to his own country, but the flame of

Italian patriotism was already spent, and no one grasped this more clearly than the Borgia Pope.

While the Romans, eager for peace, cheered his re-entry into the capital, Alexander foresaw the troubles that lay ahead. There was no hope of Italy remaining independent if the feudal lords continued to hold their armies at the disposal of the highest bidder, and at any moment a situation could arise by which the treachery of the Orsinis or the Colonnas could make a prisoner of the Pope. The only way of achieving peace was to revive the old policy of Sixtus IV, by destroying the power of the Roman barons and centralizing the states of the Church in a single principality. Secure in its temporal possessions, the Papacy could then maintain the balance of power in Italy. Such had been Pope Alexander's ambitions since the beginning of his reign. The time had now come when these ambitions could be put into execution. Though reports from Spain informed him that the Duke of Gandia was wasting his time in gambling and dissipation, the Pope persisted in regarding his favourite son as a potential military genius, and a papal Bull now summoned Juan Borgia, Duke of Gandia, to return to Italy and to take up his duties as captain of the League and Gonfalonier of the Church.

While the Pope and Cesare re-entered Rome, Lucrezia rejoined her husband in Pesaro. But after the stirring events of the past months, life with Giovanni Sforza was somewhat of an anti-climax. And before long she was back in Rome. When the Marquis of Mantua passed through the city in the spring of 1496 we hear of his paying a visit to the Madonna of Pesaro. Writing to his wife he says, 'Tired as I was I went to pay my respects to the Pope's daughter with whom I spent an agreeable evening'. These were bald words in which to record his first impression of Lucrezia Borgia in her youth, but they were written at the end of an exhausting day by a man who had probably had his fill of high-sounding Spanish compliments. Like Isabella d'Este, we are left in ignorance as to whether he saw Lucrezia merely as a figurehead, or whether he was already fascinated by those pale transparent eyes, that lilting voice which fifteen years later was to inspire him with such an imprudent and dangerous affection.

Whatever may have been his first impression, Francesco Gonzaga made no attempt to postpone his departure. Two days later he was already on his way to Naples, and among the pride of Italian chivalry which followed in his wake down the Appian Way was that unwilling condottiero, Giovanni Sforza. Did Lucrezia venture to make invidious comparisons between the virile figure of Francesco Gonzaga, the brown twisted face so attractive in its very ugliness, and her husband's anaemic pallor, or did she ignore the one as easily as she forgot the other? She is said to have cried at Giovanni's departure, but with her volatile nature tears flowed easily and dried as quickly. A courtier had only to pay her a well-turned compliment, a buffoon had only to make her laugh, and her husband was already forgotten. Once more she was free to sun herself in the adulation of her father's court, where her slightest whim was law and where the Pope's doting adoration was beginning to serve as a foil to his enemies.

Only two days after Sforza's departure for Naples, the slanderous Scalona was writing to the Marchioness of Mantua: 'The Lord of Pesaro had left Rome in despair . . . leaving his wife under the apostolic mantle'—words which, in view of future accusations, were to take on a grave significance. In another dispatch, he enlarges on the same subject: 'Maybe the Lord of Pesaro has in his own house one whom others do not suspect'.

Scalona would hardly have dared to repeat such revolting aspersions had he not been assured of a favourable reception from his mistress, who in her hatred, or rather envy, of the alien Borgias, was willing to believe the sixty-five-year-old Pope to be guilty of every crime: or was it possible that in a moment of humiliation and frustration, Giovanni Sforza had gone to the lengths of confiding in Scalona the accusations which a year later he circulated round the courts of Italy—the defence of a weakling whose manhood is put in question, the weapon of a coward avenging himself on a family who had never allowed him to possess his wife? From the very first they had come between them, though he does not appear to have been sufficiently discerning to recognize, behind the over-lifesize figure of the father, the subtler and more dangerous

9. Cover of a collection of Venetian love songs based upon the poems of Aretino, early sixteenth century. The singing of such love songs was popular at all the courts of Italy during the High Renaissance.

shadow of the brother, nor to interpret Cesare's arrogant dislike as a bitter and corrosive jealousy.

As yet Lucrezia had not fully awakened to the failure of her marriage. Dimly she realized that something was missing, that happiness such as she knew it, existed only in the intimacy of her family circle. At fifteen the depths of adult emotions were unknown to her. She was still ready to accept the standards imposed by others. But suffering lay in wait, the suffering she was to experience when her sister-in-law, Sanchia of Aragon, arrived in Rome to disrupt the harmony of her family life.

XI

URING THE past year Sanchia of Aragon had found time lying heavy on her hands. In exile at Ischia with her thirteen-year-old husband she envied those of more lowly birth who had stayed behind to welcome the French conquerors. From all accounts they were the most fascinating and chivalrous of men. And confined to a rocky island, within sight of her beloved Naples, there must have been moments when she regretted the royal blood which had married her to a Pope's bastard, an impotent child, who had cried on their wedding night. In the first year of their marriage, before the French invasion drove them into exile, she had had no reason to complain of her little husband. He was charming and docile, content to spend his days in the company of her young brother Alfonso, while she enjoyed with others the freedom of her married state. But it was not long before the scandals of her court came to the ears of her father-in-law, the Pope. And, whatever irregularities he might permit himself in his private life, Pope Alexander VI insisted on the members of his family maintaining the outward decencies. Reports from Naples told him of his daughter-in-law receiving gentlemen in the privacy of her bedchamber, while the ladies-in-waiting were kept busy in amusing her husband. And as it appeared that neither her father the King Alfonso, nor her half-brother the Duke of Calabria, nor even her grandmother, the widowed Queen, made any attempt to curb her licentious behaviour, it behoved His Holiness to assert his parental authority and to intervene as firmly as he had intervened in the case of the Duke of Gandia.

At the same time his curiosity was aroused to see what manner of woman was this daughter-in-law, whose fabulous beauty men spoke of with bated breath, and whose joyous temperament seemed so akin to his own.

But then came the French invasion, driving Sanchia's father

to abdication and to madness, forcing her half-brother, Ferrantino, to relinquish his kingdom before he had begun to reign; driving the gayest and most sophisticated court of Italy to seek refuge in monasteries and island fortresses, while in Rome, beset with his own anxieties, the Holy Father forgot all about his erring daughter-in-law. A year went by and with the help of the league Ferrantino of Aragon re-conquered his country. Calabria was the first to welcome him back. And while the court was still at Reggio, Joffré and Sanchia were suddenly summoned to the Vatican, though the chroniclers were at a loss to discover what motive prompted the Pope to invite the Princess of Squillace to take up residence in Rome.

In the marriage contract it had been stipulated that they were to reside in Naples. Their titles and revenues were derived from the Regno, and it was common knowledge that Alexander's passionate love for his children did not include his youngest son. His sudden decision was therefore open to suspicion, and there were those who speculated as to his future intentions regarding the house of Aragon, while others on the contrary maintained that in his kindness of heart, His Holiness wished to spare the young King of Naples the expenses of a second court. But those who were nearest to the truth declared 'that having been told that the Madonna Sanchia was of a surpassing loveliness, His Holiness was anxious to see and to enjoy the company of such a beautiful creature'.

That she was lovely no one could deny! 'Though it is difficult to define the secret of her beauty,' wrote Scalona to the Marchioness of Mantua. Did it lie in the contrast between the dark skin and the opaque blue eyes, the colour of the sea when the sirocco blows, or was it the contrast between the thin aquiline nose and the full sensual mouth? Did it lie in the pride of her royal bearing, the way she carried her small dark head, or in the wicked mockery of her smile? 'A wolf in sheep's clothing', was Scalona's somewhat ungallant description, and from the day of her first appearance at the Vatican both he and his colleagues prognosticated trouble.

As the daughter and sister of a king she made her official entry into the city on the 20th of May, 1496. And the dispatches of Scalona evoke that brilliant cavalcade advancing up the Appian Way, with the morning sun reflecting on silver trappings and golden chains, on jewelled bonnets and shimmering brocades. Jesters and pages, equerries and halberdiers reflected all the colours of the summer day. But in traditional Spanish fashion both prince and princess were in black. In satin doublet and hose, with a velvet beret covering his auburn curls, mounted on a jennet accoutred in silver, the fourteen-year-old prince of Squillace rode into Rome with all the pomp of royalty. Graceful and effeminate, with delicate features resembling his sister's, Vanozza's youngest son had his full share of his mother's beauty. But he had none of his father's virility, none of the robust strength of the Borgias, and it is not surprising if the Pope was sometimes led to doubt the parentage of his youngest son. The Mediterranean sun had bronzed his skin, but beneath the tan and outward look of health, the sharp eyes of the gossip-mongers detected a dissolute and lascivious look, as if too many caresses had corrupted him before he had time to mature.

As for the Princess Sanchia, she had the appearance of one who was born corrupt, while her painted cheeks and the sophisticated elegance of her black embroidered gown cut with wide sleeves in the Spanish manner made her seem older than her nineteen years. But though there were those who criticized the insolent boldness of her looks, it was universally agreed that she put the Madonna of Pesaro into the shade.

Lucrezia was already apprehensive when, at her father's orders, she rode out to meet her brother and sister-in-law at the Lateran gate. And she was naïve enough to let her jealousy transpire in public, so that Scalona was able to inform his mistress, 'the Madonna of Pesaro is not at all pleased at the thought of having a rival in the Vatican'. During the past months Lucrezia had received so much adulation that by now she must have had an exaggerated idea of her own beauty. But one can hardly blame her for her vanity, when the Roman courtesans wore silken wigs in imitation of her long blonde hair, and the poets attached to her father's court sang of 'her golden tresses.' For the first time she saw her beauty in danger of being challenged, not by a Julia Farnese, whose passing favour depended on her father's moods, but by Joffré's wife, a royal princess who might claim her place at the papal court. Never had Lucrezia dressed so carefully as on the day when in green and gold brocade and feathered bonnet, escorted by the Neapolitan and Spanish ambassadors, she rode out to the Lateran gate to meet the Princess of Squillace.

Whatever may have been her secret fears, she laid herself out to win Sanchia's confidence and affection. The ceremonial kiss of their first meeting set the seal on a relationship which, though it rested on uneasy foundations, had nevertheless all the appearance of friendship. In public the two sisters-in-law appeared to be inseparable, and before long Giovanni Sforza, who was still campaigning in the Regno, heard of his wife being associated in the scandals concerning the Princess of Squillace and her new relatives.

Sanchia of Aragon introduced a new and disturbing element into the already complicated family life of the Borgias. From the beginning both father-in-law and brother-in-law recognized her for what she was—a prostitute who had strayed into the ranks of royalty. For Cesare the outcome was obvious. Why search the brothels when in his brother's house there was a beautiful and accomplished courtesan? As for the Pope, he was in the broadest sense of the word a family man, preferring his daughter-in-law to confine her intimacies to the family circle rather than to cause trouble at the papal court. This illegitimate daughter of a king and of a Neapolitan of noble birth was a fitting addition to his family of beautiful bastards. He was pleased to have the great-grandchild of Alfonso 'the Magnanimous' for his daughter-in-law and because he liked her Spanish arrogance, he allowed her to disregard the rules of the Vatican protocol in a way which appalled the Curia officials. But even Burchard was powerless to intervene when Sanchia and Lucrezia sat ensconced on velvet cushions on the steps of the papal throne, entertaining the Pope and his cardinals with their witty sallies.

Two days after the arrival of the Princess of Squillace, Burchard was already recording in his diary the indecorous manner in which Sanchia and Lucrezia conducted themselves during the solemn Whitsuntide ceremonies at St. Peter's. The Pope and his court were assisting at High Mass. A famous

Spanish theologian was delivering the sermon, when the service was interrupted by the noisy entry of a group of laughing young women headed by Sanchia and Lucrezia. Ignoring the protests of the horrified Master of Ceremonies, they clambered into the stalls, reserved for the canons of St. Peter's, where they remained throughout the ceremony whispering and joking among themselves 'with an ignominious lack of decorum which scandalized the public', but which the Pope dismissed as an amusing incident which helped to relieve the tedium of a dreary sermon.

Before long there were graver scandals to report, scandals which Burchard did not dare to put into writing. Cesare was a daily visitor at his brother's house, and as a devoted brother and a somewhat less devoted husband, Joffré appears to have welcomed his visits, while it was rumoured that Lucrezia's apparent devotion to her sister-in-law was due to the fact that in Sanchia's company she would be sure of finding Cesare.

However amoral both by instinct and upbringing, however sensual by nature, Lucrezia was timid rather than bold in her amatory relationships. As a dutiful wife she had deployed her talents, only to find that Giovanni Sforza was incapable of appreciating the subtleties of love-making. The only real emotion she had ever experienced was the passion inspired by her brother, to whose will she had always submitted, whose demands she had never questioned. But now she was beginning to realize that to submit was not sufficient. Like Sanchia she must learn to excite and to withhold, to yield and then withdraw. Jealous yet admiring, she saw how both Cesare and her father reacted to Sanchia's presence—the Pope amused, indulgent, flattered by the attentions of his lovely daughter-in-law, and Cesare with a predatory gleam in his eye, courting her with his irresistible, all-embracing charm. But in contrast there was Joffré, bored and indifferent to the caresses of his wife, a little boy who had had such a surfeit of sweetmeats that he had lost his taste for food; spoiled, rather vicious, yet throughout it all pathetically loyal to the family who had ruined his life.

By the end of the summer Lucrezia was back in Pesaro, and there is every reason to believe that she returned of her own free will. Whether she could no longer bear to witness her brother's infatuation for their sister-in-law, or hear praise of Sanchia's beauty, or whether she was escaping from the realization of her own tormented love for Cesare, she now made a pathetic attempt to take refuge in her husband's home. But all that awaited her in Pesaro was an embittered husband and the cloying monotony of provincial life.

Conscious of the insignificant part he had played in the Neapolitan campaign, while grudging the money he had had to spend on his soldiers, Giovanni Sforza was only too ready to vent his grievances on his wife. There had been plenty of rumours in the Neapolitan camp, rumours which lost nothing in the telling, particularly when translated into the couplets of Pontano and of Sannazzaro. The story of how Sanchia and Lucrezia rivalled for the favour of Pope and cardinal was of the kind which appealed to the Neapolitan humour, but it was not likely to be appreciated by a husband whose suspicions, according to Scalona, had already been aroused before his departure for Naples.

On his return from Naples, he must have been surprised to find Lucrezia installed in Pesaro. But 'her warm embraces' were no longer sufficient to still his suspicions. On the contrary, they only served to augment them—the gestures and habits she had learnt from Sanchia, the jewels she artlessly displayed as coming from her father, the very efforts she made to please him, were all so much fuel to his jealousy. Neither reproaches nor accusations were spared her. Nevertheless, she stayed on in Pesaro, displaying such tolerance and patience that, by the time they returned to Rome, the Count and Countess of Pesaro were once more reported to 'be living in harmony with one another'.

* * * * * *

During Lucrezia's absence another event had occurred to cause further complications in the Borgia family circle. Juan, Duke of Gandia, had returned to Rome, leaving behind in Spain both his wife and his infant son. Neither the responsibilities of marriage nor of fatherhood appear to have had any sobering effect on this spoilt dissolute young man, who now came back to claim the perilous honours of 'Principe Nipote'. History has dealt kindly with Juan Borgia, portraying him as the innocent victim of his brother's ambitions, but his contemporaries judged him more severely. A 'muy mal hombre' was the reputation he had gained in Spain, and only his father persisted in remaining blind to his defects.

Pope Alexander was now ready to launch his long-planned campaign against the Orsinis and on October the 26th, Juan, Duke of Gandia, was solemnly invested with the jewelled sword and embroidered standard of a Captain General of the Church and put in command of the operations in the Campagna.

The moment was propitious, for the head of the clan, Virginio Orsini, was still a Neapolitan prisoner. And with the enemy deprived of their leader, the Borgias hoped for an easy victory. At first these hopes seemed justified. Within a week ten Orsini castles were subdued without the loss of one life. But at the family stronghold of Bracciano the papal armies came up against the assembled force of the whole clan, and for two months the massive castle on the lake resisted every onslaught. The ablest of the papal captains, Guidobaldo of Montefeltro, was wounded, leaving the incompetent Juan in charge of the operations. Then the winter rains set in and the guns borrowed from the King of Naples stuck in the mud, so that by Christmas the unfortunate young duke was still encamped beside the lake, exposing his gorgeous uniform to wind and rain, while the whole of Italy laughed at the Pope's discomfiture.

The Orsinis were not only holding out, they were also making numerous sorties into the Campagna and the dispatches of Scalona relate how

> on a hunting expedition near the *Tre Fontane*, the Cardinal of Valencia narrowly escaped falling into the hands of the enemy. If this had happened, [adds Scalona] there would have been a new Pope in Rome, for Alexander VI would never have survived this humiliation to his eldest son.

And while Cesare, fretting for active employment, was wasting his days in idle pleasure, his younger brother was heaping ridicule on the armies of the Church; ridicule so embittering to

His Holiness as to bring about one of his fainting attacks on Christmas Day.

These sudden fainting fits, which recurred with increasing frequency in the latter years of Rodrigo Borgia's life, and which his enemies erroneously referred to as epileptic fits, were in all probability the result of high blood pressure. The Pope was a heavy, full-blooded man inclined to corpulence, and the frugality of his diet may have been prescribed by doctors' orders rather than by choice. Now, when it was becoming increasingly evident that the Borgias intended to carve themselves a kingdom out of the patrimony of the Church, ambassadors and princes commented hopefully on these ever-recurring fainting fits, from which however his Holiness never failed to recover with his usual resilience.

Forced into open battle at Soriano, the papal forces suffered a resounding defeat. Guidobaldo of Montefeltro was taken prisoner and the Duke of Gandia, slightly wounded, fled the field. The Orsinis remained masters of the Roman Campagna and the Pope's humiliation was complete. But whatever might be his military defeats, Alexander VI was a past master in diplomacy. He knew that his enemies were exhausted and were not likely to exact extravagant peace terms. No time was lost in negotiating, and at the treaty signed at Bracciano on the 5th of February, 1497, the Pope restored their castles to the Orsinis on the payment of 50,000 golden florins, while the disputed fortresses of Cervetri and of Anguillara were given back to the Church. Meanwhile the Pope's faithful condottiero, Guidobaldo Montefeltro, was left to pay his own ransom, while in Naples Virginio Orsini suddenly died on the day of his release—the first of a long line of Borgia victims.

XII

'THE MADONNA of Pesaro appears to be very happy and is mad about the Lord Giovanni.' Such was the verdict of the observant Scalona when Lucrezia and her husband returned to Rome in the month of January, 1497. And in view of later events, it would be interesting to know whether Scalona's judgment was correct, or whether Lucrezia had her own motives for simulating this sudden affection. For all her air of immaturity, she was now a woman, as arrogant and ruthless as the rest of her family, while in the art of dissimulation she surpassed them all. This chameleon-like ability to adapt herself to her surroundings accounts for the passive rôle she so often plays in contemporary chronicles, where she appears to be no more than a smiling spectator of her family's crimes. Yet throughout her father's reign as Pope, this girl who was apparently so colourless, remained the undisputed mistress of the Vatican. No one, not even Sanchia, ever succeeded in usurping a position which must have required infinite tact and understanding—qualities in which Sanchia was singularly lacking.

Never had Lucrezia's 'gentle mien' been more appreciated than now, when she returned to Rome to act as mediator in her family's quarrels. But underlying the apparent gentleness and candid look was an unerring feminine instinct. Since her earliest childhood she had played on Cesare's jealousy. It had been her only weapon against his dominating egotism, and her apparent devotion to her ineffectual husband may have been no more than an act deliberately assumed to hurt her brother in the most vulnerable part of his armour, his insane and possessive jealousy. Though Sanchia was now Cesare's established mistress, the sight of his sister still tied to her ineffectual husband and apparently contented, was sufficient to arouse all the old obsessions of his childhood, turning his contempt for his brother-in-law into a hatred of which Lucrezia had not foreseen the danger. But it was not only Cesare s jealousy, which threatened Giovanni Sforza's future. Having come to the conclusion that his daughter's marriage was a failure, the Pope was planning to be rid of his son-in-law with as little scandal as possible. And he was not of a nature to allow his plans to be upset merely because Lucrezia suddenly showed affection for a man who was not even capable of giving her a child.

The events of the past year had proved that there was nothing to be gained from an alliance with the Sforzas. And robbed of his political importance, Giovanni had no other claim to the Pope's esteem. He was not only treacherous and disloyal, but as a condottiero had made no attempt to carry out his obligations either to the Church or to the league. And though there is no record as to how and when His Holiness decided to free Lucrezia from her ties, or whether having made this decision he took his sons into his confidence, the Lord of Pesaro was already a potential victim when he ventured to return to Rome, deluding himself in the belief that his wife's affection was sufficient guarantee for his security.

Outwardly the Borgias still treated him as a member of their family. Carnival was at hand and the Pope and his children threw themselves with a whole-hearted delight into a world of burlesque and masquerade. Disguised as mummers, the young Borgias mingled with the crowds, forming part of those bands of dissolute young men who, under cover of their masques, performed every form of outrage on peaceful citizens. All the traditional amusements of carnival, the races of the old men and the Jews, the battles of confetti and flowers, the giant floats representing scenes in which the mythological mingled with the obscene; the dancing and the fireworks, the comedies and songs, were all of a nature to appeal to the primitive tastes of the Borgias.

Dragging her timid husband in her wake, Lucrezia abandoned herself to the pleasures of carnival. And it was only when the last confetti had been cleared from the streets and the masks had been laid aside that she became aware of the dangers which lay ahead, realizing that Cesare's jealousy was too dangerous to be aroused, her brothers' rivalries too bitter to be placated.

The past months had brought Cesare Borgia many disappointments. He had seen Juan succeed without an effort to the military honours to which he aspired himself. And when his brother proved unworthy of these honours and came fleeing to the Vatican, with the whole of Italy laughing at his discomfiture, their father still welcomed him with the same indulgence as of old. Blind to his shortcomings, deaf to the voice of criticism, the Pope persisted in loading the worthless Juan with all the temporal riches at his disposal. And even the Spanish ambassador lodged a protest when the papal fiefs of Terracina and of Pontecorvo passed into the hereditary possession of the Dukes of Gandia. Meanwhile Scalona informed his masters that 'everything was being done to prepare Cesare's way for the Papacy'. If a rich cardinal died, it was he who received the benefices, and in the winter of 1496 there were rumours of his succeeding Ascanio Sforza as Vice-Chancellor. Only Cesare himself showed no ambition in this direction. He had no friends in the Sacred College other than his cousins, the two Borgia cardinals, both called Juan, the one known as the Elder, the other as the Younger. Apart from them and his former tutor, Juan Vera, his palace was the resort of artists and of scholars rather than of priests. All the leading poets of the day, from Francesco Sperulo to Serafino of Aquila, sang his praises; but their odes rang hollow to Cesare's ears so long as his younger brother the Duke of Gandia occupied the centre of the Roman stage.

Their relations with their sister-in-law added fuel to the flames. No sooner was Juan home from his campaign than Sanchia turned her blue eyes in his direction. There can never have been any question of love between her and Cesare. From the first it must have been a bitter unabating sex warfare, which later translated itself into hate. All the erotic practices she had learnt at the Neapolitan court (and there were those who maintained her to be versed in the acts of witchcraft) were employed to subjugate the brother-in-law of whom she had a secret fear. Juan was merely another means with which to make the teasing still more tantalizing, the risks even greater. And before long the gossip-mongers had fresh tales to tell of how 'the blue-eyed witch from Naples warmed the bed of all three brothers'.

Into this pent-up atmosphere of family hatred and intrigue Lucrezia's return introduced still further complications and intrigues. The rivalry between her two brothers in no way detracted from their mutual dislike of Giovanni Sforza. While Cesare resented his possession of his sister, Juan disputed his position at the papal court. For whatever may have been the Pope's future intentions, he still continued to honour his son-in-law in public. And Burchard records how during the Palm Sunday celebrations in St. Peter's, the Lord of Pesaro and the Duke of Gandia were the first to receive the blessed palm from the Pope's hands. But the worthy German, whose mind was concentrated on questions of protocol and ritual, was at a loss to explain why, only five days after this mark of papal favour, the Lord Giovanni should suddenly and precipitately have fled the city.

So unexpected was his departure that it could only be interpreted as flight, and even those who were more perspicacious than Burchard found it hard to unravel the mystery. Ambassadors and chroniclers filled their dispatches with conflicting reports. Some hinted at a violent quarrel between the Lord of Pesaro and the Duke of Gandia, others went so far as to say that the Lord Giovanni had been threatened with poison, and that his wife had warned him of his danger. But all that we know for certain is that in the early morning of Good Friday, March 24th, 1497, Giovanni Sforza left his wife's palace, ostensibly bound on a visit to the seven churches, 'and that twenty-four hours later he was in Pesaro'. Such are the sparse facts, from which many years later Sforza's physician, a certain Messer Monaldi, elaborated a fantastic story, in which Lucrezia was reported to have hidden one of her husband's pages behind a screen, enabling him to overhear a conversation from the terms of which she learned of Cesare's intention to murder her husband Giovanni.

Faulty and inaccurate, coloured by later events, these old man's memoirs carry no conviction; nevertheless they serve to emphasize that Giovanni Sforza fled from Rome in terror of his life, and that someone, who may well have been Lucrezia, had warned him of his danger. That his departure was contrary to the Pope's plans is proved by the many papal Bulls summoning him to return. Entrenched behind the Apennines, and supported by his cousins of Milan, Giovanni Sforza was a far more embarrassing proposition to the Borgais than if he had peacefully succumbed to a sudden attack of 'Roman fever', and from every point of view it was preferable for Lucrezia to be widowed, rather than divorced. Lucrezia's own reactions are open to question, for whereas Scalona informed the Marchioness of Mantua that 'the Madonna of Pesaro is in despair at her husband's departure', the Milanese envoy, Stefano Taberna, asserted that 'it was his wife's abominable conduct which led Giovanni Sforza to flee the city'. And reports of Lucrezia's infidelities are too persistent to be ignored. Gossip was rife as to the Borgia family relationships. Sanchia's licentious behaviour reflected on the sister-in-law who was always in her company, while Lucrezia's courtiers whispered among themselves that there was more reason to fear her brother's jealous glances than those of her insignificant husband. But if Giovanni Sforza really believed his wife 'to be no better than a whore', if he really believed her to be capable of incest, why did he make such frenzied efforts to get her back, writing her letter after letter entreating her to join him in Pesaro? Was it only on account of the dowry of thirty thousand ducats, the fact that her presence guaranteed the security of his State, or was it because in his frigid undemonstrative fashion he had learnt to love her; a love which Scalona would have us believe to have been reciprocal.

But to all these entreaties Lucrezia made no answer, and her very silence gives the lie to Scalona. Had she loved her husband, neither fear of her father nor of her brothers would have prevented her from sending him some word of comfort and affection. In silence she allowed her father to instigate proceedings for divorce, in silence she allowed her brothers to proclaim in public that they would no longer allow her to submit to the indignity of such a marriage. And in silence and to her everlasting shame she put her signature to a document in which she declared that owing to her husband's impotence, she was still 'virgo intacta', a declaration which according to the diaries of Sanudo, set 'the whole of Italy a-laughing'.

Meanwhile, nothing could have been more humiliating than

the position of Giovanni Sforza, deserted by his wife and insulted in his manhood. And with a courage born of despair he continued to resist his father-in-law's demands. When His Holiness sent the general of the Augustinians to persuade, and if necessary, to coerce him into consenting to a divorce, he refused to give an answer before consulting with his Sforza cousins. But now he was to discover that the omnipotent Duke of Milan was but a man of straw. His thorny relations with Venice and the fear that despite his pact with France, Charles VIII might at any moment return to Italy to invade his dominions, made it imperative for Ludovico to curry favour with the Borgia Pope, particularly as owing to political differences, negotiations during the past year had been somewhat strained. When the unfortunate Giovanni arrived in Milan to beg his cousin's support, he was bluntly advised that 'it would be folly to refuse a divorce, when by accepting it on his own terms he could retain both his wife's dowry and the Pope's good will'.

As to the affront to his honour and the aspersions cast on his virility, Ludovico had no other solution to offer than that he should give a public proof of his virility. Let the Pope send his daughter to the Castle of Nepi, the seat of Ascanio Sforza, and there in presence of a papal legate and the Milanese ambassador, Giovanni could demonstrate the full powers of his manhood. This suggestion, which sounds so strange to our ears, was not infrequently practised at a time when relatives and priests assisted at the consummation of family alliances. Nevertheless it seemed to impute that Ludovico had doubts of his cousin's virility. And when Giovanni refused to consider the suggestion, the Duke went even further and offered him his choice of the Milanese courtesans with whom 'he could display his physical capacities in front of the papal legate', who happened to be the Pope's nephew, the Cardinal Juan Borgia.

Giovanni Sforza may not have been a sympathetic character, but one cannot but feel for him when, humiliated and outraged, he found himself the butt of his cousin's heartless cynicism. Nervous, sensitive, fundamentally unsure of himself, the very idea of a public trial would have been sufficient to render him impotent. And indiscretion could go no further than when the

Duke Ludovico confided to the Ferrarese envoy, Costabili, 'that the fact of the Lord Giovanni having refused to submit to these tests showed that he had doubts of their success'.

Goaded beyond endurance, with his ambitions crumbling and his whole future in danger, Giovanni Sforza now defended himself by a calumny so fearful that when it was first repeated to him Cardinal Sforza 'had not dared to put it on paper'. But Ludovico had no such qualms, and when his cousin informed him 'that not only had he possessed the Madonna Lucrezia an infinite number of times, but the Pope had robbed him of his wife for no other reason than to possess her himself', he had no hesitation in repeating this atrocious accusation to every envoy attached to his court.

Had he made his accusation in a moment of anger, it could have been either forgiven or ignored. But from the dispatches of Scalona we know him to have hinted these suspicions at a time when he was still priding himself on being the Pope's son-in-law, and not only accepting but actually soliciting favours from him. Therefore, according to Scalona, Giovanni Sforza would seem to have been capable of living in harmony with a woman whom he believed to be an 'incestuous whore' right up to the moment when, goaded by fear, he struck with all the concentrated venom of a humiliated coward.

XIII

THE SCANDAL OF Lucrezia Borgia's divorce gave free rein to all the rumours which had hitherto circulated in private. Despite the protection of the apostolic mantle, the intimacies of her married life were now exposed to public comment, and scurrilous epigrams began to appear on the walls of Rome.

Two months had gone by since the Lord of Pesaro had fled the city, and threatened and harangued by her father and her brothers, Lucrezia had ended by signing the document demanding an annulment. But though she may have been secretly relieved to be rid of Giovanni Sforza, she had never envisaged he would be disposed of in this way, and that her father would force her to commit perjury by branding her husband with the cruellest and most humiliating of accusations. Whether in shame at her own action, or in open revolt against her family, her only gesture seems to have consisted in running away to a convent. And in the diaries of Marino Sanudo we read that on the 6th of June, 1497, 'the Pope's daughter arrived at the convent of St. Sixtus, *insalutado hospite*'.

For the first time Lucrezia appears to have acted against her father's wishes, for though the Pope attempted to convince the Cardinal Sforza that he had ordered his daughter's retirement to this '*loco religioso e onestissimo*', where she would stay until he had made the necessary arrangements for her to accompany the Duke of Gandia to Spain, the Cardinal had already heard other rumours of how the captain of the papal guard had been dispatched to St. Sixtus to recall Madonna Lucrezia to the Vatican, and of how angry His Holiness had been when the guard had returned without his daughter. But Ascanio Sforza kept his own counsel. As his brother's unofficial ambassador at the Vatican he had received orders to do everything in his power to facilitate the divorce.

The convent of St. Sixtus, where Lucrezia fled for refuge, is still in existence. Situated at the foot of the Aventine, it has known its periods of greatness and decline. To-day the nuns are for the most part women of the people, their pupils the children of the Roman slums. But in the fifteenth century the convent was renowned throughout Italy for its teaching, the prioresses were among the most cultured women of the Renaissance, and the inmates the daughters of the greatest patrician families.

Here Lucrezia came to face the first moral crisis of her life, seeking comfort from the nuns, who in her childhood had given her the only standards of decency she had ever known. For them her very presence was fraught with difficulties. Accompanied by her court, she introduced a disturbing influence into the even tenor of their lives. But how could they refuse hospitality to one who was not only the Pope's daughter, or rather niece (for the good nuns would never have dared to utter the word of father), but who was also the little girl they had learnt to love in the days when they prepared her for her first communion. So Lucrezia stayed on at St. Sixtus, and her father ended by respecting her wishes, while the whole of Italy reverberated to the scandal of her divorce.

But the Sforza divorce was only one of many Borgia scandals. Unpleasant stories concerning the Duke of Gandia were circulating round the town, and no young virgin or handsome page was said to be safe from his attentions. The loathing of the Roman nobles for this presumptuous Spaniard was no longer disguised. And one night at Cardinal Sforza's palace, where Juan Borgia had insulted one of the guests, the epithet of 'bastard' was hurled in his face. A brave man would have drawn his sword, but Juan went hot-foot to the Vatican to report this insult to the family honour. And the Pope, who was usually so wise and clement, acceded to his son's demands and sent his guards to arrest and summarily execute the impertinent offender.

Place-seekers were beginning to profit by the way in which His Holiness was gradually allowing his better judgment to be overruled by that of his sons. And the wary Scalona informed the Marquis of Mantua that 'if he wished to please His Holiness, he could do no better than to present his sons with the finest greyhounds and jennets in his stable'. But the princes whose states bordered on those of the Church were beginning to find that it needed more than the gift of horses and of greyhounds to placate the growing ambitions of the Borgias. The death of Ferrantino of Naples, the victim it was said of his own amatory excesses, and the succession of his Uncle Federigo, gave the Pope further opportunities for enriching his sons at the expense of Naples. And in reward for the lands and titles bestowed on the Duke of Gandia, His Holiness appointed Cesare Borgia, Cardinal of Valencia, as legate to Naples, with special powers to invest Federigo of Aragon with the hereditary succession to the Neapolitan throne.

It was on the evening of the 14th of June, 1497, two days before Cesare's proposed departure for Naples, that Vanozza dei Catanei gave an alfresco supper party for her sons in the cool of her vineyard outside the city. The tower and archway of what was once Vanozza's country house is still to be seen on the summit of the Esquiline. Trams and buses now clang through noisy streets where formerly a bridle path led through flowering orchards to the pasture fields around the Colosseum. In those days it must have been an enchanting site for a party on a summer's night and an evening made for harmony, with Vanozza, handsome and stately at the head of her laden table, and her husband dispensing his choicest wines in honour of his stepsons. Unfortunately there is little record of this supper, which in view of later events took on a sinister significance. Apart from Juan and Cesare Borgia, the only other person whom we know to have been present was their cousin, the Cardinal of Monreale. And so small and intimate a gathering makes it doubly strange that no one attempted to identify the masked figure who, after midnight, when the party was already drawing to a close, suddenly stepped out of the shadows of the vineyard, demanding to speak to the Duke of Gandia. During the past month Juan had constantly been seen in company of this same masked man. Or was it a man? We are not even sure of this. For it could just as well have been a woman in disguise, some joyous companion of his revels, who from love of adventure followed him on his nightly rounds of dissipation. Whoever it may have been, Juan's companion was taken for granted. And when the two Cardinals and the Duke left Vanozza's vineyard, the masked figure rode pillion on Gandia's mule. Laughing and singing on their way the young Borgias descended the hillside into the silent streets of Rome. It was already two in the morning when they came to a halt in the neighbourhood of what had formally been their father's palace, but which now belonged to the Vice-Chancellor Ascanio Sforza. Here they parted company, the two Cardinals crossing over the bridge into the Borgo, while the Duke of Gandia, after dismissing all his servants with the exception of one groom, and with his masked companion still beside him, turned off into the narrow streets leading to the Jewish quarter. Neither brother nor cousin appears to have warned him of his foolhardiness in venturing unprotected in a town full of his enemies. Maybe neither of them cared sufficiently, or if one of them cared it was hardly in order to safeguard a worthless and foolish brother.

The following day there were already rumours of the Duke of Gandia's disappearance. But it was only towards evening that the Pope began to grow alarmed, for Juan's amorous intrigues were of such a nature that he might well prefer to remain in hiding during the daytime rather than advertise some indiscreet affair. When night came and there were still no news of his son, the Pope began to make inquiries of the police and before long his alarm had degenerated into terror. For the discovery of the Duke's groom, lying mortally wounded and bereft of speech in an alley off the square of the Jews, left Alexander with little hope of ever finding his son alive. The Spanish guards were now called out to make a house-to-house search and, insulting the population, manhandling the Jews, they stormed through the streets, spreading chaos in their wake. The clash of their swords brought out the Colonnas and the Orsinis, till the tumult spread along the whole left bank of the river from the Piazza del Popolo to the Monte Savello.

At midnight, when no further discovery had been made, other than a riderless mule, which his attendants claimed to be that of the missing Duke, the police picked up in the neighbourhood of the Ripetto Bridge a Dalmatian wood-seller, who plied his trade on the river bank. Under threat of torture the wretched man confessed to what he had witnessed the previous night; how, after unloading his cargo, he had gone to sleep in his barge moored to the shore, when he had awakened at the sound of footsteps to see two men cautiously approaching the river. Finding it deserted, they had signalled to someone, who coming out of the shadows proved to be a rider on a white horse, carrying across his crupper what appeared to be a dead body. With the two men holding it by the head and the heels, the rider then brought his burden to the spot, from where daily the accumulated filth of the neighbouring streets was disgorged into the Tiber. Here the two attendants lifted the body from the saddle and flung it far out into the river. For a moment the rider lingered to make sure there was no trace of his victim. Then they all left as silently and cautiously as they had come.

It was a strange story as told by Giorgio, the wood-seller, and it was indicative of the times that, when questioned as to why he had not reported it before, he merely answered that 'in his day he had seen a hundred such corpses thrown into the river, without anyone troubling to ask questions'. Every fisherman in Rome was now sent to drag the river, and in the neighbourhood of the Tiber island, covered in weeds and scum, was found the body of the Pope's son. Disfigured by eight wounds, it was still fully dressed and there had been no attempt at robbery, for the jewelled collar was still intact and there were thirty ducats in the purse.

Borne in a covered barge, the remains of the Duke of Gandia were now transported to St. Angelo, where, after being washed, perfumed and dressed in robes of state, the body was seen for the last time by a despairing father. The passionate and unrestrained grief of one who till now had believed himself to be master of his own destiny, must have been terrible to behold. It was not only his favourite son, 'the very apple of his eye', whom he beheld as a mutilated corpse; it was also the crumbling of all his hopes of founding a princely line, for only a little boy in Spain, and Joffré, whom he had never regarded as his son, were now left to carry on the Borgia dynasty. Burchard describes how, when the funeral procession left St. Angelo by night bound for the Borgia chapel in Santa Maria del Popolo, above the dirges and the prayers, could be heard the heartrending sobs of the Borgia Pope coming from a lighted window in the castle.

For three days Alexander VI shut himself up in his rooms, refusing to take nourishment, while his terrified attendants clustered outside, listening to his continual weeping. By June 19th he had gained sufficient control of himself to reappear in public, and there was no one who hated him so utterly that they could not but feel sorry for him, when, looking for the first time like an old man, he mourned his son in front of his assembled court. In respectful silence, prelates and envoys heard him declare that 'had he seven Papacies, he would give them all to bring the Duke of Gandia back to life'. Grief had made of the Pope a genuine penitent. 'From now on,' he said, 'he would set no value on the temporal trappings of the Papacy but would only dedicate himself to the Church and to its government'. And in the presence of what they must have regarded as a miracle (and what to the majority must have been an embarrassing miracle), his cardinals heard him propose the long-postponed reform of the Church, with a special commission appointed to inquire into the abuses of the Curia.

Meanwhile the rumours had been gathering thick and fast. The dead Duke had many enemies, and motives for murder were not lacking. The Cardinal Sforza was suspect on account of the scene which had taken place in his palace, when one of his guests had been arrested on Gandia's orders. A certain Count della Mirandola was suspect because the Duke had attempted to seduce his daughter. Even the most valiant of condottieri, the Duke of Urbino, was accused of having revenged himself on the Borgias for the scurvy way in which they had treated him after the battle of Soriano, when they had left him to pay his own ransom as a prisoner of the Orsinis.

The nature of Borgia relationships was such that both the little Prince of Squillace and the Lord of Pesaro were included among the suspects, and in full consistory the Pope formally denied these rumours, declaring himself to be convinced of 'their innocence, and also of that of the Duke of Urbino'.

Giovanni Sforza appears to have been the first suspect, for

already on July 17th a dispatch from the Venetian ambassador reported as current Roman gossip:

> It is believed that the Lord of Pesaro has done the deed, because the Duke had intercourse with his sister, who is the Lord Giovanni's wife.

Avidly the enemies of the Borgias seized on this opportunity of connecting the Sforza divorce with the Duke of Gandia's murder. And convent walls were unable to protect Lucrezia from being involved in the scandal. So little is known of her relations with her dead brother, but in that complicated family atmosphere of mutual jealousy and fear, of love allied to hate, the impulse of a moment was sufficient to justify the satisfaction of every natural and unnatural desire. The same impulse which led Lucrezia to fire Cesare's jealousy by simulating affection for an unloved husband, may well have led her to revert to what from childhood she knew to be the most effective way of rousing his passion—by showing her preference for Juan. And if Juan, vicious and corrupt as we know him to have been, had insisted on this preference taking a tangible form, it would hardly have been in Lucrezia's nature to refuse. The Venetian ambassador repeated no more than the gossip of the day, but the fact that such gossip should have been in circulation was sufficiently incriminating to the reputation of the seventeen-year-old girl, who, in the biting couplets of Sanazzaro, was already being referred to as 'wife, daughter, and daughter-in-law of His Holiness, the Pope'.

XIV

THE MYSTERY of the Duke of Gandia's death remained unsolved, and amidst all the conflicting rumours and suspicions, the searchings and inquisitions, no one seems to have made any attempt to establish the identity of the masked figure who accompanied the young duke on his last nocturnal adventure. No second body was washed up by the Tiber. Juan Borgia met his death alone, while the companion of his revels disappeared into the night to resume whatever might have been his or her own existence. There can be little doubt that the Borgias themselves must have been aware of his identity, and for reasons of their own preferred to keep the matter secret. Barely three weeks after the murder of his son, the Pope ordered the police to stop their investigations, as if he had come to a conclusion he was frightened of making public. This reticence on Alexander's part is interpreted by certain posthumous historians as proof of the Pope having evidence of Cesare Borgia's guilt. But among all the conflicting rumours with which envoys and chroniclers filled their dispatches in the weeks which followed on the Duke's death, there is no mention of Cesare Borgia as a likely suspect, And it was not until nine months later, that a Ferrarese envoy writing from Venice in the month of February 1498, stated:

> I have again been given to understand that the Duke's assassination was the work of his brother, the Cardinal.

A rumour like so many others, but one which gradually hardened into fact, as the whole course of Cesare Borgia's destiny shaped itself in such a way as to make the murder seem not only logical but inevitable. But however circumstantial the evidence, however strong the motive, there is no definite proof of Cesare having been his brother's assassin. Fate may have conspired to bring about the circumstances, by which some nameless enemy removed the Duke of Gandia from his path, leaving him to claim what he regarded as his rightful heritage. 'Whoever did the deed', wrote the Florentine envoy Bracchi, 'it was the work of *un gran maestro*'; a curious way of describing a foul and dastardly murder, which for the moment had no other result than to gain Rodrigo Borgia sympathy even from his bitterest enemies. Even Savonarola, under threat of excommunication and at open war with the Vatican, was prevailed upon to write a letter of condolence to the Pope, whose nepotism he had publicly denounced from the altar. From Avignon came messages from the Cardinal della Rovere who, neglected and homesick at the French court, now used the Duke of Gandia's death as an opportunity for making his peace with the Borgias and preparing his return to Italy.

In his first transports of grief, the Pope banished his children from the city, as if their presence reminded him too poignantly of his murdered son. With a retinue greater than that of any visiting sovereign the Cardinal of Valencia set out for Capua, in the rôle of papal legate, accompanied by the Prince and Princess of Squillace, who had been banished to their Neapolitan estates.

Meanwhile Lucrezia stayed on at St. Sixtus, where Scalona describes her as 'overwhelmed with grief at her brother's death'. But the picture of Lucrezia as a tearful penitent at the altar of St. Dominic is hardly in keeping with certain events which took place in the early summer months of 1497. For the scandal of her divorce followed by the shock of Juan's murder which would have been sufficient to shatter a more delicate and sensitive nature, does not seem to have prevented her from finding consolation within a few weeks of her brother's death.

Little is known as to how or when Pope Alexander's favourite chamberlain, a handsome Spaniard by the name of Pedro Calderon, commonly known as 'Il Perotto', became Lucrezia's lover; whether he succeeded in winning her heart at a time when she was still the official wife of Giovanni Sforza, or whether the Pope himself brought them together by using Perotto as an intermediary between the Vatican and the Convent

of St. Sixtus. The lack of records leads to tantalizing suppositions for as a woman infatuated by her lover and longing to be
rid of her husband, Lucrezia would appear in a very different
light from the passive victim of her father's ambitions. But the
most likely conclusion is that this mysterious romance developed in the months which followed on her husband's flight
—the natural reaction of a woman at odds with herself and the
world, trying to find in some normal channel an escape from
her own obsessions. In her lover's arms Lucrezia could forget
the horror of her brother's death, her suspicion and fear of
those whom she loved the most. For the first time in her life
someone outside her family, as primitive and passionate as
herself, was able to give her a brief illusion of happiness. A
summer idyll doomed to die with the falling of the leaves, or
maybe already broken, when her brother returned from Naples
and her father, gradually recovering from his grief, turned his
attention once more to secular affairs and the final dissolution of
her marriage ties. At a time when every jurist in Italy was being
consulted over her divorce, when a special commission of
cardinals was probing into the intimacies of her married life,
when her wretched husband was being forced not only by the
Pope, but by his own relatives, to declare his impotence,
Lucrezia found herself with child by her father's chamberlain
—a man whom her family regarded as no more than a favoured
servant.

Not for this had the Pope perjured himself and his Cardinals,
asserting that his daughter's previous marriage contract to
Gasparo de Procida, Count of Aversa, had never been properly
dissolved, and that therefore her subsequent marriage was null
and void. Not for this had Cesare Borgia flattered and bribed
at the Neapolitan court, delicately letting fall that in the event
of his sister becoming free, His Holiness would have no greater
satisfaction than in seeing her married to an Aragonese prince.
For Lucrezia's divorce was not yet through before there were
plans for her second marriage, plans in which Pedro Calderon
could play no part, still less the child she carried in her womb.

Alexander was still mourning for the murdered Juan when
Cesare Borgia returned from Naples. And the fact that he was
received by his father in utter silence was interpreted by some

as evidence of the Pope having knowledge of his guilt. Others asserted that His Holiness was still so little master of himself that the presence of the son, who both in features and stature resembled his dead brother, affected him in such a way as to rob him of his speech.

But the volatile spirits of the Borgia Pope were quick to recover, and by the time the marble altar erected in memory of the Duke of Gandia, in the church of Santa Maria del Popolo, had been unveiled, the dead were already forgotten in the living. The jesters and musicians had returned to the Vatican and the Pope's interests were once more centred in his surviving children. It would have been better for Lucrezia had she been allowed to remain in the privacy of her convent. But she had no choice but to obey when a papal bull ordered her to return to the Vatican and to give public testimony on her divorce. It must have been a terrifying ordeal for a woman already six months gone with child, and one cannot but pity her when, on December 22nd, 1497, she was forced to appear in front of an assembly of envoys and cardinals on the occasion of the formal annulment of her marriage ties.

After all the resistance and recriminations, the bargainings and coercion, Giovanni Sforza had had to submit to the Pope's wishes. In a long and prosy Latin document, read aloud by one of the cardinals of the commission, Lucrezia (and one wonders whether she had the decency to blush) heard herself referred to as '*virgo intacta*'. Never had Adriana Orsini's education, her own natural powers of dissimulation, stood her in better stead, for the Milanese envoy Stefano Taberna writes that

> she comported herself with such elegance and grace, as to charm all who beheld her, while her speech of thanks to the jurists and cardinals of the commission would have served as model to a Cicero.

But for all Lucrezia's blandishments and arts, the clever draperies of her velvet gown, certain observant eyes cannot fail to have detected the secret she was at such pains to hide and once they had become aware of her condition, father and brother would have left no stone unturned to track down the presumptuous lover. It was barely two months later, on February 14th, 1498, when Burchard noted in his journal that

> the body of one of the papal chamberlains Pedro Calderon known as 'Il Perotto' has been found in the Tiber with a stone around his neck.

As usual Burchard confines himself to recording without comment, but Marino Sanudo's diary gives further details, telling of how

> Perotto has been found drowned in the river, together with a damsel of Madonna Lucrezia's court—one Panthasilea, who was known to have enjoyed the favours of the Pope.

A fortnight later a Bolognese envoy, Christopher Poggio, is even more explicit, in informing the Marquis of Mantua that 'the Pope's chamberlain is no more to be seen, after getting his master's daughter with child'.

Another and later version states that Cesare Borgia was responsible for Perotto's death, and the Venetian envoy, Paolo Capello, who arrived in Rome a year after the event, gives a dramatic account

> of how one day the Cardinal of Valencia came upon Pedro Calderon in the Pope's antechamber, and without any previous altercation attacked him with drawn sword, whereupon the terrified Spaniard fled before him till he reached the steps of the papal throne, where he begged his master's protection. But that though the Pope covered him with his own mantle, he was unable to protect his favourite from the fury of his son, who regardless of his presence drove his sword straight through the Spaniard's body, so that his blood oozed over the papal mantle and spurted into the Pope's face.

But what Paolo Capello relates as an established fact, is omitted by Burchard, who as master of ceremonies with his place behind the papal throne, would hardly have been likely to ignore a murder in the Pope's presence. Nor was there any reason for Cesare Borgia to demean himself by killing his father's chamberlain. For though Perotto was one of his favourites, Alexander would never have forgiven him the audacity of getting his daughter with child, and no sooner had he been suspected than he would have been immediately arrested.

Once she was back in her palace, and surrounded by her father's spies, Lucrezia was powerless to save her lover. One wonders whether she even tried to save him; terror of the condition in which she found herself, the humiliating subterfuges it entailed, even to the physical discomfort, may have been sufficient to kill a love which may never have been more than a physical infatuation. In the very days when Pedro Calderon was being committed to the Tiber, one of the Mantuan agents referring to her matrimonial prospects, stated that the

> Madonna Lucrezia was already showing a predilection for one of her suitors, the handsome young Duke of Gravina, of the Neapolitan branch of the house of the Orsini.

A fortnight later a cryptic dispatch from Ferrara, dated March 8th, 1498, reported as the latest news from Rome that 'the Pope's daughter has given birth to a son', the only reference to an event which the growing power of the Borgias made it wiser to forget or to ignore. And it was not until three years later that a nameless child suddenly appeared in the bosom of the Borgia family, whose identity gave rise to many strange conjectures and conclusions.

Lucrezia returned to the Vatican to find that Cesare had already usurped his brother's place in their father's affection. Little had changed and at the court, of which he had been the most brilliant ornament, Juan Borgia was already forgotten, forgotten so completely that neither the unfortunate widow nor the baby son he had left behind in Spain, appeared to be of any interest to the Pope. Maybe the Spanish princess had dared to voice aloud her suspicions of her husband's assassin. For we know her to have made a formal protest to King Ferdinand when the Cardinal of Valencia was appointed as administrator of his nephew's Italian estates. Even if she had been ordered by the Pope to bring her child to Rome, Maria Enriquez would never have obeyed him, fearing lest Juan's murderer might turn to strike her son. So the little Duke of Gandia stayed on in Spain to grow up under the tutelage of priests in the cloistered atmosphere of his mother's court, while in Rome his father's death went unrevenged, mourned for no more than a brief summer by the volatile and emotional Pope.

But if Alexander allowed the mystery of Juan's murder to remain unsolved and ordered the investigations to cease so soon after his death, it may have been a question of political expediency rather than of his own personal inclinations. Either he suspected the deed to have been instigated by the Orsinis, which would explain the inveterate hatred with which he pursued them to the end of his reign, or he had knowledge of the murderer being a member of his immediate family. And to the Borgia Pope, the unity of the family—already weakened by the loss of Juan—was too vital a part of his entire political system to be sacrificed even to the cause of justice. Outside of his family, there was no one he could trust, not one of his condottieri who would not desert him at a moment's notice. The Roman barons waged their traditional feuds under the very walls of the Vatican, with the papal guards powerless to interfere. And the consciousness of his military weakness gradually led the Pope to fall in with the plans of Cesare Borgia, when he returned from Naples fired with ambition to exchange the cardinal's hat for the standard of a captain of the Church.

In Naples, Cesare's behaviour had been neither that of a papal legate nor of a mourning brother. And within a week of his arrival he had fallen a victim to the terrible malady which had ravaged the country since the time of the French invasion, thereby deriving its name of *morbo gallicum* or *mal francese*. Rising from his sickbed to crown the king in the cathedral at Capua, 'his scarred and blotchy face and trembling knees' had made a poor impression on the Neapolitan court. Federigo of Aragon had no love for the Borgias, his family had already been made to pay too heavily for their friendship, and when with fair words and promises the Cardinal Legate offered his sister's hand in marriage to a Neapolitan prince, the King's instinctive reaction was to refuse, recognising this proposal to be but the first step in Cesare Borgia's secular ambitions.

These ambitions were now limitless. In Cesare's eyes the Aragonese dynasty was doomed, powerless to control a country disrupted by the French invasion. Now that Spanish help had been withdrawn, Federigo of Aragon was left without allies to support him, or son to succeed him, and as the price of the Borgia alliance, Cesare hoped to obtain both a kingdom and a wife. Within a month of his return to Rome, there was already gossip of 'the Cardinal of Valencia planning to relinquish his scarlet hat in favour of his brother, while in return he would have his brother's wife'.

By January the rumour had become more concrete. The Princes of Squillace were restored to papal favour and Sanchia was back on the old terms of intimacy with Cesare. Writing to the Marquis of Mantua, Christopher Poggio relates

> How every day his eminence of Valencia exercises in feats of arms and shows signs of becoming a right gallant soldier, so that it is thought that he will soon divest himself of the purple and take to wife the princess, his sister-in-law.

And the envoy adds

> However improbable this may sound I thought I had better communicate it to your Highnesses, for soon you may be hearing of a divorce between the princess and her husband, with the latter receiving the archbishopric of Valencia in exchange.

These were the rumours in circulation when Lucrezia re-appeared at the papal court. And it can hardly have been pleasant hearing to a woman who in the past months had been made to sacrifice lover and child to her brother's ambitions. With a feeling akin to apprehension she must have seen the clearing of the path to greatness, the ghosts so easily thrust aside, the alliances so easily broken—her own future once more in pawn—her own affections so casually disposed of, and for the first time her brother rather than her father acting as the arbiter of her destiny.

XV

IN THE MONTHS which followed on Gandia's death, we gradually see Alexander VI falling more and more under the influence of Cesare, allowing his own better judgment to be overruled, sacrificing his political loyalties to his son's inexorable ambitions.

With so few authentic portraits in existence and only the written word to testify to his charm, it is difficult to understand the extraordinary spell which Cesare Borgia exercised over his contemporaries, and strangest of all the hold he obtained over his father. For the Pope's relationship with his eldest son was different to his relationship with his other children. Even with Juan, his attitude had been no more than that of an over-loving, over-indulgent father. But with Cesare it was far more complicated, so that at times it seemed as if the Pope was in love with his son, talking of him by the hour to the foreign ambassadors, wooing him in public, yet curiously nervous in his presence, as if frightened of his possible reactions, recognizing in him what so many of his biographers have tended to ignore—that when Cesare came to the forefront of the political scene he was already a sick man, not always accountable for his actions. The illness he had caught in Naples, and of which the treatment was then in its first experimental stages, was to return at intermittent periods throughout his life. And it is interesting to note that one of the first medical tracts for the treatment of syphilis was written by the Pope's Spanish physician, Pedro Pintor, and dedicated to His Eminence the Cardinal of Valencia. There is no knowing what ravages this disease, which scarred Cesare's face, so that already in 1498 a chronicler was writing, 'It is not the moment for Valencia to think of marrying, as he is still marked with the *mal francese*', may not also have inflicted on his mind, making his sudden rages more difficult to control, accentuating the morbidness already inherent in his nature. Later when the disease had taken

11. Young noblemen like Cesare Borgia often settled their quarrels by the sword, as in these two plates from a fifteenth century Italian treatise on swordsmanship.

12. Young courtiers of Ferrara at the time when Lucrezia was Duchess of Ferrara. Detail from a fresco by Francesco del Cossa in the Schiffanoia Palace at Ferrara.

a greater hold on him, wild bursts of energy and of tremendous mental activity would alternate with long periods of lassitude, during which he would shut himself up in his rooms refusing to give audience even to the foreign ambassadors.

By the spring he had obtained the chief voice in his father's counsels, and the first sign of his political influence was in the change of the Pope's attitude towards Savonarola. Till now Alexander had displayed an admirable patience in his dealings with the fanatical friar, who in defiance of his ban of excommunication, preached open sedition in the Cathedral of Florence, referring to the head of Christendom 'as a broken instrument cast aside by God, whom he was not longer bound to obey'. Time after time the Pope had attempted to negotiate and even after Savonarola's conduct had forced him to resort to extreme measures, he still gave him the opportunity to make peace. But in the new year there was a sudden change in the Vatican policy. The Pope gave his open support to Savonarola's enemies and one of the two papal commissioners at the friar's trial was Cesare's old friend and mentor, Francesco Remolino, Bishop of Ilerda, who was later to become a cardinal through his influence.

Cesare Borgia's ambitions were of a nature to shock even an Alexander VI. To release the Cardinal of Valencia from his vows would entail an open quarrel with Spain. And despite his indifference to public opinion, His Holiness was aware that no Papacy could survive the scandal of an unfrocked cardinal marrying his sister-in-law. However loudly the Princess Sanchia might proclaim her husband's impotence, both a king and cardinal had witnessed the consummation of her marriage, thus making it impossible to repeat the procedure adopted with Giovanni Sforza. Nor was there the slightest chance of the King of Naples consenting to such an unholy alliance, when for the moment he was even refusing to contemplate a marriage between Lucrezia and Sanchia's brother, the seventeen-year-old Alfonso of Aragon, preferring to ally himself with his old enemy Milan, rather than have another Borgia in the family.

But circumstances favoured Cesare Borgia's plans. In April 1498, the sudden death of King Charles VIII of France gave a new aspect to Italian politics. The accession of Louis XII, the former Duke of Orleans, left Aragon and Sforza under no illusion as to the future intentions of France. For in his first speech from the throne, the grandson of Valentina Visconti solemnly laid claim to the inheritance of both Milan and Naples. The falling beam in the castle of Amboise, which had dealt King Charles his death-blow, was as fortunate to Cesare Borgia as the unidentified dagger which had stabbed the Duke of Gandia, for whereas his predecessor had never forgiven the Borgia Pope his refusal to grant him the investiture of Naples, Louis XII was willing to court the Borgias' friendship. Only through the complaisance of the Pope, could he hope to rid himself of his ugly and saintly wife, and marry in her place his predecessor's widow, Anne of Brittany, who added to her already considerable charms the dowry of the fairest province in France. To get his marriage from Jeanne of Valois annulled, Louis XII was ready to make an alliance with the Pope and to assist the secular ambitions of the Cardinal of Valencia, particularly if in encouraging these ambitions he could wean Alexander VI from his professedly Spanish sympathies.

No sooner did he receive the first news of this alliance than the King of Naples changed his attitude. And by June, his brother's bastard, the handsome young Alfonso of Aragon, was created Duke of Bisceglie and Prince of Quadrata in preparation for his marriage to the Pope's daughter.

For the second time, Lucrezia's fate was being determined by political circumstances. But this time she had every reason to rejoice, for the Roman chroniclers described Don Alfonso as 'the handsomest young man ever seen in the Imperial city'. And rumour has it that she fell in love on first sight, when unheralded and without ceremony he arrived in Rome, a hostage rather than a bridegroom.

Three days later the wedding took place in the Pope's private apartments, without any of the pomp and show in which the Borgias usually delighted. It was purely a family gathering and not a single ambassador was invited, though one of the Gonzaga confidential agents, a certain Archdeacon Gian-Lucido Cattaneo, managed to gain admittance to the papal throne room, where he witnessed the scandalous disorders which threatened to break up the wedding ceremony. No sooner had the guests arrived than a quarrel broke out between the followers of the Princess of Squillace and the Cardinal of Valencia with both Neapolitans and Spaniards drawing their swords to assert their right of precedence. The ineptitude of the papal guards was such that bishops and cardinals were involved in the fighting, which took place in the very presence of the Pope, who at one moment appeared to be in danger of being struck with a sword. It was hardly a propitious beginning for a wedding feast, but it appears to have had no effect on the Borgias. The delinquents, who were only imitating their masters' ways, were freely pardoned, and with his usual zest and gaiety, the Pope proceeded to enjoy his daughter's wedding.

This time Lucrezia appeared not as a timid but as a radiant bride. And as he bandied jokes with Ascanio Sforza, whom no false pride nor unpleasant memories had prevented from acting as sponsor to the young prince of Aragon, His Holiness was heard to say with his gusty laugh that

> at least there would be no question of an annulment, for one had only to look at the young couple to see how anxious they were to be finished with the formalities and to get on with the love-making.

Whereupon His Eminence smiled his subtle accommodating smile, for he had already been informed that the Pope's daughter had not even waited for the wedding day before giving her young husband proof of her affection.

Standing in his old place beside the bridegroom, the presence of Ascanio Sforza must have reminded Lucrezia of a day five years ago, when as a thirteen-year-old bride she had knelt beside a stranger, whom in the intervening years she had never learnt to love, still less to know. Whereas the seventeen-year-old bridegroom she had only met three days before, had never been a stranger from the time when he first smiled at her with Sanchia's eyes—those veiled blue eyes which promised long nights of love. It was easy to forget Giovanni Sforza with his fumbling, nervous gestures, easy in her present happiness to forgive him for those words, which had circulated the length and breadth of Italy, till they had reached the antechambers of the Vatican, where they had only succeeded in making her father laugh—that fat, rich laugh which now echoed through the vaulted rooms.

The setting was the same, with the Pinturicchio frescoes on the walls, the ceiling carved with the golden bull and papal crown, but so many of the protagonists had receded into the past. There was darkness beside her, where Juan once stood in his youthful pride and beauty. Five years ago he had escorted her across St. Peter's Square, acclaimed by a Roman crowd. Now he was an uneasy ghost haunting by night the fishermen on the Tiber, crying out for justice together with those other victims of St. Angelo, victims like Pedro Calderon, of whose death she had only heard spoken in whispers by her maids.

Others had vanished into obscurity, too timid or too wise to remain on the vertiginous ascent of papal favour. The Pope's familiars were few in number, being mostly confined to his relatives and the Spanish cardinals of his nomination. But even among the relatives there were now certain absentees. Adriana Orsini was still in favour, but both she and Julia were content to be matrons of Monte Giordano, rather than favourites of the Vatican. Their place had been taken by Sanchia, ever more closely linked in a complicated family relationship, in which royal and papal bastards vied with one another in their pride.

How did Lucrezia appear to a bridegroom who had come from a country where the very name of Borgia was distrusted and reviled and Sanazzaro's epigram describing Lucrezia as another Thaïs, '*Alexandri, filia, sponsa, nurus*' was generally quoted and believed. With the sensitive pride of the bastard, Don Alfonso knew that though his uncle the King had consented, even if unwillingly, to his marriage with 'this abandoned Thaïs', he would rather lose his kingdom than give his own legitimate daughter Carlotta in marriage to a Borgia. But however reluctantly he had come to Rome, by the day of the wedding, all his anger and resentment had vanished, for in those few days he had fallen under the spell of his Borgia bride and was prepared to dismiss as the foulest libel the accusations of his uncle's courtiers.

Five years had passed, but the woman who was about to

become Duchess of Bisceglie still looked as young and innocent as on the day when she first plighted her troth to Giovanni Sforza. Whatever memories had come to haunt her on her wedding day, they cast no shadow in her transparent eyes. The throat might be a trifle fuller, the parted lips more ripe for love, but she had still the same gentle mien, the '*dolce ciera*' which fascinated more than any classic beauty. A king's ransom hung about her neck in rubies, an enormous emerald glittered on her forehead, her golden robes were embossed in pearls with the arms of Borgia and of Aragon, but neither the weight of jewels nor formal stiffness of brocade could hamper her lissom grace. As one of the envoys noted: 'She walked as if on air'.

Eye-witnesses agreed that both bride and groom 'appeared to be very satisfied with one another'. Others echoed the Pope in saying that 'they could hardly control their impatience to be alone'. But some of the Neapolitan guests had an uneasy presentiment, when, conforming to an ancient custom, the captain of the papal guard extended a naked sword over the heads of the young couple. And a few silent prayers were whispered for the protection of the young prince of Aragon.

The wedding took place in private, but the festivities to celebrate the Neapolitan alliance lasted for several days with comedies and jousts and banquets, where we hear of His Holiness behaving 'like a young boy, full of gaiety and pranks', all the more surprising as it was in the heat of summer, and the atmosphere in the crowded rooms must have been so stifling as to exhaust many a younger man. The culmination to the festivities was a masque staged by the Cardinal of Valencia, in which he himself adopted the guise of a unicorn. As the mythical, heraldic beast, the emblem of virginity and pride, Cesare appeared before the assembled guests—a fabulous figure that might have escaped out of the dream-world of Pinturicchio's fantasy, strangely disturbing to those who already suspected him of coveting a royal scutcheon—a scutcheon undimmed by the shadow of the bar sinister. For now that Lucrezia was married to Sanchia's brother, Cesare had no longer any interest in securing his sister-in-law as wife. His ambitions turned to France, where Carlotta of Naples, King Federigo's daughter by a French princess, was being educated at the court of Anne of Brittany. The negotiations with King Louis had already begun, and on the success of these negotiations depended not only the future of Cesare Borgia, but the whole future of the House of Aragon.

Lucrezia and Alfonso were married, but from the first night, her brother's shadow loomed over their bridal bed. The Aragonese alliance rested on frail foundations, and Neapolitans in Rome still kept their swords unsheathed. Only the young lovers, passionate, sensual, and absorbed in one another, allowed themselves to be drugged into an illusion of safety. Lucrezia was at peace, for with a husband fashioned in Sanchia's likeness she lost her jealousy of Sanchia and of Cesare. It was as if for the first time she were meeting her brother on equal terms and could find it in her heart to pity him his restless discontent. They were constantly in one another's company, living in that closed intimate circle where even a Roman patrician found it difficult to gain admittance,

In the parks and gardens, open to their pleasure (for in those days every Cardinal had a casino in the surroundings of the city), the young Borgias indulged in those pastimes, which though they may have seemed primitive to a Giovanni Sforza were of a nature to appeal to a prince of Aragon. And in the letters of the Mantuan agent Cattaneo, we read of how one day in the park of Cardinal Ascanio's villa, in the neighbourhood of the Tiber island, the Cardinal of Valencia staged a vast bullfight

> in honour of his sister, her husband and the princess, his mistress, where together with fourteen other Spaniards he performed such miracles of valour that eight bulls were killed in the course of an afternoon.

Cattaneo's dispatch dated August 18th, 1498, shows that the bullfight must have been to celebrate the events of the previous day, when for the first time in many months, the Cardinal of Valencia made an appearance in the consistory to lay his case for dispensation before the Pope and the Sacred College. Forewarned of his demand, only half of the usual number of cardinals were present, the rest preferring to absent themselves rather than to be identified in such a scandal, or as Cattaneo writes,

> not wishing to give their sanction to an event which was bound to bring disaster to Italy by giving free rein to the ambitions of France.

As a humble suppliant the haughty Cardinal begged hearing of his colleagues, reciting in his soft persuasive voice the speech he held written in his hands, reminding them that it was not of his own free will that he had entered the Church, for which he had never had any vocation. 'It was his conscience', he told them, 'that now left him no other choice than to throw him-·self on their mercy and to crave their forgiveness, so that out of the love he bore them all they might see fit to release him from his vows. No sooner was he free', he assured them, 'than he would dedicate himself to the service of Italy and of the Holy Church, and first and foremost of his tasks would be to work towards a better understanding with France who had been the cause of all their miseries, and for that purpose he proposed to go himself to Louis XII as an ambassador of peace'.

No words could have been more fairly spoken, but they left his listeners under no illusions as to the Borgia's future intentions. Realizing that the speech had been written under the Pope's direction, the cardinals deemed it wiser to defer to the judgment of the Holy Father, who with all the sophistry at his command now set out to deceive an audience who had already interpreted his thoughts.

> The demand of the Cardinal of Valencia [said Alexander VI] was too grave a matter to be decided without deliberation and discussion. The problems and difficulties arising from such a question were manifold and much thought would have to be given to it before an answer could be made.

As Cattaneo remarked:

> No one was surprised to hear that Valencia was to keep his benefices until he had made sure as to what compensation he

was likely to receive from France both in the way of a dukedom and a bride.

King Louis had already been informed of the heavy price
he had to pay for the bill of dispensation which would rid him
of his unwanted wife. And the very afternoon, while Cesare
was demonstrating his prowess in the bull-ring and Cardinal
Ascanio's park re-echoed with excited Spanish voices, an
ambassador from France landed at Civita Vecchia, bearing the
letters in which his most Christian Majesty King Louis XII
presented his well-beloved cousin, Cesare Borgia, ex-cardinal
of Valencia, with the dukedom of Valence, 'a fine city on the
Rhone, bringing in a revenue of ten thousand scudi a year'.

With such a brilliant settlement in view the Pope could
spare himself any further deliberation, and not many days
elapsed before the Cardinal of Valencia was released from his
vows, His Holiness having come to the conclusion that this was
the only way of saving his immortal soul. And writing to the
Marquis of Mantua, Cattaneo commented with irony: 'Beware
of the designs of the father and of the son, for it appears as if
the Holy Ghost has very little to say in the matter.'

XVI

AT HEART, THE POPE was not feeling very happy about the French alliance. Whatever may have been his quarrels with the King of Spain, whatever angry words may have passed between them, as when King Ferdinand had asserted his right to be consulted on the choice of Spanish Bishops, the Borgia Pope was first and foremost a Valencian, distrusting both French and Italians with all the xenophobia of the Spaniard. The temporal weakness of the Papacy had led him to fall in with the plans of his ambitious son, even at the risk of incurring the open enmity of Spain. Nevertheless he continued to view Cesare's proposed journey to France with a certain distrust, and the pride with which he regaled the Cardinals with tales of Cesare's future greatness was partly in order to convince himself of the wisdom of his policy. In secret he brooded over Cardinal Ascanio's warning, who, when he boasted to him of how the King of France had requested his son's presence, answered half in jest,

> Beware, O Holy Father, for though your son is a proper man, well versed in feats of arms and clever into the bargain, if the King wants to have him near him it is for no other reason than that he does not trust you. Your Holiness may think him content to be the instrument of your plans, but take care lest you and your son may not be reaching too high, and that in falling down, you may not receive some very unpleasant knocks.

So spoke the wily Milanese Cardinal in words calculated to give the Pope many a sleepless night. But in opposition to Ascanio Sforza was his old rival Giuliano della Rovere who had come to the forefront of the political scene as the principal intermediary in the negotiations between King Louis and the Borgias. Since the invasion of Naples, della Rovere had been neglected at the French court, and now was ready to make his peace with the Pope by acting as sponsor to his son.

Alexander may have had doubts as to the wisdom of his policy, but Cesare had subjected him to an extent that he was ready to spend the most fantastic sums on impressing the King of France. The Pope who till then had prided himself on his tolerance, now resorted to the most shameful expedient to raise money for Cesare's retinue. And a fine levied on the Spanish Jews to whom he had given refuge from the Inquisition contributed to the cost of 'the pages dressed in cloth of gold, the horses shod in silver and the mules harnessed with golden chains, each separate chain a masterpiece of Italian work-manship!' Nothing was too good for the Duke of Valence, even the most private articles of his toilet down to the vase and urinal had to be fashioned of solid silver. In his anxiety to impress King Louis, the Pope betrayed himself for the first time as a parvenu. Fortunately, he was never to hear the King's sarcastic comment, 'that it was all too much for a little Duke of Valence'.

Meanwhile the other members of his family watched and marvelled, believing him to be bewitched by Cesare. And Lucrezia, who was as venal as her father, saw with regret the finest jewels from the papal treasury set aside for an unwilling bride. Alfonso and Sanchia had told her that their uncle the King of Naples would never consent to the Princess Carlotta marrying a Borgia, and she was subtle enough to notice that even her father seemed to have his doubts of the success of Cesare's enterprise. She saw the efforts he was making to overcome his natural revulsion when Cesare introduced French fashions at his court, his insistence on an escort of Spanish nobles accompanying his son to France by way of stressing his Spanish origin. But whatever Lucrezia noticed the die was now cast, and like the others her only duty was to applaud. As for the ambassadors, they also watched and marvelled, though not all were confident of Cesare's success. An unpleasant eruption on his face still marred his beauty, for though his illness was now dormant, it had left him pitted as with the smallpox, which was not likely to commend him as a suitor to the fastidious Carlotta of Aragon.

On October 1st, 1498, Cesare Borgia, ex-Cardinal of Valencia and now Duke of Valence, set out from Rome. But this time there was no triumphal procession down the Via Lata. The French alliance was still too much of an uncertainty to be proclaimed in public and only three cardinals saw Cesare off when he left the city by way of the Vatican gardens. He must have cut a gallant figure in the autumn sunlight, mounted on his bay mare, wearing a white satin doublet slashed in gold, a black velvet cloak and plumed bonnet. The deep tan on his cheeks helped to hide the tell-tale marks, a wig covered the remains of his tonsure, so that he still appeared to be in the full strength of his virile beauty. But for all his self-confidence and pride, his departure gave rise to uneasy apprehensions.

> Valencia has left for France, [wrote Cattaneo] and the ruin of Italy is confirmed. When he returns it will be at the head of an army, if indeed he returns at all, for it is not for the sake of his beautiful eyes, that the King loads him with favours, but because he can be useful to him.

For those who remained behind in the Vatican, Cesare Borgia's departure inaugurated a period of peace. And no one can have been more aware of this than Lucrezia, to whom the shuttered windows in her brother's palace meant freedom from his watchful eye. For the first time she must have been secretly relieved at his departure. It was not that she loved him the less, but that for the moment she was free of her obsession. It was now Sanchia's turn to be jealous, humiliated in her pride to be cast aside in favour of her cousin Carlotta. And Sanchia's bitterness against the Borgias, and more particularly against Cesare, was to have a disastrous effect on Lucrezia's married life. Beautiful, vicious, utterly corrupt, the Princess of Aragon was one of those women born to make trouble, and it was largely through her influence that her young brother first became involved in politics.

From the Pope's own testimony we know that Don Alfonso had neither ability nor brains. He was just a charming, good-looking young man, content to spend his days in hunting and his nights in love. As such, his father-in-law took pleasure in his company, delighting in his daughter's happiness, informing his ambassadors with pride that the Duchess of Bisceglie was already pregnant.

But however ardent a lover, Alfonso had no head for politics and his young wife was too dazed with happiness to notice the pitfalls which lay ahead, or to realize that the Spanish and Neapolitans who formed their court were gradually making it into a centre of opposition to the French alliance, while acting as mentor to the young couple, and more dangerous even than the Princess Sanchia, was Ascanio Sforza. Despite their public quarrels in consistory when the Milanese Cardinal did not hesitate to accuse His Holiness of handing over Italy to the French, and His Holiness did not hesitate to answer that no Sforza had a right to criticize his actions, when Ludovico had been the first to call the French into Italy, pope and cardinal were still on sufficiently intimate terms for Ascanio Sforza to hope that 'he might yet prevent Alexander VI from becoming the chaplain of the King of France'. So Cardinal Sforza continued to haunt Lucrezia's palace, teaching Alfonso of Bisceglie lessons in politics it would have been wiser he had never learnt.

Meanwhile, a French galley had landed Cesare Borgia at Marseilles, and in the papal palace of Avignon he had his first meeting with Giuliano della Rovere: two ambitious spirits, who for the time being had need of one another. Riding through Provence, the Pope's son paraded the luxury of Italy and Spain before the astonished eyes of the French peasantry. Was it for this, the people murmured, that they gave their contributions to the priests and bought their indulgences at so dear a price—so that this red-haired Spaniard could ride on horses shod in silver and dress the meanest of his lackeys in cloth of gold.

Coming from a country where all the petty princelings vied with one another in magnificence, borrowing from one another the golden plate and jewels for state occasions, Cesare Borgia failed to understand that in France, particularly at the court of Louis XII, where the parsimonious King was rarely to be seen wearing anything else but a beaver bonnet and woollen cloak, excessive luxury was looked upon as vulgar and out of place. The Duke of Valence's journey across France and his arrival at the court of Chinon aroused both wonder and comment, but it was the kind of comment which is aroused by a travelling circus, rather than a royal progress. The halberdiers dressed in red and yellow, the colours of the French King, the trumpeters sounding their silver trumpets, the sacred reliquaries carried by pages dressed in brocades such as had never been seen at court; above all the fantastic appearance of the young Duke himself, a-glitter with jewels from his bonnet to his boots of which even the leather was sewn with pearls, while round his neck was what a contemporary rhyme describes as:

un collier, pour en dir le cas que valait bien trente mille ducats . . .

None of this was of a nature to appeal to a generation who had fought at Fornovo, and who saw in this beautiful vainglorious figure no more than a priest's bastard. Della Rovere might write to the Pope, that 'the Duke of Valence is so filled with modesty, prudence and skill, and endowed with so many physical and moral attributes that he is the envy of everyone'. But to French eyes there was an element of the ridiculous about an unfrocked Cardinal in search of a wife. At the request of the King of Naples, five monarchs including Henry VII of England had written to the French King protesting against a Royal princess being coerced into marriage with an upstart Borgia. And though King Louis was ready to flatter Cesare as an ambassador from Rome, who brought with him the Bull of dispensation, which would rid him of his pious wife and make Anne of Brittany for the second time into a Queen of France, he made no serious effort to overcome King Federigo's opposition to his daughter's marriage. For what interest had Louis of France in encouraging an alliance, which would make of Cesare Borgia a claimant to the Neapolitan throne?

The Pope, who was usually so well informed, was for the first time kept in ignorance of the truth, for he only heard of the honours and the compliments, never of the rebuffs, when with studied insolence the French courtiers ignored the Duke of Valence and his Spanish gentlemen. While della Rovere assured His Holiness that his son was 'in high favour with the King and that everybody loved and esteemed him', certain

Spaniards in Cesare's suite were sufficiently indiscreet to hint the truth. A young cousin of Cardinal Lopez wrote back to Rome 'that though the King rode pillion with the Duke the honours paid him were somewhat like those paid to Christ on the Mount of Olives, for any day now they might be ready to crucify him'. And though Cesare himself would have been the last person to admit the possibility of failure, he had been unable to withhold the papal Bull of dispensation until King Louis had complied with his part of the bargain. His only compensation had been to dance at the King's wedding, where Carlotta of Aragon figured among the loveliest of Queen Anne's maids of honour.

Certain chroniclers report that so great was Cesare Borgia's fascination, that the proud princess of Naples melted before his ardent glances. Nevertheless she seems to have made no attempt to oppose her father's wishes, and she was still heard to say 'that for nothing in the world would she be known as La Cardinala'. Outwardly the King of France gave Cesare every opportunity to pursue his courtship, and when a Neapolitan embassy arrived in Chinon with a letter from their king, in which Federigo refused to sanction an alliance between his daughter and the Duke of Valence, the embassy was officially banished from court. But only a few months later, King Louis bestowed his blessing on the marriage between the princess Carlotta and one of his Breton Barons, and on this occasion the princess appears to have had no difficulty in obtaining her father's consent. It was to be an evil day for the House of Aragon when Cesare discovered that the King of Naples preferred giving his daughter in marriage to an unknown Frenchman rather than to a Borgia.

King Louis was married to his predecessor's widow, and in the French provinces troops were already being raised in preparation for the second Italian expedition. But still Cesare Borgia remained without a wife and Rome was rife with rumours. Men now dared to repeat in Lucrezia's presence what they would never have ventured to say before her father, and neither her husband nor sister-in-law were at any pains to hide their delight in Cesare's reverses. Was it true, as they asserted, that the brother whom Lucrezia had hitherto regarded as irresistible was ignored at the French court, not only ignored but actually mocked and that the Paris students had staged a burlesque of 'A Cardinal in search of a Wife'.

For the first time Lucrezia was made aware that there were certain families in Europe who refused to contaminate their blood with that of a Pope's bastard, and that though the King of France had assured Cesare that he had only to take his choice among the French princesses, the princesses themselves, or rather their fathers, were not showing themselves over-anxious for a Borgia marriage.

Also the Pope was beginning to have doubts of his son's success, suspecting that 'the French king was exposing him to universal ridicule'. And more dangerous than ridicule was the suspicion that the Cardinal Ascanio might have been right in warning him of the danger of Cesare becoming a French hostage. A pact between France and Venice, signed at Blois in presence of Cardinal della Rovere and of the Duke of Valence, at which the two negotiating powers agreed to divide among themselves the spoils of the duchy of Milan, was a clear intimation that Louis XII intended to carry out his plans with or without the co-operation of the Papacy.

'If his son had not been in French hands,' writes Cattaneo, 'there is little doubt but that the Pope would have made a counter-alliance with Naples and Milan'. In the Vatican Ascanio Sforza was once more in favour, the Duke of Milan was informed that the Pope would not tolerate any infringement of his territory, and despite King Federigo's intransigent attitude, the Aragonese party was still in the ascendant.

Lucrezia was happy and about to become a mother. As Cesare's hopes of providing him with a royal grandchild dwindled, the Pope made elaborate plans for the future of his daughter's unborn son. Both he and Lucrezia appeared to have forgotten the baby who had made its indiscreet appearance in the previous spring. But this time her pregnancy was less fortunate. Those high spirits which at moments led both Lucrezia and her father to behave as irresponsibly as children brought about a miscarriage. While romping with one of her damsels in Cardinal Lopez's garden (romping is the word used in the dispatch), Lucrezia slipped and fell, pulling the girl down on top of her. She was carried home and that night gave birth to a stillborn child.

At first the Pope appears to have been inconsolable at her loss. But sorrow with the Borgias was of a short duration. Barely a week later, during carnival, Alexander and his daughter were to be seen on the balcony of the Castle of St. Angelo, watching the traditional procession of mummers passing across the bridge. It was a spectacle in which they both delighted, and it was as characteristic of the fifteenth-century Romans to parade their pornographic masques and obscenities under the eyes of the Holy Father, as it was of the Borgia Pope to encourage his daughter to take pleasure in sights which most fathers would have preferred their daughters to avoid.

The pilgrims, who in expiation of their sins had walked barefoot the road to Rome, can hardly have been edified at the spectacle of the head of Christendom shaking with laughter at a procession of 'mummers travestied as priests exposing their secret members'. Nevertheless, the appearance of the Borgia Pope was still sufficiently magnificent to arouse the enthusiasm of the Roman crowds. His tall massive figure in his white and gold vestments, outlined against the background of Hadrian's fortress, appealed to their innate love of the theatrical, while his daughter with the smile that asked all men to love her, and the winter sunlight tangled in her hair, was so beautiful as to make even the most critical forget the scandals which of late had been gathering round her name. Their gay sensual faces reflected no doubts or fear, their laughing eyes held no unpleasant memories. Conscienceless themselves, they forced others to forget, yet it was in this very fortress that the Pope's own secretary Bartolomeo Floreo had recently died after being arrested on the charge of forging papal Bulls, and it was rumoured, that it was not so much the forging which had led to his arrest, as the fact that he had not handed to his master a full share of the profits. In the past few weeks Pedro d'Aranda, Bishop of Calahorra and former master of the papal household, had been flung into prison on the false charge of having secretly reverted to the ancient Hebrew faith, while his immense revenues had been sequestrated to contribute towards the cost of Cesare Borgia's journey. Wealthy prelates were beginning to absent themselves from Rome, so as to avoid exposing themselves to the Pope's cupidity. But to the general public Alexander still appeared as a kindly beneficent figure, father to all mankind, whose very failings only made him more tolerant and understanding of their own.

In carnival week, the Pope was capable of behaving as if he had not a care in the world. Yet worry and irritation were combining to rob him of his sleep. Both Spain and Portugal had sent special embassies to protest against the French alliance. Their ambassadors had not hesitated to use violent language in presence of His Holiness, to which he had replied in kind, even going to the lengths of casting aspersions on the reputation of the virtuous Queen Isabella, and threatening to have them thrown into the Tiber for their impertinence. But at heart Alexander was too much of a Spaniard not to regret the situation, and humiliation could go no further than when the Spanish ambassador taunted him in public—telling him the day would come, when as a lackey of France, 'he would be lucky if he succeeded in escaping in a rowing boat to Spain.'

But at the moment when papal prestige was at its lowest and the Pope was giving free vent to his bitterness against both France and Spain, came the news that Cesare Borgia had secured a wife. Louis XII had kept his promise by marrying the Duke of Valence to his own cousin, Charlotte d'Albret, daughter to the King of Navarre. Partly through bribery, partly through coercion, Alain d'Albret had consented to his lovely sixteen-year-old daughter becoming the bride of an ex-cardinal, and the wedding bells which rang out at Blois on May 12th, 1499, sounded the death knell to the Aragonese dynasty in Naples and the end to Lucrezia's peace.

XVII

IT DID NOT take long for Lucrezia to recognize her brother's marriage as a threat to her happiness. And never were her powers of dissimulation so strongly taxed as when, seated in her usual place on the steps of the papal throne, she listened to a seven-hour recital of Cesare's triumphs.

Travelling by night and day, a messenger had covered the distance between Blois and Rome in four days, and as a special concession he was allowed to sit in the papal presence, while, with the eagerness of a child, His Holiness questioned him on every detail of his son's courtship. It seemed as if the Pope could never tire of hearing of the honours paid to Cesare—of the rich presents given him by the King and Queen of France, and the alfresco wedding banquet on the banks of the Loire, where Cesare had entertained King Louis's court in a vast tent hung with tapestries and damask, while musicians played to them from a raft anchored in the river. 'An idyllic setting,' said the messenger, 'for the beauty of bride and groom, for never was a fairer couple seen in the whole land of France.'

But to Lucrezia, seated at her father's feet and pregnant for the second time within a year, every word of the recital spelled danger for her husband's future. Even if Charlotte d'Albret was reputed to be lovelier than Carlotta of Aragon, Cesare would never forget the insult received from the King of Naples. However much in love with his young bride, she knew her brother well enough to know that even at his wedding feast he would have found time to notice Carlotta of Aragon dancing with her Breton baron. Her father might profess to be delighted with the news, reading out in front of his assembled court the letter in which Cesare gave the most intimate details of his wedding night; roaring with laughter as he regaled his cardinals to the postscript in which King Louis congratulated him on his son's virility, admitting himself to be more than beaten in this field, by one whose sexual prowess was such 'as to have broken six lances in a single night'. But none of his audience were under any illusion as to the implications of the French alliance, and the humblest official in the Curia was aware that in giving Cesare Charlotte of Navarre for wife, Louis XII had tied his hands far more effectively than by assisting his marriage to a Neapolitan princess. For better or for worse the Papacy was now the ally of France. And Louis XII had made no secret of his plans, of which the two primary objects were the conquest of Milan and Naples. Cesare Borgia could no longer hope to satisfy his ambitions at the expense of Naples, and the fact that he had nothing further to gain from the House of Aragon, made Lucrezia and the Neapolitan party fear for the future.

The bonfires which blazed on the seven hills to proclaim the marriage of the Pope's son, 'to the scandal' writes Burchard, 'of both the Church and the apostolic seat', served as beacons of warning to both Milan and Naples. By the beginning of July the first French outriders had crossed the Alps and Ludovico Sforza discovered that in the whole of the peninsula he had not a single friend. Even his ally Naples remained neutral in the vain hope that the French might content themselves with the despoiling of Milan; while at the Vatican Cardinal Ascanio realized that he had exhausted his powers of persuasion, and that His Holiness was ready 'to sell the keys of St. Peter in return for a kingdom for his son'. So after handing over to the Pope the safe custody of his palaces and castles, and no doubt uttering a few last words of warning, the Cardinal set out from Rome, to take part in the defence of Milan.

By his departure Alfonso of Bisceglie lost his one friend and adviser. And if the powerful Vice-Chancellor of the Church deemed it wiser to absent himself from Rome, how much graver were the dangers which threatened the young Aragonese prince, whose uncle had dared in the face of Europe to insult the Borgias. We are left in ignorance as to what motives prompted Don Alfonso's flight, whether he was acting on orders of Naples or the advice of Milan. But barely a week following the Vice-Chancellor's departure, Lucrezia woke one morning to hear that under cover of the night her husband had fled the city. On August 4th a Venetian envoy informed the Signoria:

> the Duke of Bisceglie, Madonna Lucrezia's husband, has secretly fled and gone for protection to the Colonnas at Genezzano. He has deserted his wife, who has been with child for six months and she is constantly in tears.

Whether Lucrezia was taken into her husband's confidence or left in ignorance of his plans, her plight was equally pathetic —pathetic and ludicrous at the same time. Once more she found herself exposed to the shafts of ridicule and slander, and her first reaction to the news appears to have been an outburst of hysterical laughter. But the laughter was soon superseded by tears, the tears of a pregnant wife deserted by her husband, forced to escape from what he justly or unjustly believed to be the persecution of her own family. If it was Cardinal Ascanio who advised him to leave with the intention of embarrassing the Borgias, then those intentions were thoroughly successful for Lucrezia was miserable and her father was furious. It was in vain that the Pope sent messengers to fetch Don Alfonso back, in vain that he complained to the Milanese ambassador, suspecting it to be the work of Ascanio Sforza. All his elaborate pretence of maintaining neutrality, his efforts to temporize with Spain by granting ecclesiastical privileges to King Ferdinand, were set at naught by his son-in-law's sudden and inexplicable flight, which proved to the outside world that even their nearest relatives did not dare trust the Borgias.

Lucrezia's tears only added to the Pope's irritation. For once his family had failed him. In place of their usual light-hearted gaiety there were nothing but scenes of hysteria. Joffré, the youngest, and hitherto the most colourless of all the Borgias, so colourless in fact that his father was inclined to doubt his own paternity, was making up in dissipation for what he lacked in character. Emulating the unfortunate Juan he masqueraded in the streets at night in company of a band of dissolute companions, involving himself in drunken brawls, and fights with the police, 'with the result', writes Cattaneo, 'that one night he narrowly escaped his elder brother's death'. But the scandals of

Joffré, and the screams of Sanchia, who raged like a miniature fury through the Vatican, because her father-in-law refused to 'take action against the police who had acted in interests of the peace' were less embarrassing to the Pope than the tears of his beloved daughter.

For once Alexander was unable to distract Lucrezia by the gift of brocades or pearls. In her sad and lonely pregnancy she drooped and wilted before his eyes, making none of her usual attempts to amuse him with witty sallies or Spanish songs. It was as if the blue-eyed prince of Aragon had stolen away her wits. So obsessed was she with his image that her father even suspected her of planning to escape. And when his spies intercepted a letter from Don Alfonso begging her to join him in Neapolitan territory, His Holiness placed his daughter under guard.

Lucrezia was now bitterly aware of how little she could count on her father's love. It was not even in her power to alleviate Sanchia's lot, when in a fit of rage against the daughter-in-law whom he had always suspected of being a trouble-maker, the Pope banished the Princess of Squillace to Naples, without so much as defraying the expenses of her journey, declaring to the Milanese ambassador

> that if the King of Naples was so anxious for his nephew's safety as to place him under the protection of the Colonnas, then he could also enjoy the safe-keeping of his niece and pay the fabulous bills of her court.

'Let each man have his own,' said the Pope, and while Sanchia returned to Naples, Joffré remained behind in Rome to keep his sister company. But Pope Alexander was beginning to feel that Rome was not a very safe place for Lucrezia in her present mood. And in fear lest she might attempt to escape, he appointed her to the incongruous position of Regent of Spoleto. In bestowing on her this public honour, he removed her to a safe distance from Neapolitan intrigues, and it was characteristic of him to ignore the scandal of a nineteen-year-old girl being given a position which by right belonged to a cardinal, and of which the venerable priors of Spoleto would be the first to disapprove. Whether Lucrezia took pride in her strange appointment, or recognized it as an attempt to imprison her in a network of onerous duties, she appears to have accepted it in the only way in which it was possible for her to accept it—as a proof of her father's love and confidence.

On the morning of August 8th, 1499, the crowds gathered early in St. Peter's Square to see the Duchess of Bisceglie and the Prince of Squillace set out on their journey. His daughter's appointment had been proclaimed by Alexander with all due pomp and ceremony and as usual he was on his balcony to give the paternal blessing. But it was not so much a paternal blessing as an official benediction to the Governor of Spoleto on taking up her new duties. Every member of Lucrezia's escort had been specially chosen, for they were to serve not only as courtiers but as jailers. And at the head of a procession of priests and nobles, preceded by fifty mules carrying her baggage rode a woman six months gone with child, not daring to droop or falter before her father's watchful eye.

St. Peter's Square shimmered in the white glare of the August sunlight, the banners wilted in the windless sky and the crowds gathered round the fountains trying to borrow some coolness from the spray. But on his loggia the sixty-eight years old Pope stood firm and erect in his heavy vestments and as they passed beneath his palace Lucrezia and Joffré made every effort to emulate their father's bearing. Only later, when they had passed out of the gates of Rome, would Lucrezia be able to relax in the litter the Pope had ordered for her comfort, a litter lined with scarlet satin, with embroidered curtains and cushions of ivory damask, where hidden from public gaze she could dream her secret thoughts and plan for Alfonso's future.

Bravely she smiled at the cheering crowds, gaily she chattered to her brother and the Neapolitan ambassador, who accompanied them to the entrance of the Borgo, deliberately treating them in public as princes of the House of Aragon, rather than as Borgias, but at heart she must have been sick and frightened, and the road which led northwards to the Apennines only took her further from Alfonso. By now she can have had little faith in her father's promises, and when five days later she saw the fortress of Spoleto outlined against the elms of

Monteluco, not even the refreshing green of the Clitumno valley nor the serenity of the Umbrian landscape could rid her of the feeling that she was not so much a governor as a prisoner.

In reality the Pope was as anxious as his daughter to put an end to an embarrassing situation. In the last days of August the captain of the Papal Guard, a Spaniard by the name of Juan Cervillon, noted for his loyalty to both Aragons and Borgias, was dispatched to Naples to assure the sceptical king not only of the Pope's goodwill, but of his absolute neutrality in Italian affairs. Federigo of Naples allowed himself to be persuaded that it was still possible to come to terms with the Borgias, and Lucrezia had barely been in Spoleto a month before she was joined by her husband. For a few days the grim fortress of Gil d'Albernoz re-echoed to their happy laughter, while the staid old priors of Spoleto basked in their regent's smiles. But only for a few days, for on September 25th a messenger from the Pope summoned the Duke and Duchess of Bisceglie and the Prince of Squillace to a family council at Nepi, the castle which Ascanio Sforza had been sufficiently unwise to leave in custody of the Pope.

In France the last days of Charlotte d'Albret's married life were drawing to a close. For over four months she had lived happily with her husband. And as far as it was possible for Cesare Borgia to feel affection for any woman other than his mother or his sister, he may be said to have loved his wife. He not only loved her, but what is even stranger, he trusted her, as is proved by the fact that when he left for Italy, he appointed her as sole administrator and trustee of his lands in France. Valencia had become Valence and by a trick of fate, or at his own request, so as not to lose a title to which 'he was seemingly so attached' the signature Valentino remained unchanged. But there was no more question of Cesare Borgia settling down in his dukedom of Valence than there had ever been of his visiting his Spanish see. When he left his wife to accompany King Louis on his triumphal entry into Lombardy, he was still in search of a kingdom and he had no intention of renouncing his ambitions even for the sake of the most charming of wives. When Charlotte d'Albret wrote to her august father-in-law, telling him with all the ingenuousness of her sixteen years, 'of her love for her husband and her contentment with her married state', she did not realize that to the Borgias she was already no more than a name inserted in a treaty of which the principal clause was a military pact with France.

For the sake of the French alliance, His Holiness had risked incurring the enmity of Spain and Portugal. In the past months he had had many anxieties and doubts. But no sooner did he hear of the first French successes in Italy and of Ludovico Sforza's flight to the Tyrol, than he knew the moment had come when he could put forward his own claims.

Lombardy had welcomed the French, Cremona had fallen to the Venetians, who now hurried into action to make sure of their spoils. Florence, Siena and Lucca all hastened to join the winning side. And on October 6th, 1499, Louis XII entered Milan, not as a conqueror but as its rightful sovereign by virtue of his grandmother Valentina Visconti. In his train rode Cesare Borgia and Giuliano della Rovere, the one so young and hand-some—'so handsome' writes Baldassare Castiglione 'that both by his natural beauty and the adornment of his person, he out-shone all others', and in contrast, the middle-aged Cardinal with his strong rugged features and powerful frame more fitting to a suit of armour than a priest's gown—a man whose ambitions were as limitless as those of Cesare, but who unlike Cesare could still afford to wait.

At Nepi the Pope celebrated the fall of Milan in characteristic fashion by dispossessing Ascanio Sforza of the town and castle he had given him in reward for his services, and handing them over to his daughter and her heirs. Lucrezia thereby became the ruler not only of Spoleto, but of vast lands and baronies, including both a bishopric and castle situated on the strategic highway between Rome and Viterbo. To the neighbouring barons this fresh example of papal nepotism served as a warning, that if the Pope bestowed these lands upon his daughter, what limit had his ambitions for his son?

The extent of these ambitions was first revealed at the family council at Nepi, when in the presence of Cesare Borgia, who had ridden down from Milan, the Pope outlined the plans he intended to carry out with the assistance of his French allies.

They were founded on what had been his policy since the days of his accession—the suppression of the Roman barons, followed by the destruction of the states of the independent vicariates of the Romagna, and the centralization of the states of the Church under a single government. It was only in one respect that these plans had changed. From now on the whole temporal power of the Papacy was to be centred in the person of Cesare Borgia. As Lord Lieutenant of France and Captain of the papal armies he was to take the field against the rebellious vicariates of the Romagna, and in the rôle of Gonfalonier of the Church, conquer for himself a kingdom.

XVIII

O<small>N HER RETURN</small> to Rome from the family council at Nepi, Lucrezia began to take an active part in politics and to appear in open opposition to her brother. Till now she appears to have been unconscious of the way in which the various elements opposed to the French alliance were making her court into the focal point of their intrigues. But at Nepi she realized the extent to which the Papacy was committed to the French alliance, and how dangerous it was both for her own and her husband's future. The time had come when she had either to fight of her own accord or be sacrificed to Cesare's ambitions. Her love for Alfonso and the terror of losing him gave her an added strength and force of character. And in those last weeks of pregnancy, when a woman's normal instinct is to relax in peace, she continued her daily visits to the Vatican, wooing her father by all the means in her power, flattering his vanity, pandering to his tastes by bringing to his notice all the youngest and prettiest of her maids of honour. So well did she succeed that the ambassadors noted that 'Donna Lucrezia is more than ever in her father's favour'. Before long her sister-in-law Sanchia was summoned back from Naples, and the Pope, who at heart was so much more at home with his Aragonese relatives than with the French, sought refuge from politics in the pre-eminently Spanish atmosphere of his daughter's court.

Her pregnancy was another factor in Lucrezia's favour. When on the 1st of November she gave birth to a son named Rodrigo after his grandfather, the Pope is reported to have 'been nearly hysterical with joy'. With regard to his grandchildren Alexander VI appears to have been as inconsistent as in the rest of his behaviour. He openly neglected the little Duke of Gandia, declaring him to be the responsibility of the King of Spain. When Charlotte d'Albret gave birth to a daughter, neither he nor Cesare displayed much interest, but when it was a question of Lucrezia's son, then he showed himself a doting and loving grandfather. And through Rodrigo, Lucrezia hoped to save both her husband and the Aragonese dynasty.

As Cattaneo writes in one of his dispatches:

> The Pope is so mixed up with his family alliances and relationships, that he gives promises first to one side, then to the other and as the result is distrusted by all.

Even now the Mantuan agent had the impression that, left to himself, the Pope would willingly have broken off his alliance with France. But Louis XII was in Milan, the Sforzas had fled to Germany, and in the French camp Cesare Borgia was impatiently awaiting the arms with which to begin his campaign.

Only a few days after the Pope had returned from Nepi a Bull was issued from the Vatican, proscribing the tyrants of Imola, Forli, Pesaro, Faenza and Rimini for having omitted to pay the census due to the Apostolic See and thereby forfeiting their rights to act as vicars of the Church. Simultaneous with the publication of this Bull the papal armies marched into the Campagna to attack the fortresses belonging to the Gaetanis, who as hereditary vassals of Naples were to be the first of the Roman Barons to be despoiled of their lands.

The baby Rodrigo was born to the sound of the soldiers parading in St. Peter's Square, soldiers about to march against the allies of his house. And in contrast to the trumpets of war, the hammers of the stonemasons completing the new road leading from the St. Angelo Bridge to St. Peter's, which the Pope was to inaugurate on the first day of the Jubilee year of 1500. All the leading senators and cardinals assisted at his christening which took place with royal honours in the Sistine Chapel. The Cardinal of Naples officiated, assisted by Francesco Borgia, Archbishop of Cosenza, an illegitimate son of Pope Calixtus III, and all day long the courtiers came and went in the palace of Santa Maria in Portico, where pale and exhausted from a long and difficult confinement, Lucrezia lay in her great bed of state, under a canopy embroidered with the royal arms of Aragon. But though in her present state of weakness she

would willingly have dispensed with the presents and the compliments, she was too much her father's daughter not to appreciate the importance of these ceremonies. No ally was too
humble, no acquaintance too casual to be ignored at a time
when the Vatican was already full of her brother's spies. This
pompous christening in the presence of the foreign ambassadors
gave her the courage to believe that her father had not yet
decided to sacrifice the Aragonese alliance, that at heart he was
still too much of a Spaniard not to resent and distrust the pretensions of King Louis of France. When he visited her bedside
beaming with pride at the baby Rodrigo, declaring like any
other doting grandfather, that 'already he saw a likeness to
himself', Lucrezia's natural resilience may have reasserted
itself sufficiently to enable her to envisage the future with
confidence.

As the ambassadors and cardinals gathered round her bed,
offering their rich gifts, she may have remembered that other
christening, two years ago, when hurriedly and secretly by
night, her father's cousin, Francesco Borgia, had baptized an
unwanted child. As the Pope promised her honours and titles
for Rodrigo, she may have reminded him of the other promises
he had made when she clung to him in fear and shame. But
she was still so young that instinctively she may have thrust
into the background both the unpleasant reminders of the
past and the uneasy fears for the future, gathering comfort
from her father's pride and the knowledge of her husband's
love.

Prodigal with her smiles she listened to the compliments of
the ambassadors, the eulogies of the poets, those men who
earned their living by wandering from court to court, heaping
extravagant praise on the patron of the day. They were all
there—Serafino of Aquila, Bernardo of Arezzo, known as
'l'unico Aretino', Francesco Sperulo, Evangelista Capodiferro
uniting in their praise of the Pope's daughter, 'who was chaster
than the Lucrezia of old, daughter not of man but of Jove'.
Lucrezia was cynical enough to accept the panegyrics of the
poets for what they were worth, knowing that the same pen
which composed the Petrarchan odes, was equally capable
of concocting the scurrilous libels which circulated round the

taverns, but for the moment she had need of both flatterers and friends.

Rodrigo of Aragon was christened and barely a week later Cesare Borgia paid a secret visit to Rome, introducing a disturbing element into the family idyll of the Vatican. The sight of the Pope fondling his baby grandson and of Lucrezia's affection for her Aragonese husband were not calculated to please a man who had made too many sacrifices on the altar of his ambition to tolerate any human weakness on the part of his family; while the continued presence of Alfonso of Bisceglie only served as an unpleasant reminder of an obsolete alliance. Personal envy may also have played a part, envy of Lucrezia's happiness, the happiness he denied himself when he parted from the young wife to whom for a short while he appears to have been devoted, for the letters to Charlotte d'Albret written in the first year of their separation are those of a loving and considerate husband. Whether his affection was sincere, or merely part of his diplomatic flattery of France, he gradually let her fade out of his life, another of those human ties which only served to impede his plans.

Among the madrigals which circulated round Florence in the early days of the sixteenth century, is a song reputed to have been a favourite of Il Valentino's and which may well have been inspired as a tribute to his absent wife.

> *Donna contro la mia voglia,*
> *Mi convien da te partire*
> *E non creder per fuggire*
> *Del tua amore mai mi spoglia.**

So runs the refrain of a song, light-hearted even in regret, a song which can have brought little comfort to a young wife left lonely and pregnant in her castle in the Dauphiné. But there were certain ties Cesare could never ignore and the jealousy which was the most human part of his character now flared into being at the sight of his sister's happiness.

> * *Lady if against my wishes,*
> *I am forced to leave you now,*
> *Do not think, that the escaping*
> *Will divest me of my love.*

For the first time he recognized Lucrezia as an opponent, detecting her wiles, the subtle way in which she manoeuvred so that only her friends and allies should enjoy the favours of the Pope; the ability with which she had already persuaded him to hand over to her son the properties confiscated from the Gaetanis, as if any woman, let alone a princess of Aragon, had the right to own such extensive territory in the neighbourhood of Rome. The curious thing was that as an opponent, Lucrezia appears to have fascinated her brother more than in the days when she submitted meekly to his wishes—for with Cesare, jealousy was an essential part of passion. All his hatred was now concentrated against Alfonso of Aragon and his Neapolitan entourage, who openly proclaimed their distrust of 'Il Duca Valentino'. They had good reason to fear, for already Cesare had given proof of how easily his enemies could be eliminated. The Spanish Captain who had accompanied the Duke to France, and who on his return had spoken too freely of the rebuffs suffered at the French court, was one night committed to the Tiber. Only a few weeks after he had carried the baby Rodrigo to the christening font, Juan Cervillon was found stabbed outside the house of his nephew, Don Teseo Pignatelli. Some said his death was caused by his having spoken dishonourably of the Princess Sanchia, but it was more generally believed that after asking for leave to return to the service of the King of Naples, Cervillon was rendered suspect to the Borgias as a man who knew too many of their secrets.

While Alexander VI sat in council with his cardinals, discussing the Jubilee celebrations, and the Roman craftsmen put the last touches to the golden door which according to time-honoured tradition, the Holy Father was to open on Christmas Day, envoys and agents accredited to the papal court were beginning to refer to the mysterious disappearances and sudden deaths of those who had ventured to incur the despleasure of the Pope's son. And the laconic phrase of '*Ha bevuto*' made its first appearance in dispatches.

But if the Borgias used poison as a silent and efficacious means of ridding themselves of their enemies, it was a habit they acquired not so much from their Spanish ancestors as from their Italian contemporaries. Coinciding with the news of a certain white powder with slow-working but deadly effect, which was being administered to the prisoners of St. Angelo, came the news of a bold and desperate attempt to poison the Pope, said to have been instigated by Caterina Riario Sforza, whose two cities of Imola and Forli were first on the proscribed list of the vicariates to be won back for the Holy See.

It was towards the end of November when the peace messengers from Forli arrived in Rome, and by their suspicious behaviour attracted the attention of the police. They were arrested and put to the question, when they confessed that the letter they carried in a hollow stick carefully bound up in cloth, and said to be a petition to the Pope from the citizens of Forli, was in reality impregnated with a deadly poison.

One can picture the consternation in the papal entourage, the terror of the Pope's children, who having always regarded their father's person as inviolate and sacrosanct, now saw on what perilous foundations rested their own security. For though the Borgias, in common with the majority of their neighbours, might look upon poison as a legitimate weapon, till now not even the most hardened of sinners had dared to plot against the life of the Vicar of Christ. Caterina Sforza however had been nurtured in a hard school. The natural daughter of Duke Galeazzo Maria Sforza, she had seen her father assassinated on the steps of the Cathedral of Milan. At sixteen she had been married to Pope Sixtus's nephew, the brutal and sadistic Girolamo Riario, Count of Forli, to whom she brought as dowry the neighbouring town of Imola. A few years later he also fell a victim to the fury of the mob who in her very presence hurled his naked body out of the castle window of Forli. With a savage determination she had avenged his death and maintained her power, only to see her second husband, Gia-jacomo Feo, assassinated in the same castle. This time her vengeance had spent itself in blood lust. Pursuing the assassins to their homes, she had every man, woman and child in the village hacked to pieces.

Of such mettle was the female warrior who was to be Cesare Borgia's first opponent in the Romagna, described by her contemporaries as 'a cruel virago, but a great-hearted

woman, equally ardent in love and war'. Posthumous historians have tried to prove that Caterina had no part in the
attempt on the Pope's life; that it was nothing more than a
fabrication of the Borgias to justify Cesare's behaviour against
a woman, whose courage won her the admiration even of his
French allies. But in reality the granddaughter of the Condottiere Francesco Sforza was both in cunning and in martial
prowess fully a match for the ex-cardinal, who till now had
never seen a battle. Her weakness was that she could only rely
upon herself and a few devoted lieutenants, whose loyalty she
rewarded by inviting them to bed. The people as a whole
detested her, and the name of Riario was execrated throughout
the Romagna, so that before Cesare's armies had crossed the
Apennines the citizens of Imola were already preparing to
surrender.

Louis XII returned to France, leaving a French governor
in Milan and, in accordance with his treaty with the Papacy,
two of his ablest captains in command of the eighteen hundred
cavalry and four thousand infantry which were to be placed at
the disposal of the Duke of Valence. Cesare was now ready to
take the field, and by one of those dramatic coincidences of the
Borgia reign, he entered Imola on the same day that in Rome
the papal court was gathered in St. Peter's to give thanks for
the safe deliverance of the Pope. Both the Duke and Duchess
of Bisceglie are recorded as being present on this occasion,
accompanied by the Neapolitan ambassador, who still stayed
on in Rome, hoping by the Duchess's influence to retain
the Pope's neutrality.

It must have been half in relief and half in fear that Lucrezia
saw her brother depart for the Romagna, not knowing as to
what his success might bode for the future. As the woman who
had attempted to assassinate her father, Caterina Sforza inspired her with nothing but revulsion. As a child she had
listened in terror to the guns of St. Angelo booming across the
Tiber, and been told of the redoubtable Amazon who was
holding out against the cardinals. As Countess of Pesaro, at the
time of the French invasion, her husband's cousin had been the
first among their neighbours of the Romagna to raise the
standard of revolt against the Apostolic See. So now she felt no

14. A court lady of Ferrara, from a series of sixteenth century Italian prints illustrating the coiffures of the different courts of Italy.

15. An allegorical fresco from the Salon of the Months in the Schiffanoia Palace at Ferrara, painted by Francesco del Cossa, provides a glimpse of the court ladies of Ferrara in Lucrezia's time.

pity for the Countess of Forli in her unequal struggle against the combined forces of the Papacy and France.

Nevertheless she feared that every success gained with the arms of France was another blow at Naples. And when in the early dawn of November 28th the whole of the papal court was woken up to share in the Pope's joy at the news of the taking of Imola, it must have been with a heavy heart that Lucrezia and her husband crossed over to the Vatican palace to offer their congratulations.

All her talents as a woman were now deployed to sustain the Neapolitan party. Every rumour of trouble in Cesare's camp, of quarrels between her brother and the French captains, was eagerly seized upon and repeated. But for once it seemed as if Cesare were able to curb his violent temper, and men spoke of the miracles he was accomplishing in smoothing over the difficulties between the French soldiers and his own Italian mercenaries. A week after the fall of Imola, he was already administering justice in the town, and on Christmas Day he entered Forli in triumph, while in the fortress above the town Caterina Sforza prepared her last desperate resistance.

XIX

ON JANUARY 1ST, 1500, the bells of a hundred churches rang in the year of jubilee, promising redemption to the pilgrims who were flocking into Rome from the four corners of the world.

First among the pilgrims to inaugurate the Holy Year was the Pope's daughter, who in company of her husband the Duke of Bisceglie and the Prince and Princess of Squillace passed in solemn procession from St. Peter's to the Lateran. All the Spanish blood of the Borgias asserted itself on these occasions, combining piety and pomp, devoutness and superstition. Not on foot but on horseback, not in sackcloth but in velvet, preceded by a cavalcade of two hundred Roman and Spanish noblemen, escorted by her chaplain and the captain of the Papal Guard, Lucrezia appeared as the fairest and most indulged of penitents. But at heart she may have been as sincere as the humblest pilgrim who had trudged the way from Germany or France. The buoyant optimism she had inherited from her father had helped her to retain throughout the vicissitudes of her life the simple unquestioning faith of her childhood. Scrupulous in their observance of the outward forms of religion, rigidly adhering to the dogma of the Church, neither Pope Alexander nor his daughter appear to have had any doubts as to their ultimate salvation. And the Romans, who delighted in the public show of a religious festival, cheered Lucrezia Borgia in the rôle of penitent, as they would have cheered the leading actress in a favourite play. The beauty of Alfonso and Lucrezia, their ready smiles, their easy wit made them the favourites of the Roman crowds. Past scandals were gradually forgotten at the sight of this young couple, so charming and so in love, and with that showmanship natural to all the Borgias, Lucrezia lost no opportunity of exploiting her popularity.

Some verses of Aretino dating from these days show her in the rôle of peacemaker, presiding at a banquet in the Vatican, seated between the Neapolitan and French ambassadors, who were both rivalling for her favours, and in the words of the poet, 'content to conquer with her eyes, where they had to resort to arms'. The whole of Europe seemed to be flocking to Rome in the first weeks of Holy Year, and at those interminable audiences, where even Burchard grudgingly admits that 'the Pope never spared himself', Lucrezia was to be seen seated on her golden cushion on the steps of the papal throne. Whether sunning herself on the loggia of her palace, with her maids dressing her hair in public, or mingling with the pilgrims in St. Peter's Square, or praying as a penitent at the tomb of the Apostles, Lucrezia was always careful to keep herself in the forefront of the scene. And her ever-growing popularity was noted and reported by her brother's spies.

Spies and counter-spies—Spanish—French—Neapolitan— most of them accredited to the Curia in some capacity or other —the Vatican teemed with these silent unobtrusive figures who delved into the secrets of St. Angelo and probed the mystery of many an unsolved murder. Rome was beginning to have an increasingly unhealthy reputation, and a growing fear of the Borgias was preventing some of the neighbouring princes from making the accustomed pilgrimage. The Pope's ambitions for his son were now known to be limitless, and there was not a lord in the Romagna or the Marches who did not fear lest he might be the next on the proscribed list.

A letter from the Marquis of Mantua to his sister, the Duchess of Urbino, begging her to renounce a pilgrimage 'so fraught with dangers', is characteristic of the attitude even of those who outwardly professed to be on friendly terms with the Borgias. The letter arrived when the Duchess had already set out on her journey, 'which could not be abandoned without affecting both her own and her husband's honour'. But apart from visiting the four Basilicas she appears to have ventured into Rome as little as possible, deeming it wiser to stay under the protection of the Colonnas in their stronghold of Marino. The ruthless manner in which the Gaetanis had been dis-possessed of their castles and flung on false charges into prison, had frightened the Roman barons into living in a perpetual state of siege. For whatever might be their own personal relations with the Pope, whatever promises he might make them in his soft and lisping voice, they remembered how Onorato Gaetani had been flattered and caressed, to the day when he was suddenly arrested and committed to the dungeons of St. Angelo.

But none of these princes, who in their secret correspondence showed such a loathing for the Borgias, made any attempt to assist Caterina Sforza in her unequal struggle against Il Valentino and his French allies. And in the mud and sleet of the Romagna, the heroic defence of the citadel of Forli was entering its last phase. Treachery from within the fort forced Caterina to surrender three weeks after the city had opened its gates to the conqueror. But even in defeat she still displayed the cunning natural to her house, in deliberately stirring up trouble between the allies by declaring herself to be the prisoner of France, rather than of the Pope. Not only was it against the laws of French chivalry to hold a woman as a prisoner, but the French captains and in particular the cavalry commander, the impressionable Yves d'Allegres, who on a former occasion had shown such courtesy to another beautiful prisoner, Julia Farnese, was already half in love with the intrepid Amazon and determined to protect her from falling into Cesare Borgia's hands.

The dissension among the allies was assuming serious proportions. While every French captain was said to be 'as arrogant as if he were the king of France himself', the Duke Valentino was reported to hold his allies in particular aversion on account of the appalling behaviour of the troops, who behaved as soldiers in a foreign country, pillaging the peasants and ransacking their homesteads. Cesare on the contrary adopted the attitude not of a conqueror, but of a liberator, out to reclaim the lands which by right belonged to the Church and to establish his authority by a just and magnanimous government. With this aim in view, he was tireless in his efforts to discipline the motley army of foreigners and hired mercenaries, punishing looting by death and thereby arousing the natural resentment of the French soldiers who knew that, but for the alliance of their King, he would be no more than an unfrocked priest in Rome.

Yves d'Allegres might admire the Junoesque beauty and intrepid heroism of a Caterina Sforza, but to Cesare Borgia she was a fierce virago, who, not content with trying to poison his father, had on more than one occasion profited by an hour of truce to attempt to lure him to his death. Nevertheless, in homage to the French or maybe as a tribute to her courage, he appears to have treated the Countess of Forli with the utmost chivalry, sending her satins and brocades with which to replenish her wardrobe, and claiming her custody, not as a prisoner, but as 'an honoured guest of His Holiness the Pope'.

Even if it were true that he exacted the *droit de seigneur* when by the fortunes of war she fell into his hands, there is no record of any complaint on the part of the victim. Passionate, sensual, unbridled in her appetites and already verging on middle age, Caterina may well have succumbed to the dangerous fascination of the twenty-five-year-old conqueror. As for Cesare, he was sufficiently young and sufficiently perverse to enjoy a physical victory over this female condottiere. The very fact that she hated both him and his family probably added to her fascination. And had he met her when she was younger, this woman as strange and complex as himself might well have inspired him with a genuine passion. But she was no longer the arrogant beauty who from the battlements of Forli had once bared her body to an insurgent mob. Prematurely aged and coarsened by her numerous pregnancies, she had become so vast that Cesare was probably in all good faith when he declared that 'on capturing the citadel of Forli, he had found the Countess to be pregnant'.

The last act of the drama of Forli is open to conjecture as to what happened after Il Valentino had transported the Countess to his headquarters at Cesena and lodged her in his own palace, in apartments adjoining his own. The documents are missing— those letters in which Cesare must have regaled his father with the same intimate details he had described when recounting his wedding night with Charlotte d'Albret. Indiscreet as usual, the Pope appears to have repeated these details, with the result that before long the rumour of Cesare's relations with the redoubtable Countess had spread to the papal antechamber.

149

And the eagerness with which the various envoys circulated the story proves that very few of her contemporaries believed Caterina Sforza to have been the unwilling victim of Cesare Borgia's lust.

'Every good tiding has its reverse' said the Pope when on the day following the capture of Forli came the news of Cardinal Borgia's death. Universally beloved, of a charming and amiable disposition, Juan Borgia, known as the 'Younger', was one of the few people to enjoy the confidence both of the Pope and of his son. As Papal Legate to the Romagna and the Marches his diplomatic skill had smoothed the way for Cesare's campaign. And it was a sad day for the Borgias when this valued counsellor and devoted friend was struck down with a fever, while on his way from Cesare's camp to Rome. Letters from Urbino, where he was taken ill, tell of how he lay abed with a flux, when he received the news of the storming of the fortress of Forli, and against the advice of his physicians insisted on attempting to return to camp, with the result that he caught a chill and died within a few hours. Despite the fact that Cesare was devoted to his cousin and in no way benefited by his death, as the young Cardinal left nothing but debts, there were the usual sinister rumours of Juan Borgia having died by poison administered in Cesare's camp. This baseless story was the more readily believed as in those very days one of the Borgias' confidential agents, a Portuguese Bishop by the name of Ferdinando d'Almeida, was suddenly found dead after having partaken of his patron's wine. In the past d'Almeida had acted as a go-between in Cesare's marriage negotiations, and some said his death was caused owing to his having opened his mouth too wide in claiming reward for his services. Others asserted that he was one of King Louis's spies, and Cesare Borgia was not a man to tolerate being spied on, even by his allies.

Cardinal Borgia's death was only the first of a series of reverses. In the last days of January, a letter from Ascanio Sforza, ostensibly condoling with the Pope on the death of Juan Borgia, gave him the first news of Duke Ludovico's triumphal entry into Milan. With the help of the Emperor Maximilian the Sforzas had reconquered his dukedom. And it must have given much pleasure to the former Vice-Chancellor to inform the disloyal Pope, who had profited by his downfall to rob him of his benefices and castles.

The return of the Sforzas came as a shattering blow both to the Pope and to Cesare. The French were now compelled to rush reinforcements into Lombardy, and the first soldiers to be recalled were the troops on loan to the Pope. The news reached Cesare when he was already on his way to Pesaro, where Giovanni Sforza's state was to be his next objective. But now all plans had to be postponed. The departure of the French contingent left him with only a small band of Spanish and Italian mercenaries, barely a sufficient number with which to garrison the conquered towns. But he had learnt a valuable lesson, that in the future he would have to rely upon himself and the troops under his direct command. For the present there was nothing to be done but to return to Rome and to concentrate on the raising of funds for the levying of fresh recruits. And on February 26th, 1500, accompanied by four prisoners, among them Caterina Sforza, the Duke Valentino announced his arrival at the Vatican.

Here the news of his return was received with mingled feelings of joy and of misgiving. While the Pope worked himself into a fever of excitement, planning such an elaborate reception as to give rise to sarcastic comments as to whether 'the four prisoners were to be dragged in golden chains behind Cesare's triumphal chariot', Lucrezia envisaged her brother's return with a nervous dread, lest in his thwarted ambition Cesare might vent his vengeance on the House of Aragon and force their father's hand.

Burchard has recorded every detail of the strange and gloomy cavalcade with which Cesare Borgia set out to impress the Roman populace. In public deference to his dead cousin and guided by his unerring theatrical instinct, he had his entire retinue dressed in mourning. Surfeited by the pomp and glitter of religious processions, the Romans poured out into the streets to see Cesare's soldiers march by in utter silence, without sound of pipe or drum, preceded by a hundred wagons draped like catafalques. From the Duke's black velvet doublet to the ostrich plumes in the bonnets of his Swiss mercenaries, there was not a single note of colour other than the banners of the captured towns and the golden pennants flaunting the Lilies of France and the Borgia Bull. In the winter evening, lit by a thousand torches which reflected in the armour, the whole procession took on an even more fantastic aspect.

Had Cesare chanced to overhear the King of France referring to him as an overdressed young upstart? So that now in the rôle of conquerer he appeared in a simple black doublet wearing no ornament other than the golden chain of the Order of St. Michael, no weapon other than the sword, which with a curious insight into the future had been forged by Messer Ercole Fideli, the most famous goldsmith of the age, in the days when as Cardinal Legate he had crowned Federigo of Aragon at Capua. Engraved with the legends of his famous namesake, this sword had opened the way to a new and more adventurous life. '*Cesare aut nihil*'—already he had adopted the motto as his own. And the cardinals and ambassadors who followed in his wake down the Via Lata knew that so long as the Borgia Pope occupied the Roman See, loyalty to his son was essential to their safety.

The cannon boomed in welcome from St. Angelo. Fireworks blazed over the Tiber, illuminating in sheets of flame the Castle bastions where the Pope stood watching Cesare's triumphal arrival. All the emotion, one might almost say hysteria in Alexander's dual nature, was now apparent in his relations with his son. He was as obsessed and uncontrolled as in the days when he was dominated by his passion for Julia Farnese. Eye-witnesses describe how in greeting him he cried and laughed at the same time, breaking off into the Valencian dialect, as was his habit in moments of excitement. Cesare answered him in the same tongue, but what was forgiven in an emotional old man, was interpreted as deliberate insolence on the part of the young duke. The Borgias addressing one another in an alien language in front of a curious, and for the most part unfriendly court, was not calculated to improve the relations between the Pope and the Italian cardinals.

From the balcony of her palace, Lucrezia saw the procession go by and joined the crowds in cheering for the conqueror. In the flickering light and shadows of the torches, Cesare's figure towered above his captains, his face took on a cold, inhuman quality with hair and beard gleaming in separate tongues of flame. And riding at his side, Alfonso of Bisceglie, who at the Pope's orders had been forced to escort his brother-in-law into the city, appeared to be no more than an adolescent, with the soft and poignant beauty of those who are too fair to live.

Brother and husband turned towards the balcony where in the sophisticated elegance of her fur-trimmed gown, with the torches shining on her hair, waking mysterious shadows in her eyes, Lucrezia represented to the one a jealously-guarded present, to the other an even more jealously-guarded past.

XX

CESARE BORGIA's return to Rome coincided with the first day of carnival week, which revolved in a series of festivities celebrating his military triumphs. No praise was too fulsome, no flattery too blatant to find favour with the Pope. Mythological allegories compared Cesare to Apollo and to Mars. A vast stage set in the Piazza Navona depicted the victories of Julius Caesar, while one morning the pilgrims on their way to St. Peter's found that the entire square had been railed off in preparation for a *corrido* in which the Pope's son took the part of toreador, killing five bulls in the course of an afternoon. The fact that it was Holy Year had no restraining effect on the carnival festivities, which had never been more brilliant than this year, with Cesare Borgia in the forefront of the scene. The first procession of mummers had not crossed the St. Angelo Bridge before he had discarded his mourning for his cousin and was out in the streets, the leader of the wildest revels.

For the last time, Borgias and Aragons shared in the pleasures of carnival, forgetting their mutual antagonisms and jealousies in the devising of masques and the composing of songs. Once more, brother and sister performed their Valencian dances in front of the Pope and his cardinals; once more the Duke Valentino and the Princess of Squillace provided material for the gossip-mongers and we hear of a public duel on the Monte Testaccio in which the rival combatants, a Frenchman and a Burgundian, were supported, the one by Cesare and the other by Sanchia.

But though the wanton charms of his sister-in-law might lead Cesare to abandon Caterina Sforza in her prison in the Belvedere, they were not sufficiently powerful to alter his determination to rid Lucrezia of her Aragonese husband. As the Florentine envoy wrote:

There are in the Vatican so many causes for grudges both old and new, so much envy and jealousy both on public and private grounds, that scandals must necessarily arise.

If Cesare ever ventured to suggest to the Pope that his sister's husband were better out of the way, he would have made it into a political issue, declaring that Don Alfonso's continued presence in the Vatican was an unfriendly act towards their French allies. But His Holiness was in no way enamoured of those allies, 'who could conquer but could never govern'. And it was only after the French forces had recaptured Milan and beaten the Sforzas in decisive battle at Novara, that the Borgia Pope resigned himself to the fact that from now on, for better or for worse, King Louis XII was a force to be reckoned with in Italian politics.

A French duchy was in the possession of his son, the lilies of France were emblazoned on his scutcheon, but the Pope still derived pleasure from seeing the royal arms of Aragon above his grandson's cradle and he still had a certain tenderness for his beautiful young son-in-law. Unfortunately, Don Alfonso did little to assist his cause, being hot-headed and impatient and quick to take offence. When, at the instigation of France, the Pope granted the King of Hungary the annulment of his marriage to his Neapolitan queen, Don Alfonso was heard to protest in public against an act which was 'both a scandal to the Church and an insult to the House of Aragon'. Rash words to utter, when it was common knowledge that the enormous sums paid for the annulment had helped to secure fresh troops for Il Valentino.

This spring, fortune smiled on the Borgias. The French reconquest of Milan smoothed the way for Cesare's next campaign. The Sforza brothers were now the prisoners of France, and though Alexander VI made a half-hearted attempt to intercede on behalf of his former Vice-Chancellor, he ended by allowing the man who more than anyone else had been instrumental in making him Pope to languish in a French prison. In Rome, Cesare Borgia was the undisputed master of the city; within a month of his return his father had presented him with the order of the Golden Rose and created him Gonfalonier of the Church. He lodged now not in his own palace, but in the Vatican, in rooms immediately above the Pope's private apartments, and his troops kept order in the city. The letters of the pilgrims who crowded into Rome during the Easter Week celebrations, describe the horror of passing by the public gallows on the St. Angelo Bridge, where as many as twenty corpses were seen hanging on one day. Yet the dread inspired by the Pope's son only served to contribute to his ever-growing reputation. Attracted by his personality as much as by his generosity (the extravagance deplored by his more cautious father), soldiers of fortune from Italy and Spain were flocking to enrol themselves under his banner. Even the Venetian Signoria, who viewed with a suspicious eye the Borgia ambitions in the Romagna, were beginning to make friendly overtures to one whom their ambassador, Paolo Capello, assured them 'had all the requisite qualities for success, and if his father lived, would be one of the first captains in Italy'.

'How long will the Pope live?' was the question people were beginning to ask themselves; how long could this seventy-year-old Spaniard retain his tenacious hold on life? 'His Holiness grows younger every day', wrote Capello, and even Burchard paid tribute to his unflagging energy in carrying out the multiple duties of Holy Year. Yet every now and then there would be some reference to 'His Holiness suffering from one of his usual fainting attacks', and one day in the last week of June a rumour went round the town that the Pope was dead.

It was the eve of the Feast of St. Peter and a violent thunderstorm raged over the city. The Pope was in his private apartments in company of one of his cardinals and a secretary, when lightning struck a chimney of the Vatican, sending it crashing through the roof, wrecking the room below, killing three attendants, and causing a great pile of masonry to fall into the Pope's chamber. The cardinal and secretary saved themselves by rushing to the open window, and seeing the Pope's chair covered in ruins, cried out that he was dead. But when the rubble was cleared away, Alexander VI was found unconscious, but alive, with only a few superficial wounds on his head and arms. The beam in the ceiling immediately above his head had been clamped with iron to an outside wall, so that though broken in two, it had not fallen, but had bent in such a fashion as to form a protective screen. No wonder that even his enemies began to believe in the charmed life of the Spanish Pope, and nothing can have been more galling to the tyrants of the Romagna, who nightly prayed for deliverance from the Borgias, than to hear that not only had His Holiness escaped from death, but that Il Valentino had only just left the room in which the three attendants had been killed, while in another half an hour the entire Borgia clan would have been gathered in the papal apartments to celebrate the Feast of St. Peter.

'The Pope sees no one but his family and his doctors', wrote one of the Mantuan agents. And it was in those first days of convalescence, when they were all gathered at their father's bedside, that Cesare's resentment of his brother-in-law came to a head. Did he really suspect Alfonso of plotting with the Colonnas, or did he merely use that as an excuse to justify any further action on his part? Maybe the young prince had been foolish enough to become embroiled in some political conspiracy. He was barely nineteen at the time, and since the departure of Ascanio Sforza had been left with no other advisers than his Neapolitan entourage, men who were for the most part as hot-headed and incautious as himself. His feelings towards Cesare were based on a reciprocal dislike, and all Lucrezia's attempts as peacemaker had been unavailing, only serving to augment Alfonso's jealousy and Cesare's suspicions. Her brother had not forgiven her for obtaining from their father the confiscated properties of the Gaetanis, and the fact that she was officially stated to have paid eighty thousand ducats to the Apostolic See, for what he knew to have been a free gift on the part of the Pope, only made him the more bitter, seeing how the rich lands of the Gaetanis might have enabled him to raise more troops for his campaigns. On recovering consciousness, the Pope's first words were for his daughter, she alone was allowed to nurse him, and these signs of Lucrezia's growing ascendancy over their father found no favour in her brother's eyes.

The Pope's accident showed Cesare how easily all his ambitions might have come to nothing, and made him all the more determined to hurry on his plans. There was no senti-mentality in his relations towards his father; it is doubtful whether he even felt any affection for him, but for the moment his whole future depended on him. And we hear of the Venetian envoy being received in audience when the Pope was barely convalescent—an audience arranged by Cesare for no other reason than to recommend himself to the good graces of Venice.

A dispatch of Paolo Capello describes the Pope sitting-up in bed, surrounded by his family and despite his bandaged head and arm, as cheerful and loquacious as ever. Not only Cesare, Joffré and his nephew the Cardinal of Capua assisted at this interview, but all his womenfolk appear to have been present, including Lucrezia, Sanchia and one of Lucrezia's maidens, a certain Valencian named Caterina, who was the latest papal favourite. Each in turn set out to charm the Venetian envoy, Lucrezia by 'her sweet and gracious ways', her father by 'his fair and honeyed words', and Cesare by 'that air of modest diffidence' he could assume at will. As usual there were vague promises of assisting Venice in her struggle against the Turks, before His Holiness came to the main point which was to 'recommend his well-beloved and highly-considered son to the favour of the Signory'. The envoy was polite but reserved; it was the time for friendly overtures, but not yet for definite commitments. And when, on leaving, Cesare accompanied him out of the room and taking his arm, confided in him 'that recent events had shown him how dangerous it was to rely on the protection of the Pope, and that he had no greater wish than to place himself at the service of the republic', the envoy replied, 'You are very wise, my lord duke, for should the Pope die, you would be reduced to nothing within four days'.

Capello's dispatch shows how the Borgia Pope was in the habit of conducting his political negotiations in front of his entire family. On this occasion, the only missing member was Alfonso of Aragon who had probably been excluded on Cesare's orders. The young prince must have been feeling very lost and friendless in those weeks, when Lucrezia was spending not only her days, but also her nights, in the Vatican, sleeping in a room adjoining the papal apartments. And this very loneliness may have led him to embroil himself with the rasher and more foolish elements in his Neapolitan entourage, thereby rendering him even more suspect to his watchful brother-in-law.

It was the night of the 15th of July, when Alfonso of Bisceglie accompanied by two of his gentlemen was returning home from the Vatican after supping with his wife—a clear summer's night with St. Peter's Square deserted except for what appeared to be a group of pilgrims sleeping on the steps of the church. All unsuspecting, the young prince advanced towards them, when they suddenly sprang to their feet, revealing themselves to be armed men, who fell on him with daggers. Though severely wounded in the head, he still tried to fight his way through to his palace, only to find the entrance barred by other armed bands, and had it not been for the gallantry of his companions he would never have escaped alive. The noise of the fighting brought out the papal guards and no sooner had they appeared than the assassins fled in the direction of the Tiber.

Covered in blood, his doublet cut to ribbons, Alfonso of Aragon was brought to the papal apartment, where his wife and sister were still sitting-up with the Pope. An eye-witness records that before losing consciousness, he openly accused his would-be assassin, and that on hearing her brother's name, Lucrezia fainted in her father's arms. At first the prince's condition was so desperate that a cardinal was summoned to administer the last sacrament. And there is no greater indictment of the atmosphere of suspicion prevailing in the Vatican than that His Holiness should have called the Neapolitan ambassador to witness his own doctor dressing his son-in-law's wounds 'so as to make sure that there was no suspicion of poison'.

It is difficult to envisage the full horror of Lucrezia's situation, when, on recovering consciousness, she saw the cardinal administering to her husband the last sacraments. Even when hope revived and the doctors said Alfonso might recover, there was still the constant anxiety and dread lest the would-be assassin might strike again. Her father promised to protect Alfonso's safety, he was lodged in the rooms adjoining the Pope's apartments and a strong guard was placed outside his door. The Neapolitan ambassador was instructed to write to his king inviting him to send his own personal physicians. But whatever Lucrezia's father might promise in his expansive, emotional way, however distressed he might be, not only by her grief, but by the deplorable effect on public opinion, his subjugation to Cesare was such that he made no attempt to institute a public inquiry into the crime.

Assisted by Sanchia, she kept watch over Alfonso's bed, preparing his food for fear of poison, never sparing herself despite a fever brought on by her nervous state and the excessive heat of those summer days spent in an airless sickroom. The King's physicians arrived from Naples, together with Don Alfonso's mother. And finding himself surrounded by his own people, the young prince took heart and the natural resilience of youth re-asserted itself.

Outside the sickroom, the Pope was profuse in his apologies and explanations. But as a Mantuan agent writes:

> The fact that such a thing should have happened in such a place, to one who was not only a royal prince, but a Pope's son-in-law, shows that the author of the crime was one who was even more powerfully placed.

The murder of the Duke of Gandia was recalled and the Venetian ambassador asserts:

> It is not known who wounded the Duke of Bisceglie, but it is said to have been the same person who killed the Duke of Gandia.

The only one who explicitly names Cesare Borgia as the assassin is the poet Vincenzo Calmeta, who in a letter to the Duchess of Urbino states: 'The Duke Valentino is universally believed to have instigated the attack'.

Cesare himself made no attempt to deny the deed, beyond informing the Venetian ambassador, 'I did not wound the Duke

Alfonso, but had I done so, it would have been no more than he deserved'. And the same ambassador describes how the Pope, after assuring him of Il Valentino's innocence, ended by admitting that if the Duke Valentino had really been guilty of such a crime it meant that Don Alfonso had done something to deserve it. Cesare had already succeeded in persuading his father either into believing in his innocence or in acting as an accomplice in presenting him as the victim of Neapolitan aggression. Did he really suspect a plot against his life, when he ordered that under pain of death, no man was to carry arms between St. Peter's and the St. Angelo Bridge, or was it merely an excuse for forcing his father's hand? The answer may be found in one of the Mantuan dispatches written a few days after the attempted assassination.

> If Don Alfonso dies, the Pope will have no other alternative than to give himself entirely to France, for the House of Aragon will never forgive him such a grievous injury.

Time was pressing and Cesare could no longer afford to wait on his father's vacillations. The summer days passed by in an atmosphere laden with suspicion and intrigue, yet the patient in the Borgia tower continued to make good progress, and by August 18th he was already convalescent, able to walk about the room and sit by the open window which in those days gave out on the terraces of the Pope's private garden. Perhaps it was true that on that fatal morning Don Alfonso caught sight of the tall arrogant figure of his brother-in-law walking, unguarded and alone, in the gardens below, and in a moment of despairing hatred either he or one of his devoted and foolish Neapolitan gentlemen seized a bow and arrow and deliberately took aim with intent to kill. Such was the story as told by Cesare Borgia to justify his later action—a story duly repeated by the ambassadors, but not so easily believed.

That afternoon, Lucrezia and Sanchia were keeping Don Alfonso company, listening to the songs of their Neapolitan buffoon, and with the inherent optimism of youth, already making plans for the future, for the Pope had promised that as soon as the prince was out of the doctors' hands, he would be free to return to his Neapolitan estates, when suddenly there was the sound of armed men coming up the stairs, the clash of swords in the ante-chamber and Cesare's assassins burst into the room, overwhelming the guards. When Lucrezia heard the order of arrest she knew that this time it was the death warrant. In the first moment of panic both she and Sanchia had only one thought—to rush to the Pope to seek his mercy and beseech his intervention. His Holiness was absent, whether by accident or by design. By the time they had returned, they were too late. The entrance to the room was barred by Cesare's soldiers and thrown across the bed lay Alfonso's strangled body.

XXI

IFTY MILES north of Rome in the shadow of Mount Soracte lie the ruins of the castle of Nepi, a vast pile of ivy-entangled stones merging into the cracked volcanic landscape. It is a wild, desolate country of tufa rock and scrub and dwarf oak, rent by great chasms, honeycombed by caves, the tombs of the ancient Etruscans. A heavy melancholy permeates the land, as if it were gradually atrophying into death. And in this slow and lingering death the passing of five hundred years is of little account, castles may rise and crumble amidst the ruins of an older world, but the intrinsic sadness remains the same. And when Lucrezia Borgia came to Nepi in the first months of her widowhood, she found in these desolate highlands of Etruria, a melancholy equalling her own.

Whether she came of her own free will, or banished at Cesare's orders, her plight was equally pathetic. Friendless and defenceless, she was left to face the first great tragedy of her life. People might pity her, but no one dared openly to condole, for fear that in showing her too much sympathy, they might find themselves in the position of those loyal Aragonese, who were awaiting trial in the dungeons of St. Angelo. The whole of Italy was shocked by the murder of Alfonso of Aragon, but no one turned in loathing from Il Valentino when he openly proclaimed himself his brother-in-law's assassin. Even the Pope's attitude was one of embarrassment rather than of horror. 'His Holiness is embarrassed,' writes Cataneo, 'partly on account of the King of Naples, partly on account of his daughter, who is in despair.' But, dominated by Cesare, Alexander VI had no other choice than to listen to his son's excuses and defend his conduct. Envoys were informed that the Duke of Bisceglie had tried to murder the Duke Valentino and had paid the penalty for his rashness. To prevent them from asking uncomfortable questions, the Pope promised to publish a full report of the results of an inquiry into this crime.

163

No report was ever published, but those who valued their lives deemed it wiser to let the matter rest, and Naples was the only court to break off relations with the Vatican. Meanwhile, Alfonso of Aragon was buried secretly by night, with as little ceremony as if he were a humble page, rather than a royal prince, and the only Borgia who attended his funeral was the kindly old Archbishop of Cosenza, who but a few months previously had officiated at the pompous christening of his son. Cesare Borgia made no attempt to leave the city, and the day after the funeral was holding his customary audience in the Vatican.

Cruellest of all was Cesare's behaviour towards his sister, for when Lucrezia, racked with fever and half crazed with grief, was brought back to her palace, she had still to submit to the presence of her husband's murderer. The records are silent as to whether Cesare came to beg forgiveness or to threaten, but with his guards camped in the ante-chamber, the latter seems the more likely explanation. Maybe he was sufficiently callous to bargain for his sister's future by holding to ransom the safety of her baby son, sufficiently perverse to enjoy this last victory over a man to whom even now he grudged his sister's tears.

We know nothing as to what passed between them—whether Lucrezia indulged in reproaches and recriminations, or merely sat in frozen silence, but after this one interview Cesare seems to have made no further attempt to intrude upon her grief. Five days later the French ambassador arrived in Rome with fresh proposals from King Louis. And at the instigation of his son, the Pope began to plan another marriage for Lucrezia. Faced by a grief beyond his comprehension, embarrassed by her mourning weeds and swollen, tear-stained face, her father's sympathy for Lucrezia was rapidly changing to irritation at what he considered to be the obstinate persistency of her sorrow. As the Venetian envoy wrote, 'Alexander VI is a man on whom cares never weigh for more than a night, who loves life, has a joyous nature and does whatever turns out to be most useful to himself.' His son-in-law's murder was to him no more than an unpleasant incident, the desecration of the Vatican was a matter to be forgotten as quickly as possible. And Don Alfonso was barely in his grave before His Holiness was already weighing the widow's matrimonial prospects.

'There is talk of the Pope marrying his daughter to some important personage in France, but it is said that she refuses to go there,' wrote the gossip-mongers; and Lucrezia's refusal to act according to his wishes, coupled with her melancholy looks, succeeded in alienating her father's affection at a time when she was in the greatest need of it. Surely it must have been to her father that she referred in that unhappy letter addressed from Nepi—a letter undated and written partly in code, in which she says,

> All the time when I found that Farina neither answered nor wrote to me, I was able neither to eat nor to sleep and wept continuously. God forgive Farina, who could have made everything right, but did not do so.

Only so long as she continued to play her part as a carefree young woman whose radiant smiles attracted fresh matrimonial prizes into the Borgia net—only so long as she kept her emotions within the bounds of family interests—could she hope to find favour with the most capricious and tyrannical of fathers.

The Pope was irritated by Lucrezia's tears and it was in Cesare's interests to have his sister out of Rome, lest public sympathy with the unfortunate young widow might prejudice his chances at the next Consistory, when twelve new cardinals of his choosing were to be put up for nomination. And whereas Burchard asserted with his usual caution that the Pope was sending his daughter to Nepi 'to seek solace in her grief', public opinion interpreted the journey as a decree of banishment.

Neither father nor brother could forgive Lucrezia her love for her murdered husband. They even deprived her of Sanchia's company, fearing that the fiery Aragonese princess might incite her to open opposition. And the two young women who might have comforted one another in mourning the husband and the brother they had been powerless to save, were banished, the one to her Neapolitan estates, the other to the castle of Nepi.

Nothing remains of Lucrezia's sojourn at Nepi, other than

some stones carved with the arms of Borgia and of Aragon. To find records of these lonely, tragic months, we must travel to Modena, where buried among the Este archives lies a slim bundle of letters—no more than four or five in all—referring to the days when Lucrezia Borgia was not yet the 'triumphant Duchess of Ferrara', but still 'the unhappy princess of Salerno', haunted by the memory of a horrible crime, not daring to write to her servants except in cipher, for fear of the letters being intercepted by her brother's spies. Addressed to the master of her household, Vincenzo Giordano, these letters must have been still in his possession when he accompanied her to Ferrara, or else have been handed back to her as too confidential to fall into stranger hands. For the most part they are concerned with purely domestic affairs, yet they enable us to envisage the appalling loneliness of the twenty-year-old widow, whose only friends were servants, whose only consolation her religion. But even in this hour of tragedy, she had too much of her father's buoyancy and natural optimism to renounce her tenacious hold on life. Her letters from Nepi, though impregnated with melancholy and filled with misgivings, are those of a woman who is already making an effort to reshape her future. Underlying every letter is a note of fear. There are constant injunctions for secrecy and names written in cipher, to which unfortunately we do not possess the key; though when she writes of 'how Farina could have made everything better, but had failed to do so', and impresses on her servant 'on no account to let the letter fall into Rexa's hand', it would seem as if Farina stood for the Pope, and Rexa for Cesare.

Apart from her servants, her godfather the Cardinal of Lisbon and her father's cousin, the Archbishop of Cosenza, appear to have been the only ones who made any attempt to alleviate her distress. Old friends were curiously absent. Where was Julia Farnese, who in the past had used her as a stepping-stone to power, and Adriana, who professed to love her as a mother? Where was her own mother, Vanozza, whose natural instinct should have been to comfort her widowed daughter? Not one of them came to Nepi. With their habitual caution, Julia and Adriana deemed it wiser to identify themselves as

Orsinis, the new friends and allies of the Pope, whose sons were now fighting in Cesare's armies. As for Vanozza, she would have been the first to believe that Cesare had killed his brother-in-law in self-defence. The daughter she had barely seen since childhood had little claim on her affection in comparison with the son who had exalted her in his triumphs and made her into one of the wealthiest and most respected women in the capital.

Summer turned to autumn, and the fickle Roman public was already beginning to lose interest in the scandal of Alfonso's death. Cesare Borgia ruled the city, dreaded but withal respected, and at the Consistory of September 28th the twelve new cardinals of his choosing were elected without a note of opposition. No secret seems to have been made of the fact that each cardinal had to pay for his nomination. Burchard goes so far as to name the exact amount. And Marino Sanudo writes of how the Duke Valentino visited all the old cardinals and openly asked them to support his nominees, so that he might be supplied with sufficient funds to finance his campaign in the Romagna. He adds that at the magnificent banquet to which the Duke entertained the successful candidates, 'one hundred and twenty-thousand ducats was collected as a token of their gratitude'.

Ludovico Sforza was now King Louis's prisoner in France and French troops were free to return to the Romagna. But Cesare was no longer willing to be dictated to by foreign captains. His armies, financed by the papal treasury, now included some of the finest condottieri in Italy, men such as Vitellozzo Vitelli, tyrant of Citta di Castello, Gian-Paolo Baglioni, Lord of Perugia, and the two Orsini brothers, Paolo and Giuliano. Under the pressure of France, at the instigation of their ambassadors, the Signory of Venice, withdrew their protection from the threatened states of Pesaro, Rimini and Faenza. And not even the Estes, proudest of all the Italian princes, dared to refuse the offer of Cesare Borgia's friendship, when the most exclusive nobility of Europe welcomed him into their ranks, 'as an honorary citizen of Venice'.

Courted and flattered, his ante-chambers crowded with supplicants, the young duke, who turned night into day and received ambassadors in the small hours of the morning, who rode masked through the streets and rarely appeared at any public function, was rapidly becoming a legendary figure in his father's capital. In this jubilee year of 1500, Rome gave hospitality to Martin Luther and to Copernicus, to Bramante, and to Michelangelo. Yet they only passed across the background of the stage on which Cesare Borgia stood illumined in the full light of his sinister fame.

By the end of September his armies were ready for action, and pilgrims to St. Peter's could see the Pope's son reviewing his Spanish troops under the walls of the papal palace, while his father looked on from the loggia above the entrance. Placed under the ban of excommunication, the Lords of the Romagna prepared themselves for resistance or for flight. But it was useless for Giovanni Sforza to count on the support of his relatives of Mantua; useless for Pandolfo Malatesta to journey to Rome, to present the census money so long overdue; useless for the young Manfredi of Faenza to believe that the loyalty and bravery of his people was sufficient to withstand the onslaught of an army trained and equipped in professional warfare. It was all equally useless, for across the Mediterranean the Kings of France and Spain were plotting to invade the Neapolitan Regno, and to divide the spoils. But to ensure the success of their enterprise and to reconcile the Pope to having two such powerful neighbours on his frontiers, it was first necessary to placate the ambitions of Cesare Borgia by giving him a free hand in the Romagna.

Would the fate of Naples have been the same, had King Federico consented to his daughter Carlotta becoming Cesare Borgia's wife? Would Spain have been content to remain aloof, while the Borgias reigned as princes in the Regno under the benevolent hegemony of France? Ever since the days when Alfonso 'the Magnanimous', King of Aragon and the two Sicilies, had bequeathed his Italian inheritance to his illegitimate son, Ferrante, the Spanish monarchy had viewed their Neapolitan cousins with a secret jealousy. Nevertheless, when it was a matter of diplomatic negotiations with other powers, and more particularly with the Papacy, Spain had till now identified herself with the Aragonese princes of Naples. The fear of repercussions in his own country had on more than one occasion prevented Alexander VI from embarking on a war with Naples. Now Spain had suddenly changed her policy, and filled with ambition for her own aggrandisement, had succumbed to the blandishments of France. The Treaty of Granada was not yet signed when Cesare Borgia set out on the Via Flaminia, but the fate of Naples was already sealed, and Cesare could congratulate himself that by the murder of the Duke of Bisceglie he had forestalled any awkward complications which might have arisen, had his father been tied by sentimental considerations towards Lucrezia's husband.

Ruthless and single-minded, overriding all opposition, Cesare Borgia drove on towards his goal. And it was characteristic of a nature which never knew remorse, that he should have halted his advance on Pesaro, where his former brother-in-law was already contemplating flight, in order to claim his sister's hospitality at Nepi.

Not only did Cesare Borgia spend the night of October 4th, 1500, as Lucrezia's guest, but she herself contributed to his entertainment, and as a six weeks' widow, consented to meet her husband's murderer, and to sit at table with him, eating off earthenware, as prescribed by Spanish mourning, while he fed off golden plate. Somehow one refuses to believe that only fear constrained her to see him. The picture of a grief-stricken, frightened girl represents but one aspect of her character. On the other hand is a woman, voluptuous, sensual, still desperately missing the husband she had loved with a purely physical passion, still filled with revulsion against an unnatural brother —but already though maybe still unconsciously trying to forget—knowing that in forgetting lay the only hope for the future. When the heralds blew their silver trumpets outside her gates and the red and yellow banners of her brother's armies appeared on the horizon, it was as if she were being summoned back to life. The marching-songs of Italy and Spain and the laughter of fighting-men, the shiver of steel and the neighing of horses—all the confusion and bustle of an army on the move, combined to reawaken senses numbed by grief and to rekindle old desires. For the first time she saw her brother as a condottiere, surrounded by his devoted captains, a brother gay and confident, happy in a life of action, looking at her with clear, conscienceless eyes as if the past were no concern of theirs, speaking to her only of the future, which opened full of glorious possibilities before his limitless ambition. Did she wish to share in that future, or bury herself with the dead? Did she wish to identify herself with the triumphs of the Borgias or merge into the dust of the ruined house of Aragon? The autumn skies were blue and clear, sunlight flooded the Campagna, and suddenly her widow's weeds looked drab and dusty beside her brother's shimmering brocades. Life was waiting for her, harsh and pitiless, bereft of tenderness, yet withal so infinitely precious. And barely a month after Cesare Borgia's visit to Nepi the widowed Duchess of Bisceglie returned to Rome.

XXII

NO SOONER WAS Lucrezia back at the Vatican than the ambassadors were busily speculating as to her third husband. Some clung to the belief that Cesare would still succeed in marrying his sister to the King of France. Others asserted that the Pope had reverted to his old idea of sending his daughter to Spain. Meanwhile the Colonnas were trying to make their peace with the Papacy, by suggesting an alliance with one of their sons, and for the second time the Orsinis put forward as a candidate the young Duke of Gradina. But for the moment the widowed Duchess of Bisceglie showed no intention of embarking on a third marriage. When the Pope brought up the matter for discussion, she informed him in front of his court, that she would never marry again. When questioned as to the reason she quietly replied: 'Because it is better to remain single, when one brings bad luck to one's husbands'.

With Cesare already enthroned in the Sforza Palace at Pesaro and Alfonso of Aragon in his grave, one would have thought these words were sufficient to damp the enthusiasm of the most ardent suitor. But ambitions countered fear and Lucrezia's dowry combined with the privileges attached to a Pope's son-in-law provided too tempting a bait to be ignored. Though Lucrezia might declare her aversion to another marriage and for the moment believe herself to be sincere, the Pope merely laughed at these assertions, knowing his daughter well enough to realize that she would be the last person to refuse the chance of a really brilliant marriage. And by 'brilliant' the Borgias no longer implied a royal bastard or petty princeling; they now aspired to the scions of ruling houses, firmly and legitimately planted on their thrones; to families, who through fear, were beginning to accept their overtures of friendship.

The unfortunate Alfonso of Bisceglie was still alive when Cesare Borgia, in search of allies, set out to win the favour of the

Estes. One of the oldest and proudest families of Italy, established in the valley of the Po since the days of the Lombard
kings, the Estes by their subtlety and statesmanship succeeded
in ruling Ferrara as hereditary vicars of the Church and Modena
as a fief of the Empire. A family of self-willed individualists, of
humanists and soldiers, they inspired, one might almost say
created, a native school of artists and of poets who transformed
a little town in the mud-flats of the Po into one of the great
centres of European culture. From the beautiful Lionello
painted by Pisanello, who endowed Ferrara's university and
library, to his brother Borso, the magnificent patron at whose
orders the walls of medieval palaces came to life under the
brush of a Cossa or a Tura; from the reigning Duke Ercole II,
with his passion for the theatre and his cult for the classical
drama to his daughters Isabella and Beatrice, who corresponded
in Greek and Latin with the humanists, the Estes were fitting
representatives of the most brilliant aristocracy of Europe. But
underlying their erudition and refinement, they were as hard
and ruthless as their neighbours, matching and even outvying
the Borgias in their avarice and ambition. Now fear controlled
their pride and dominated their ambition, for rumours had
reached them of the Pope having sounded the reactions of
Venice, as to the possibility of Cesare Borgia extending his
dominions in the direction of Ferrara. Venice had always been
a jealous neighbour, and to protect themselves from the
pretensions of 'these Spanish upstarts', the Estes had nothing to
rely on but the traditional friendship of France. They had been
the first to welcome King Charles VIII on his passage through
the north of Italy and were privileged to wear the *fleur de lys*
emblazoned on their escutcheon, but now Louis XII was too
immersed in his plans for the re-conquest of the Neapolitan
Regno, to offer them anything beyond advice. And an unfortunate combination of circumstances had made Alfonso
d'Este, heir to the reigning Duke, into a widower shortly before
the Prince of Aragon fell a victim to Cesare Borgia's assassins.

Lucrezia was free, and the whole of Italy knew that her
father was ready to sell her to the highest bidder, but the Estes
had not yet envisaged the possibility of marrying into the
Borgia family. As the bastard of a Spanish priest, tainted in

172

their eyes with every natural and unnatural vice, Lucrezia was hardly likely to appeal to a family who exacted a high standard of virtue and honour in their women, and when they failed to live up to these ideals punished them by death. The accusations of Giovanni Sforza, the scandals of the Princess Sanchia, the murder of Alfonso of Aragon, all reflected on the twenty-year-old widow, who within a month of her re-appearance at the Vatican had recovered her looks and spirits to an extent as to make it seem as if her mourning robes were merely to enhance the exquisite texture of her skin and the sheen of her golden hair. Some may have noticed that the cheeks were more painted than of old, the hair a trifle brighter, but the general effect was still that of a young and artless girl, and the descriptions of Lucrezia Borgia as a widow differ very little from those of the thirteen-year-old child who was married to Giovanni Sforza, or the eighteen-year-old bride of Alfonso of Aragon.

> She is of medium height and slender figure [writes Nicolo Cagnolo]. Her face is somewhat long. She has a good profile, golden hair, light eyes. Her mouth is rather large with dazzling teeth. Her throat is smooth and white and charmingly rounded, and her whole being radiates gaiety and laughter.

This is a curious description of a woman, who in her short life had witnessed so many tragedies and shed so many tears. But even the most consummate actress can hardly have simulated that radiant quality, which springs from the very joy of living. When Lucrezia abandoned the loneliness of Nepi, she had already come to terms with life. Memories might still prevent her from responding to her father's plans for her future, but Alfonso's death had drained her of the little strength she had gathered from his love. The image she had presented to his eyes was unable to survive alone, it belonged to the world of troubadours where lovers die in youth; alone she reverted to the woman, whom both brother and father knew so well that they were able to exploit her weaknesses, recognizing her as one of themselves, sensual and venal, holding out her hands for her share in the Borgia fortunes. Gradually she lost the very will to resist, seeking forgetfulness in the orgies of her father's court, falling a victim to her old obsessions, though except for that one night in Nepi she was to see nothing of her brother till the summer, by which time her future had already been decided.

There were many tentative hints at an alliance with the Estes before the Borgias made a direct proposal. From Pesaro, where Cesare made a triumphal entry during the last days of October, a Ferrarese envoy wrote to Duke Ercole, repeating as the current gossip of Valentino's camp that 'The Pope intended giving Pesaro as a wedding portion to his daughter, and that he had found for her a husband, an Italian, who would always be able to retain Valentino's friendship'. Two weeks later the Venetian ambassador to Rome overheard in the ante-chambers of the Vatican 'some talk of Madonna Lucrezia marrying the hereditary Prince of Ferrara', but it was not until three months later in the first days of February 1501 that the Estes received a letter through Pope Alexander's trusted friend and adviser, the Cardinal of Modena, containing direct reference to a marriage 'which would be of the greatest material advantage to Ferrara'.

As in the case of the King of Naples, Duke Ercole's instinctive reaction was to refuse. For the moment the bravery of the young lord of Faenza and his loyal subjects had halted Cesare Borgia in his whirlwind drive. Pesaro, Rimini and Cesena had hailed him as a liberator, but Faenza stubbornly resisted, immobilizing his armies throughout the winter, while the rest of Italy looked on in wonder and in shame. But then came the spring bringing fresh reinforcements to Cesare and forcing Faenza to capitulate. Duke Ercole changed his tune. With Borgia troops already encamped on Ferrarese territory and neither France nor Venice offering a word of protest, he ordered his son to accept Cesare Borgia's invitation to witness the final assault on Faenza and to lend a favourable ear to the question of a matrimonial alliance.

Alfonso d'Este resented his father's change of heart. As a proud and loyal soldier he felt humiliated at having to witness the dying agony of the town, which time after time had implored Ferrara for assistance, and even after his visit to Cesare's camp, after he had been shown the portraits and heard the poems praising Lucrezia's beauty he still remained so

174

bitterly opposed to the idea of marrying a Borgia, that he told his father 'if he wanted whores he could find them in the brothels of the town without bringing them into the palace'. His sister Isabella was even more outspoken in her condemnation of an alliance which would be a disgrace to the family, but Duke Ercole remained unmoved, secretly hoping that by protracting the discussions to the uttermost, by bargaining and then withholding, some merciful providence might remove the Pope and his Spanish spawn before he was irrevocably committed.

Meanwhile Lucrezia was beginning to take an interest in these new plans for her future. Partly from pride, partly from the desire to escape from old and painful associations, she was willing to become for the third time the pawn of her family's ambitions. For Cesare the Este marriage was no more than a political manoeuvre necessary to secure his northern frontiers and to enable him to maintain the balance of power in his relations with France and Venice. But to the Pope it presented a far more personal aspect. He was childishly delighted at the thought of marrying his daughter to a ruling prince, and all his love and pride in Lucrezia revived at the prospect of her brilliant future. His enthusiasm was contagious, where she had begun by being indifferent she ended by being as excited as her father over becoming the Duchess of Ferrara. Neither father nor daughter seems to have resented the obvious reluctance with which the Estes were consenting to negotiate. Throughout their dealings with Duke Ercole the Borgias give the impression of being over-eager and slightly vulgar in their willingness to pay their way into the Este family.

Maybe Lucrezia was never aware of the horror with which her name inspired her future husband, or even if she was aware of it she may have considered it to be of little account, trusting to her charm and beauty to disarm all opposition. Just as she had no longer the strength to resist, so she may no longer have had the strength to feel. All that was soft and lovable in her character was buried with Alfonso of Aragon. Outwardly she had changed so little, but at heart the woman who returned from Nepi bore little resemblance to the light-hearted girl, who, heedless of the consequences, had submitted to her family's will. If she still submitted it was only in order to provide a loophole of escape, for the desire to escape from Rome was her dominating thought, making her ready to abandon her child and to ignore the fact that the very foundations of the Este marriage were raised on the ruins of the Neapolitan house of Aragon.

The whole question of Lucrezia's marriage revolved round French support, and King Louis's attitude was dictated by the Pope's reactions to the Treaty of Granada. The far-sighted politician in Alexander VI had recoiled at the thought of having the forces of France and Spain on the borders of the Papal States, but of late the doting father had triumphed over the sagacious Pope, and he was ready to make French support of the Este marriage the primary condition for granting Louis XII the investiture of Naples and the assistance of Cesare's troops. So though the French King had no wish to facilitate the conquests of the Borgias and was watching with a jealous eye their expansion towards the north, he nevertheless had no other alternative than to urge his old ally, the Duke of Ferrara, to consent to this marriage and to be sure to exact the most favourable terms.

When it came to bargaining Duke Ercole was more than a match for the Pope. If he had to sell the honour of his house, he was determined to sell it at the highest price. With cool effrontery he demanded the fantastic sum of 200,000 ducats for Lucrezia's dowry as well as the remission of the annual dues payable by Ferrara to the Apostolic See. Money, benefices and castles, there was nothing the Duke was not prepared to ask as the price of his condescension. Yet as he declared with malicious irony to the King of France, 'There was no question of blackmail nor of simony, for though he was no Pope, but merely a sinful layman, he would never stand out for more than his legitimate rights.' A delicate way of reminding His Majesty of France that he knew him to have succumbed to both bribery and blackmail.

Someone more sensitive then Lucrezia might have been disgusted by the months of sordid bargaining which preceded the signing of the marriage contract. But far from being disgusted, she was beginning to take an eager interest in every detail,

16. Francesco Gonzaga, Marquis of Mantua, warrior and lover of Lucrezia. Detail from *Madonna della Vittoria*, by Mantegna.

17. Alfonso d'Este, Duke of Ferrara and husband of Lucrezia Borgia, with his son, Ercole d'Este, from an Italian miscellany of the sixteenth century.

supporting the Duke of Ferrara in his exorbitant demands, doing all in her power to remove the obstacles which stood in the way. 'She is already proving herself to be a good Ferrarese', wrote the Duke's ambassador, and Lucrezia's sound common sense, her practical knowledge of finance, were beginning to make a favourable impression on her future father-in-law who declared that 'if his son persisted in his refusal, he would end by marrying her himself'.

By the summer the Pope was discussing his daughter's marriage in Consistory, and every effort was being made to convince the Estes that Lucrezia was worthy of entering into their family. The neglected widow of a murdered prince was once more the triumphant favourite of the Vatican. And the Mantuan agents, who were always ready to regale their gossip-loving mistress with the smallest details of the Borgias' private lives, noted that 'Madonna Lucrezia had taken her silver out of store and was no longer eating off earthenware'. Curiously enough none of these vigilant observers were concerned with the incident related by Burchard, who tells us with his usual terseness that at the end of July 1501, His Holiness the Pope set out from Rome on a brief tour of the Papal States, and

> that shortly before departure he handed over his palace and his business affairs to his daughter Lucrezia, authorizing her to open all letters in his name, but in all matters of importance to consult with the Cardinal of Lisbon.

The picture of a twenty-year-old girl as regent of the Vatican conferring with cardinals and presiding at Consistories has become incorporated in the Borgia legend. And the brief tenor of Lucrezia's regency has been depicted as one of the major scandals of the Borgia reign. But to her own contemporaries there appears to have been nothing particularly strange or shocking in Lucrezia administering the Papacy during her father's absence. It was the usual custom for Italian princes of the Renaissance to leave their wives as regents in their absence. Acting as a secular prince Alexander VI was merely following the example of his neighbours. As a Pope he had already irrevocably transgressed and the world that had accepted his children was now ready to accept his daughter as a regent. With her grace and tact, her readiness to defer to the wishes of her elders, Lucrezia neither antagonized nor offended the members of the Sacred College. In the same way as she had gained the respect of the Priors of Spoleto, so now she gained the affection of the most austere of cardinals. Her godfather, the noble and high-minded Cardinal of Lisbon, was heard to declare before his assembled colleagues that he supported the remission of the dues payable by Ferrara to the Church, merely because of his devotion to the future duchess. Enthroned in the Vatican, Lucrezia was already winning her first victories for Ferrara, writing to Duke Ercole on paper stamped with the papal seal, 'that she had no greater wish than to love and to serve him as a daughter'.

XXIII

WHILE THE POPE and the Duke of Ferrara were wrangling over the question of Lucrezia's dowry, Cesare Borgia was going through an anti-climax to his earlier triumphs. The fall of Faenza had made him master of Romagna, and the Pope had formally granted him possession of all the lands, which stretched southwards to the outskirts of Sinigallia up the Adriatic coast as far north as Cesena, extending westwards to the borders of Bologna and of Tuscany and the southern limits of the Ferrarese. Faced by a conqueror so favoured by fortune, both Bologna and Tuscany trembled for their safety. His forces had only to cross into Bolognese territory for the Bentivoglios to surrender to his demand by ceding him the important frontier town of Castel-Bolognese, and though ostensibly under the protection of France, even the Signory of Florence lacked the courage to resist when, urged by his condottieri, Il Valentino demanded the right to march through Tuscan territory. Twelve years ago under the rule of Lorenzo de' Medici, Florence had held the balance of power in Italy, now she humbly and abjectly submitted to Cesare Borgia by offering him a condotta at the fantastic salary of 36,000 ducats. But the anti-climax was to come and for once it was the Pope who put a curb on his son's ambitions.

Alexander VI was sufficiently clear-sighted to realize that Cesare was playing a dangerous game in giving in to his unruly captains. The King of France would never allow Tuscany to fall into Borgia hands. And at a time when the first French troops were already passing through Rome on their way to Naples and the first Spanish ships were landing at Civita Vecchia, it was imperative for the Vatican to remain on good terms with those who were about to become its nearest neighbours. A Papal Bull summoned the new Duke of

Romagna back to Rome, to take part in the conquest of Naples. But despite the fact that 'he was welcomed in Rome with as much enthusiasm as if he had conquered the lands of the infidel and not of the devoted subjects of the Holy See', Cesare Borgia appeared to be so discontented and morose that the chroniclers were not slow in interpreting his mood as one of resentment at being forced to subordinate his plans to those of France. Serving under the banners of the Valois, the all-powerful Duke of Romagna was no more than any other vassal of King Louis. And throughout the Neapolitan campaign Cesare Borgia's frustrated ambitions vented themselves in an orgy of savagery and lust.

Even if he were not directly responsible for the appalling massacre of Capua, nor for the kidnapping of the forty Neapolitan virgins, who according to Guicciardini were transported to Rome to be reserved for the Duke's pleasures, he nevertheless behaved with such sadistic cruelty that the chivalrous French knights turned in disgust from one whom they no longer regarded as *gentil compagnon et hardi homme*.

Apart from his humiliated pride Cesare Borgia may well have resented leaving the Romagna at a time when the Emperor Maximilian, enraged by the Treaty of Granada, was threatening to descend into Italy to destroy Il Valentino's puppet kingdom, and prevent an alliance between the Estes and the Borgias. Fortunately for the Pope, Maximilian's habitual lack of funds prevented him from carrying out his threat, and in the end the Duke of Ferrara was the only one to profit by the situation. As a vicar of the Church and a vassal of the Empire, he exploited his defiance of Maximilian as a means of obtaining still further concessions from the Pope.

While her brother was helping to drive her former relatives from the throne of Naples, Lucrezia Borgia's marriage contract was finally signed in the Este castle of Belfiore. After being accused by the Pope of behaving like a tradesman, the Duke of Ferrara had succeeded in obtaining his demands, though the dowry itself had been converted to 100,000 ducats in gold, with the remaining 100,000 to be paid out in jewels and in precious objects. Satisfied with his bargain, Duke Ercole could afford to be amiable, writing to the Pope 'that God himself had illuminated the heart of His Holiness in allowing him to condescend to mingle his blood with that of the Estes'. With what cynical laughter Alexander VI must have read this letter in private, even though in public he praised the Duke of Ferrara 'as the noblest and most high-minded of men'!

As for Lucrezia, her joy at the signing of her marriage contract was frank and unashamed. The news reached Rome on the evening of September 4th, and already on the morning of the fifth she had set out on a pilgrimage of thanksgiving to the Borgia church of Santa Maria del Popolo. Escorted by three hundred knights and ladies of her court, flanked by the ambassadors of France and Spain, she rode through the streets to the cries of 'Long live Pope Alexander VI'—'Long live the Duchess of Ferrara'. The cannon boomed in triumph from St. Angelo, the bells of the Capitol rang out in pride as if they were announcing the advent of a new Pope rather than the betrothal of a Pope's bastard. Yet the very vulgarity with which the Borgias advertised their parvenu delight in their good fortune, fitted in to the general picture of gaudiness and grandeur, of sordidness and beauty which composed the Rome of the Renaissance. Their superb showmanship appealed to a people who cheered their torchlight processions and their bullfights as formerly they had cheered the gladiators in the arena, and on this glittering summer day acclaimed Lucrezia as once they had acclaimed Poppea.

It was part pilgrimage, part masquerade, with the priest giving way to the buffoon. For when Lucrezia had said her prayers before the marble altar raised by Alexander in memory of his murdered son and had returned in state to the Vatican, the friends and followers of the Borgias continued their noisy demonstrations throughout the night. Eye-witnesses recount that according to a custom of the day Lucrezia presented her favourite fool with the magnificent golden robe she wore during the procession, and that with ribald laughter and obscene gestures the clown went running through the streets, flaunting it as a banner and crying out, 'here goes the illustrious Duchess of Ferrara'—a characteristic picture of that curious world in which the Papal Keys and a jester's cap and bells were so closely interlinked.

Though the Duke of Este had put his signature to the marriage contract, he was determined that not a single member of the bridal escort should leave Ferrara before every ducat of the dowry was safely in his hands. Two jurists versed in every aspect of Canon and Roman Law were sent to Rome to prevent the Pope from going back on his promises. And their letters to Duke Ercole describing life at the papal court shows us a new aspect of Lucrezia's character. We see her day after day assisting at the lengthy discussions of the notaries, perusing every document with care and on many an occasion persuading her father to give in on some legal point. 'The future Duchess of Ferrara,' writes one of the envoys, 'is both intelligent and capable and appears to be more interested in business than in pleasure.' They were impressed if somewhat shocked at the freedom with which she moved in and out of the papal apartments with Cardinals and Ambassadors begging the honour of escorting her to her usual place on the steps of her father's throne. The Pope appeared to have no ears or eyes except for his daughter and would break off in the midst of the gravest discussions to order some item for her trousseau.

The warehouses of Venice and of Florence were once more rifled to provide their embroidered velvets and brocades; the merchants of the Levant were once more summoned to the Vatican to display their stores of pearls. Lucrezia's wedding chests were the talk of Italy. She was said to have a dress trimmed with golden fringe estimated at 15,000 ducats and a hat—one of those enchanting hats laden with jewels and feathers such as we see in some of Pinturicchio's frescoes, costing no less than 10,000 ducats. But the fabulous trousseau was not sufficient to impress the Estes. The Archbishopric of Bologna had to be robbed to provide them with the frontier castles of Cento and of Pieve; the remission of the census had to be granted not only to the reigning Duke but to Alfonso and his heirs. Their avarice amounted to extortion, but though the Pope now and then allowed himself to give vent to his indignation, Lucrezia had always to show herself resigned and sweetly reasonable. Inwardly she must have been as angry as her father at the way in which Duke Ercole was deliberately procrastinating in order to delay the marriage. His flattering letters praising her wisdom and sagacity, calling her his most brilliant advocate, could not blind her to the fact that from her future husband she had received no more than a few formal lines dictated to a secretary. Only her longing to leave a city where the dead still claimed her from the living led her to dissimulate her pride and to play in front of the Ferrarese envoys the part of a patient and submissive daughter-in-law.

Maybe her longing to get away was accentuated by the fact that Cesare was back in Rome. After a riot of dissipation in conquered Naples he had been taken ill with his old complaint and had returned to the Vatican sick not only in body but in mind. On many an occasion we find the Pope apologizing for what he called 'the strangeness of his son', while he openly condemned his behaviour in keeping the Ferrarese envoys waiting for an audience. When they were finally received they found the Duke Valentino lying fully dressed on his bed, utterly exhausted from having danced through the night. The seventy-year-old Pope's capacity for sitting up till dawn and his delight in watching his children dance seems to have told on the health of both Cesare and Lucrezia for Duke Ercole is informed that 'Madonna Lucrezia is ailing and greatly fatigued, though she has no chance of resting so long as she is forced to sup with her father every night and dance or sing till three or four in the morning'.

What was fatiguing to Lucrezia must have been agony to a man racked by a painful disease, and many of Cesare's sudden acts of violence may have been caused by the breaking down of an iron self-control. The massacres of Capua had added to his already sinister reputation. There was not a murder committed in the city for which he was not held responsible. Every ageing prelate who in the summer heat succumbed to malaria or to apoplexy was regarded as one of his victims. Yet even his enemies fell under the spell of his magnetic personality and the masked figure of Il Valentino, a mask adopted no longer as a caprice but in order to hide the ravages of the *mal francese*, dominated the Vatican.

The letters of the Ferrarese envoys prove that in negotiating with Duke Ercole Cesare showed himself more liberal than his father. But though he regarded his sister's betrothal as a

diplomatic triumph, at heart he must have hated the Estes—
hated them for their superb self-confidence, their frigid insolence
which transpired through their courtly manners. And to a
mind warped by disease the natural outlet for his hatred was to
find some way to humiliate and to besmirch the proud façade
with which the Estes faced the world. If we accept this sup-
position, then we can accept the picture of Lucrezia being
deliberately debauched by her brother in the months before her
marriage. For there is no denying that she was present at the
feast which took place in Cesare's apartments in the Vatican on
the night of All-Hallows Eve, 1501. Burchard is too explicit in
his facts and the German Master of Ceremonies is no scandal-
monger. Time after time he ignores incidents which the other
chroniclers relate with pleasure. But for once the ponderous
Latin of his *diarium* leaves us under no illusions as to what took
place when Cesare invited his father and his sister to a banquet
with fifty of the lowest prostitutes in Rome. 'And after supper
the aforesaid women entertained them with singing and
dancing of a licentious character, gradually divesting themselves of all their clothing.'

At a time when the Ferrarese envoys were already lodged in
Lucrezia's palace and the ambassadors of friendly powers were
writing to Duke Ercole praising 'the sweetness, the amiability
and above all the intrinsic virtue' of the future Duchess of
Ferrara, Lucrezia was taking part in the Ballet of the Chestnuts,
a ballet which for all we know may have been of her own
devising, when holding lighted candelabras in their hands the
naked prostitutes grappled on the floor for the roasted chestnuts
flung from the papal throne. The difficulty with which the
drunken women brandished their candles and retrieved their
nuts only added to the general merriment, and both the Pope
and his daughter appear to have sunk to the depths of applaud-
ing Cesare's lieutenants while they gratified their lusts on the
naked women. Burchard relates no more than the barest facts,
but the very coldness of his style only makes the facts more
incriminating, showing how Cesare profited by his father's
unbridled sensuality and by his sister's weakness to assert his
own supremacy. Never was he so completely the master as
when he degraded the head of Christendom into a coarse and

lecherous old man and brought his sister to the level of a whore.

There have been attempts to prove that Lucrezia was an unwilling participant at this feast, but not even Cesare would have dared to force the future Duchess of Ferrara to attend against her will. If she came, she came of her own accord, because both by nature and by upbringing she delighted in such spectacles. Parties of this kind must have been common in the Vatican though Burchard only draws attention to the banquet on All-Hallows Eve and to a curious incident which took place a few days later, when with 'obvious pleasure and much laughter' the Pope and Lucrezia watched from the windows of the Vatican four champing stallions released from the papal stables disputing the favours of two terrified mares. It was hardly an edifying sight to be witnessed by father and daughter and it is difficult to reconcile the Lucrezia who took pleasure in such obscenities, with the Lucrezia who questioned the Ferrarese envoy with an ever-growing anxiety as to when the bridal escort was arriving to take her away. Maybe she was frightened of the woman whom she knew herself to be, frightened of succumbing entirely to Cesare's influence. On the other hand she may have been sufficiently conscienceless, sufficiently her father's daughter, to regard these erotic pastimes as a natural outlet for her passions. One side of her nature craved for admiration and respect, but the other dominated by her senses held her chained to an inheritance from which she could never escape. It was as natural for Lucrezia to take part in the Ballet of the Chestnuts as to preside at a Consistory of Cardinals, as natural for her to forgive her brother for her husband's murder as to order perpetual masses to be said for Alfonso's soul. She was probably never so sincere as when she told the Ferrarese envoys that the Vatican had become hateful to her, but with the Borgias hate and love were so closely interlinked that at times they hated what they loved the most.

XXIV

MONG THE many delicate matters to be discussed between the Borgias and the Estes was the future of Lucrezia's son. The little Duke of Bisceglie was only a year old and the Estes feared that his mother might insist on bringing him to Ferrara. But in this, as in all other matters, Lucrezia showed herself willing to conform to her father-in-law's wishes. So reasonable does she appear that one might almost accuse her of superficiality and heartlessness. For one searches in vain for a proof of her having made some effort to retain the child to whom she was said to be so passionately devoted. According to one of the Ferrarese envoys the subject was barely mentioned before she informed them that her son was remaining behind in Rome. The little Rodrigo was present at this interview, though fortunately too young to understand the full purport of his mother's words. And Lucrezia, who by now must have realized that to talk of sentiment to the Estes was merely a waste of time, went on to assure her father-in-law's ambassador that the Duke of Bisceglie was well provided for with a revenue of 15,000 ducats. In other words her son would never be a financial embarrassment to the Estes.

The Pope's adoration of his grandson had survived the downfall of the house of Aragon. And curiously enough Cesare raised no objection to a princely settlement being provided for Alfonso of Bisceglie's son. In the splitting-up of the Neapolitan Regno the Duchy of Bisceglie and the town of Guadrata had fallen to the share of Spain, and in an access of conscience at the way in which they had treated their Neapolitan cousins, the Spanish monarchs had allowed the Princes of Aragon to remain in possession of all their private estates. But besides his father's inheritance, the little Rodrigo was now invested by the Pope with all the territories confiscated from the Gaetanis including the Duchy of Sermoneta and the twenty-eight castles which two years previously had come into Lucrezia's possession. Not only Cesare but also the Estes seem to have raised no objection to this handing over of Lucrezia's property. No doubt they preferred to have the dowry paid in golden ducats rather than in stolen land.

Richly endowed, with two cardinals for his guardians, one of them the kindly old Archbishop, now Cardinal of Cosenza, who had assisted both at his christening and his father's funeral, Rodrigo of Bisceglie took his place as a Prince of the House of Borgia. He was not the only child to profit by Lucrezia's marriage, for it was towards the end of this summer of 1501, that the mysterious *Infante Romano* made his first appearance at the Vatican. No one seems to have made any attempt to explain the identity of this three-year-old boy, till a Papal Bull on the 1st September, 1501, decreed that 'the noble Giovanni de Borgia, natural son of the Duke Valentinois and of a Roman spinster, should by special apostolic authority be made legitimate and granted the same privileges as other members of his family'. Had the Pope been content to settle the child's identity by the publication of this one Bull, posterity would never have thought of questioning his parentage and Giovanni Borgia would have gone down to history as one of Cesare's numerous bastards. But in his anxiety (or maybe someone else's anxiety) to secure Giovanni's future, the Pope put his signature to a second, and this time secret, Bull, in which he contradicted his previous statement and declared that

the aforesaid Duke was not responsible for the defect in the child's legitimacy, and though in the future the said Giovanni Borgia might be described in deeds and documents as the son of the Duke Valentinois, this was in no way to prejudice his rights, he being in fact the child not of the Duke, but of himself, Pope Alexander VI, and of the same Roman spinster.

From these two contradictory Bulls it would seem either as if the Pope were attempting to protect Cesare's bastard son against the claims of his legitimate children, or that Cesare had consented to act as a cover to his father's errors. But there was no particular reason why either of them should have denied the parentage. Till now Alexander VI had conducted his private affairs regardless of public opinion. The Pope who in the first year of his reign had received his cardinals' congratulations on the birth of Julia Farnese's daughter, and who at the age of seventy-one openly boasted of having rendered one of his mistresses pregnant, would never have stooped to all this elaborate concealment on his own account. There must have been some other reputation to safeguard, some reputation which at the moment was of vital interest to the Borgias. And involuntarily one thinks of Lucrezia, remembering her brief and tragic love-affair with her father's chamberlain, the rumours circulating round Italy in the spring of 1498, which crystallized into one cryptic dispatch emanating from Ferrara and giving as the latest news from Rome that 'the Pope's daughter had given birth to a son'.

Long before the Estes had contemplated the possibility of a Borgia marriage, the Ducal chancellery appears to have been in possession of Lucrezia's secret, and it is hardly likely that anyone as perspicacious as Duke Ercole would have failed to draw his own conclusions from the fact that if he were still alive, the child born in the spring of 1498 would be exactly the same age as the three-year-old boy who had now come to live in the Vatican. But whatever may have been Duke Ercole's suspicions, neither in his correspondence with the Gonzagas, nor in his private dispatches to his ambassadors in Rome, does he make any reference to the possible identity of the *Infante Romano*. With admirable restraint he refrains from commenting on the Pope's curious behaviour in endowing Cesare's natural son with one half of Lucrezia's possesssions in the Roman Campagna, including the town and castle of Nepi and thirty-six other baronies and fiefs.

Cesare had several children, some acknowledged, others ignored, but till now there had been no attempt to make any of them into princes. The case of the *Infante Romano* was the one notable exception, all the more notable as the Bull of his legitimation was dated on the day when Lucrezia announced her engagement to Alfonso d'Este. From then right up to the time of the Pope's death, Giovanni Borgia and Rodrigo of Bisceglie were the two cherished children of the Vatican, doted on by Alexander VI, taking part in all public processions as acknowledged heirs to the Borgia fortunes. When the Duke-dom of Camerino fell to Cesare Borgia's armies, the child in whom he himself never showed the slightest interest was created by order of the Pope, Duke of Nepi and of Camerino. But if Cesare showed little interest in the boy, who after the Pope's death was at first known as his son and later as his brother, Lucrezia was for ever bestirring herself on the child's behalf, and so well did she succeed, that though the Estes never permitted Rodrigo of Bisceglie to visit his mother in Ferrara, Giovanni Borgia was later allowed to reside at Alfonso's court.

His presence in Ferrara may account for the fact that the two conflicting Bulls regarding his parentage are to be found not in the Vatican archives but among the Este records at Modena. But would they have been so carefully preserved in Lucrezia's private chancellery, unless they had been of some vital interest to her? And what other interest could they have, unless she happened to be the mother? All the evidence points to this conclusion, but the question as to who was the father still remains unanswered. There are some who will not accept the more normal explanation, and who refuse to admit that Cesare's murder of Pedro Calderon proves the Spanish cham-berlain to have been the father of Lucrezia's child. They argue as to whether the Borgia Pope would have been at such pains to legitimize the result of his daughter's passing fancy for a handsome servant, and whether Lucrezia herself would have shown so much concern for a child whose very existence must have caused her both embarrassment and shame. Cesare may have shown no affection for the *Infante Romano*, nevertheless he allowed the Pope to invest him with his own conquest of Camerino. Their arguments carry weight, creating the horrible picture of a seventeen-year-old girl who in the seclusion of a convent indulged in incestuous relations with her brother and allowed an innocent and love-sick servant to serve first as a screen and then as a victim of her crime. It is a picture so monstrous as to seem scarcely credible. Instinctively one denies it, but whatever may be one's suppositions, the mystery of the *Infante Romano* remains unsolved, more disturbing to posterity than to his contemporaries, who accepted his presence at the Vatican as they had accepted so many other Borgia scandals.

The time had come when even the Estes had to ignore these scandals. Duke Ercole wrote to the Emperor Maximilian

> that though he had hoped that the coming of the winter might prevent Lucrezia from leaving for Ferrara, the Pope's determination to hurry on the marriage meant that short of having an open quarrel with the Vatican, he had no other alternative but to dispatch the bridal escort.

And on December 9th, the brilliant cortège headed by Cardinal Ippolyto, and his two younger brothers Don Ferrante and Don Sigismondo d'Este, started out from Ferrara, on what was then a thirteen-day journey to Rome. Now that he was irrevocably committed, Duke Ercole was determined to impress Italy with the importance of the marriage. The retinue of five hundred knights who accompanied his sons to Rome included some of the greatest names in Ferrara and the vassal states—Strozzis and Rangonis, Mirandolas and Corregios, all magnificently dressed wearing the indispensable golden chains, the hall-mark of a well-dressed nobleman.

Trusted counsellors of the House of Este guarded the jewels which Duke Ercole was presenting to the bride. But even in the matter of his gifts, the Duke was taking no unnecessary risks, for Cardinal Ippolyto was instructed not to give them as a personal present but to word the presentation in such a way, that in the case of Lucrezia's death or even of her divorce the jewels would be returned to the Ducal treasury. But it was sufficient for the Pope to know that his daughter was to be crowned with the fabulous Este jewels, and once the bridal escort had left Ferrara, Alexander's enthusiasm knew no bounds. He was continually laughing, continually making jokes, at times of a puerility to make his courtiers marvel, as when he questioned one of the Ferrarese envoys as to 'who was the taller, himself or Duke Ercole', insisting on standing up to measure himself with the ambassador, and delighted when he was told that he was the taller by an inch. At other times he would start making plans, as if he were still a young and active man.

'Nothing,' he said, 'would prevent him from visiting Ferrara in the spring. It had always been one of his favourite cities.' And he would recall the days when he was a young and brilliant cardinal on a visit to Duke Borso's court. The Ferrarese envoys were worn out by his inexhaustible vitality, his youth and zest were a continual source of wonderment, though they could not refrain from commenting that 'at his time of life it would be wiser if he changed his ways and did not venture out of his palace before daybreak,' from which it would seem as if the Pope still kept to his old habits of seeking nocturnal adventures in the byways of the city.

There can have been little time for these escapades now that there were nightly festivities in the Vatican where Lucrezia occupied the centre of the stage, with her father forever drawing attention to her beauty and her grace. 'Look at your new Duchess,' he would say, 'you see she is not lame'. But the new Duchess had already conquered the hearts of her future subjects, serious and practical with the one, gay and confiding with the other, enchanting them by her eagerness to please, her willingness to conform to their customs and their ways. They were touched by the concern she showed when Duke Ercole fell ill. 'She has only one wish,' they wrote, 'that she were already in Ferrara, so that she could nurse your Highness as she nursed His Holiness at the time when the roof of his palace fell in'. Well might Lucrezia pray for her father-in-law's recovery, for if the Duke died, Alfonso might still refuse to ratify the marriage contract. But at last her doubts and anxieties were at an end. For on the morning of December 23rd she woke to the salute of the guns which announced the arrival of the bridal escort.

After weeks of sleet and rain, the sun glittered in a cloudless sky, as if even the weather participated in the triumph of the Borgias. Since dawn the crowds had been converging towards the north of the city, taking up points of vantage along the Flaminian Way, from where the Este princes were to make their public entry into the city. By the time they had crossed the Milvio Bridge, it was an unending procession of senators, ambassadors and cardinals, outvying one another in the splendour of their retinues, culminating in the Piazza del Popolo with the arrival of Cesare Borgia, 'a vision breath-taking in its magnificence, ablaze with gold and jewels, riding a horse which seemed to have wings'. Today there was no trace of the ravaged invalid, the sadistic pervert of whom it was said that even the Pope now lived in fear. Smiling and benign, beautiful as a demi-god, he appeared at the head of a cavalcade of four thousand men. The Este princes were handsome, vigorous young men, their escorts the flower of knightly chivalry, but as usual, it was Cesare who was the cynosure of all eyes. However humbly he might defer to the French ambassador riding beside him, however graciously he might dismount to embrace the Cardinal Ippolyto, it was for him alone that the bay and myrtle were thrown in homage, that the cries of 'Duca! Duca!' rent the air.

It took over four hours for this vast unwieldy procession to reach the Borgo, and the short winter day was nearly over by the time the Este princes were brought to the papal palace. In this carefully studied pageant, where every Borgia had a part to play, Cesare now made way for his father, and the over-life-size figure of Alexander VI took the stage, gracious, condescending, prodigal in his compliments, combining in his inimitable fashion dignity and *bonhomie*, ineffable charm and sublime majesty. Then when the last of the Ferrarese knights had kissed the papal mule, came the moment for which princes and pages had been waiting with the same impatience, the arrival at Lucrezia's palace.

It was a moment on which so much had been staked, where everything depended on the first impressions. Cardinal Ippolyto already knew his sister-in-law, remembering her from the days when with her blue-eyed Neapolitan husband she had led the revels in the gardens of the Vatican, but to the grave old counsellors of the House of Este this was the moment to judge and to record. Lucrezia knew she was on trial, that the slightest gesture was important. For weeks—for months—she had been planning for this day. So many words of welcome had been composed and then re-written, so many dresses had been chosen and then rejected. No actress could have calculated her entrances with a greater attention to detail, yet the final effect was one of spontaneous modesty.

She was waiting to greet her guests at the foot of the great staircase lit by torches, leaning on the arm of a venerable white-bearded Spaniard, the perfect foil for her blonde fragility. All the elegance for which she was justly famous had come into play today. The warm flattering tones of her gold and mulberry gown and heavy velvet mantle lined with sable, the headdress of emerald gauze enmeshed with pearls, the enormous rubies gleaming on throat and forehead were all calculated to enhance her delicate colouring and small exquisite figure. And if in contrast to their voluptuous strong-limbed women, she might strike some of the Ferrarese as insignificant and cold, it was not long before she had reassured them by the warmth of her manner and the candour of her smile. From the impressionable Don Ferrante to the gravest of Duke Ercole's counsellors, it was one long paean of praise. Even those who had been deputized to criticize and to record could only write: 'she is an intelligent, lovely, and exceedingly gracious lady, of whom it is impossible to believe anything but good'. And one who prided himself on telling his master the truth added: 'in short her character is such, that it is impossible to suspect anything sinister of her'. From which it would seem as if even at the eleventh hour Duke Ercole still harboured uneasy doubts as to his daughter-in-law's good name.

XXV

I T WAS NOT only in Ferrara that every detail of Lucrezia's appearance and behaviour was being eagerly discussed. In the neighbouring court of Mantua, Duke Ercole's daughter, the Marchesa Isabella, was avidly collecting information on the sister-in-law who with her limitless resources threatened to outvie her in the realm of elegance. Endowed with a masculine intellect, Isabella had the longing to be admired for her feminine charms. She would spend hours in devising some new fashion, thinking out some way of making herself appear to be taller and slenderer than was natural to her. For though her courtiers might describe her as 'ethereal as a nymph' she was in reality short and squarely built, inclined to plumpness, and only the majesty of her bearing and the rhythm of her movements helped to give her the illusion of grace.

Lucrezia was frail and slender, she moved 'as if on air', and most galling of all, she appeared to be even younger than her twenty-one years. Unless Isabella looked to her laurels, and exploited by art what she lacked by nature, it seemed as if in the coming festivities at Ferrara she would find herself outrivalled by the new Duchess. The slightest detail of Lucrezia's wardrobe was of interest to her, and because neither her brothers nor her envoys were able to satisfy her curiosity, she dispatched one of her own spies to Rome, who, travelling in the suite of a Ferrarese nobleman, was able to introduce himself into the inner circle of Lucrezia's court. It is to this curious Shakespearean character, half familiar, half buffoon, who signs himself with the pseudonym of 'El Prete', that we are indebted for those minute descriptions of Lucrezia's dresses and appearance, both on the journey to Ferrara and in the days which immediately preceded her departure. Whether or not he was in reality an unfrocked priest, as his signature would imply, he seems to have possessed an uncanny talent for insinuating himself into the intimacy of the bedchamber and in unlocking the secrets of the confessional. He was not boasting when he asserted that he could follow 'the most excellent madonna like her own shadow, and what his eyes could not see, he would ferret out with his nose'.

Through the eyes of El Prete we follow Lucrezia in the endless round of festivities which celebrated her third marriage. We see her one evening at an impromptu reception in her own palace, leading the dance with one of the Este princes, graceful and animated in her *camorra* of black velvet with gold borders, cut in the Spanish fashion with tight cuffs and slashed sleeves. For no woman could be more explicit than El Prete in describing the details of Lucrezia's gowns; her taste for coloured furs as trimmings on overskirts and sleeves; her feminine coquetry in inserting in her low-cut bodices finely-pleated vests of gauze and cambric; the deliberate simplicity with which she dressed her hair, as on her wedding day, when in contrast to her pompous robe of crimson velvet lined with ermine, the splendour of rubies and pearls, she let her long curls fall about her shoulders confined by no other ornament than a velvet band.

A marriage by proxy had already taken place in Ferrara, but the Pope insisted on the service being repeated in Rome. So, on the morning of December 30th, 1501, Lucrezia dressed as a bride for the third time. This time it was the two young Este princes who led her by the hand across St. Peter's Square with all the Ferrarese nobles and their retainers following in her train. Fifty maids of honour carried garlands of myrtle; twenty pages dressed in cloth of gold bore aloft the standards of Borgia and of Este, while stationed on the steps of St. Peter's, a band of musicians accompanied the procession to the sound of viols.

El Prete waxes lyrical over the beauty of the background and the beauty of the bride. But inwardly Lucrezia can hardly have been feeling like a radiant bride. However insensitive by nature and by upbringing, however ready to forget the past, it must have been impossible for her to ignore that the musicians stood on the very spot which barely eighteen months ago had been stained with her husband's blood. So long as she remained in Rome the ghost of Alfonso of Aragon could claim her back and she would see him, as she had seen him the night when they brought him bleeding and unconscious to the Vatican, or that summer's day when she found him lying across the bed, with his blue eyes wide open looking at her, in the way their child had looked at her of late, frightened and insecure. Today she was on her way to receive all that Cesare had promised her at Nepi, security, power and a firmly-established throne, a position where slander could never attack her, nor envious hands reach up to pull her down. 'Long live the illustrious Duchess of Ferrara.' The crowd cheered in the winter sunlight and in front of the papal palace the master of ceremonies was waiting to escort her to her father's presence.

Was it at Lucrezia's wish that this time the ceremony, instead of being held in the intimacy of the Borgia apartments, took place in the Sala Paolina, where El Prete tells us that 'the Pope, the Duke of Romagna and thirteen cardinals, including Ippolyto d'Este, as well as all the foreign ambassadors, with the exception of that of his Imperial Majesty, assisted at the service'. There is no mention of Joffré nor of Sanchia. Having seen her brother murdered before her eyes and her family overthrown with the deliberate connivance of the Borgias, Sanchia would hardly have been a tactful guest at the Este wedding. And in order to avoid unpleasant incidents Alexander VI may have deemed it wiser to keep his tempestuous daughter-in-law out of Rome.

The marriage service was reduced to the barest essentials, and when the Bishop of Adria attempted to deliver an address, he was cut short by the Pope, who had a horror of long and tedious sermons. Lucrezia appears to have played her part with her usual grace, accepting the ring presented by Don Ferrante with a proper show of modesty, but she showed neither enthusiasm nor animation till it was time for the presenting of the wedding gifts. This was the part entrusted to the Cardinal Ippolyto, who, combining a herculean frame with an almost effeminate elegancy of manner, appears to have been so diplomatic in the handing over of the jewels, which were in reality no more than a loan, that he was congratulated by the Pope 'on having added to the beauty of the presents by the charm of his manner'.

The shrewd eyes of the Borgias appraising the value of the jewels estimated them to be worth no less than seventy thousand ducats. Here were the fabulous rubies, worn by the late Duchess, the gentle and lovely Eleanora of Aragon; diamonds and emeralds from the furthest Indies brought home by Venetian traders; pearls faultlessly matched in colour and in size, and even more beautiful than the stones themselves, the settings—golden filigree as fine and soft as silk; enamels vying in lustre and in colour with the gems. All the loving craftsmanship of the greatest Ferrarese goldsmiths had gone to the setting of the Este jewels, making each coif and necklace into a separate work of art. With his plump white hands the Pope displayed their beauties to his daughter, who was now all smiles and radiance, suppresssing her natural instinct to dwell on the size and lustre of the stones in order to show the proper appreciation of the craftsmanship. Already Lucrezia had taken her first lesson in those artifices of refinement demanded of a Ferrarese princess.

The company then repaired to the so-called 'Chamber of the Parrots', where dancing marked the culmination of the festivities. From the *Danses Basses*, in fashion at the courts, to the *Morescos*, the ballets which were usually part of a masque, dancing was the natural outlet for the Italians of the Renaissance. But with the Borgias it amounted to a passion. Their blood pulsated to a dancing rhythm, as if some anonymous gypsy ancestor had bequeathed to them a legacy of haunting lilting tunes, which betrayed themselves in the manner of their walk, the turn of their head, the feline grace of their movements. Their joys, their triumphs, their very lusts expressed themselves in dance; even the ageing Pope got restive as soon as his musicians began to play. And El Prete relates that no sooner was Alexander seated on his throne with the cardinals on his left, and Lucrezia, Ippolyto d'Este and Cesare on his right, than he ordered the revelries to begin and his son and daughter to lead the dance, 'which they did with the utmost grace, delighting His Holiness who was in continual laughter'.

There appears to have been an element of hysteria in 'this continual laughter', for Alexander was too highly strung and emotional not to feel the impending separation from Lucrezia. Despite his boasting of visiting her in Ferrara in the spring, inwardly he must have known that this was the last time he would ever see his children perform together the dances they infused with their vitality and life. Lately he had been relying more and more on his daughter's company; there were times when he, the superb, arrogant and perennially youthful Pope, felt himself to be no more than a tired lonely old man, frightened of Cesare's limitless ambitions, frightened that the moment might come when in his insensate pride, his son might try to measure himself with God and no longer regard the Papacy as necessary to his plans. But Alexander's love, or rather obsession, for his children had reached a point where no act was too unscrupulous if it served to further their careers; when subjugated by Cesare's evil genius, he was ready to tolerate and even to connive at crime. The callousness with which he would seize on the goods of dying cardinals without any attempt to conceal his pressing need of money; the curious coincidence by which several of the richest members of the Sacred College had died in the past year, led his enemies to accuse him of poisoning his Cardinals in order to finance his son's campaigns. Nobody trusted the Borgia Pope, and unlike Cesare, Alexander wanted to be loved. He enjoyed life and wanted others to enjoy it with him. But the ruthlessness with which he pursued his own ends only made his joviality and graciousness the more inhuman to those, who like the Gaetanis and the Colonnas had suffered from his extortions. It was characteristic of the distrust he inspired, that he had the greatest difficulty in collecting a suitable retinue to accompany his daughter to Ferrara, for too many of the Roman barons feared that he might profit by their absence in order to expropriate their lands. And the majority preferred to trust Il Valentino rather than the Pope, for as a soldier Cesare had a reputation of loyalty towards those who served him well. The people who cheered the Borgias in the streets and the nobles who danced at Lucrezia's wedding were paying homage not so much to the power of the Papacy as to their fear and respect for Cesare Borgia.

Finally the notaries and ambassadors had settled the last legal details; the Curia officials had given their unwilling consent to concessions which would involve the Apostolic See in many thousands of ducats; and the hundred and fifty mules carrying

Lucrezia's wedding chests were duly loaded. The emotion of leave-taking does not seem to have stopped her from profiting by her father's generosity, who against the advice of his lawyers had refused to have an inventory taken of her property. As a worthy daughter-in-law to Duke Ercole, she stripped her palace of everything that was movable. No sense of shame prevented her from packing the superb dinner service stamped with the Sforza arms, presented by Cardinal Ascanio on the occasion of her first marriage, nor the magnificent Flemish tapestries and jewelled reliquaries of the House of Aragon. 'In objects alone she possesses a mountain of gold and silver', wrote the rapturous ambassadors to the Duke of Ferrara.

But the link between Lucrezia and her father-in-law was not entirely venal. The most curious side of Duke Ercole's complex character was his leaning towards mysticism. Disappointed in the failure of the reforms promised by the great Ferrarese preacher, Savonarola, disillusioned in the non-fulfilment of the prophecies, Ercole d'Este had thrown himself heart and soul into the revival of the cult of St. Catherine of Siena. Perhaps the strangest phenomena of the closing days of the fifteenth century, were the nuns who appeared in convents all over Italy, bearing on their hands and feet the marks of the stigmata, professing to be in constant spiritual intercourse with St. Catherine, and imitating her way of life. Of all these miracle-working nuns, whose ecstatic visions were so carefully studied by the Duke of Ferrara, the one who acquired the greatest hold over his imagination was a certain young Dominican nun, known as Sister Lucia of Narni. Nothing less would satisfy him than to remove her from her nunnery in Viterbo in order to settle her in a new and magnificent convent in Ferrara and to found an order dedicated to her patron saint, St. Catherine. Sister Lucia appears to have accepted his offer with alacrity, but neither the town authorities of Viterbo nor the other inmates of the convent, who lived in the reflected glory of Sister Lucia's miracles, would allow her to leave; and in the end the proud Duke of Ferrara had to resort to the somewhat ignominious method of smuggling his prophetess out of Viterbo in a laundry basket. But no sooner was she settled in Ferrara in her magnificent new convent decorated by all the leading masters of the Ferrarese school, than the little Umbrian nun began to feel homesick. Conscious of her power over her adoring patron, who treasured as sacred relics the cloths stained with the blood of her stigmata, Sister Lucia demanded that a number of her former friends and relatives should be made to leave their convents and their native villages in order to join her in Ferrara.

It was in the delicate matter of persuading a lot of unwilling and frightened women to transfer themselves to an unknown destination, that Duke Ercole counted on his daughter-in-law's tact and powers of persuasion. In a letter to Lucrezia he wrote, 'No sooner had we thought of using the means and favour of your Ladyship in this matter, than we knew that we had gained our object'. And it was not difficult for Lucrezia to cajole her father into sending Papal Bulls to the Governors of Viterbo and of Narni, threatening the nuns with excommunication unless they came immediately to Rome. The Pope appears to have been vastly amused by Duke Ercole's obsession for his holy women, and one wonders whether Lucrezia was already too much of a good Ferrarese to share in her father's laughter. Probably she was irritated rather than amused when in the midst of preparing for her own departure, she had to comfort and persuade a group of stubborn countrywomen, who as soon as they arrived in Rome, spent their time in soliciting audiences, and in inventing every possible excuse in order to defer their departure.

It must have been with the utmost relief that she finally saw them safely bundled into their carriages, covered with tarpaulin to protect them against the weather—a thoughtful attention due to her own generosity rather than to her father-in-law's religious fervour.

And now the hour had come to make her own farewells. There was a visit to Vanozza, though mother and daughter were so estranged that they can have had little to say to one another. Alexander's former mistress was now a wealthy and respected matron, the owner of some of the richest vineyards and the most prosperous inns in the city. But apart from her love for Cesare, she seems to have had little interest in either her daughter or her grandson, and she was as remote from Lucrezia now that she was Duchess of Ferrara as when she was an unhappy and neglected widow. But while Vanozza remained estranged, others were quick to profit by Lucrezia's good fortune. After carefully absenting herself from Nepi, Adriana Orsini now came forward to offer her services. And because it suited both Lucrezia and her father to produce in front of the Estes an Orsini relative, the shrewd and worldly Spanishwoman was put in charge of the bevy of delicate beauties who were to accompany their mistress to Ferrara.

January the sixth 1502 dawned grey and bleak. There had been a slight snowfall during the night. Dressing by candlelight in the palace which had been her home for ten years, unhappy memories must have assailed Lucrezia on every side. There were the last goodbyes to her little son, the last injunctions to his tutors, the last visit to Alfonso of Bisceglie's tomb. And already her father was waiting for her in the papal throne room. The interview between the Pope and his daughter lasted for over an hour, and not even a secretary was present to overhear the secret counsels and instructions for the future, the loving promises and tender words with which Alexander softened the harshness of goodbye. However much Lucrezia may have longed for a new and different life, this must have been the moment when she clung to her father, when all the terrors of the past years were forgotten in the security of his presence, the warmth of his affection. For the last time he took her in his arms and she was conscious of that massive strength, that superb self-confidence from which she derived her own stamina and pride.

The antechambers filled with a throng of glittering courtiers. The Este princes were waiting to take their leave, and from his place behind the papal throne, Burchard noted that as Lucrezia left the room, the Pope called after her in a loud voice, speaking in Italian, so that all might understand, telling her 'to be of good cheer and to write and ask him for whatever she might want, for all he had done for her in the past was nothing compared to what he would do for her in the future'. Then he went to the window and watched her mount her white jennet bridled in gold, surrounded by all the magistrates, ambassadors and cardinals in Rome. Over a thousand people were assembled in St. Peter's Square waiting to accompany Lucrezia to the city gates. His Holiness had decreed that his daughter should be paid the honours due to a queen, and there was no cardinal so aged and infirm that he had not braved the elements at papal orders. A hand lifted in a last salute; a face turned upwards with a smile an old man's eyes could no longer see, and the great cavalcade was on the move with Lucrezia riding between her brother and the Cardinal Ippolyto, who were accompanying her on the first stage of her journey. Gradually the last of the trumpeters and musicians, the last of the swaying carriages filled with nervous women, the last of the hundred and fifty mules vanished out of sight. A cold grey emptiness settled over the square, but still the Pope kept running from window to window of his palace, straining his eyes for a last glimpse.

XXVI

THE JOURNEY was long and tedious. Bad roads and inclement weather held up the travellers, while the elaborate receptions in the various towns through which they passed only caused further delay and an extra strain on already exhausted nerves. Lucrezia was of a delicate constitution, and neither she nor her ladies were used to the saddle. On the seventh day, by which time the party had only reached the Umbrian town of Foligno, one of the Ferrarese councillors was already informing Duke Ercole:

> although we wrote to your Excellency from Narni, that we would travel from Terni to Spoleto, and from Spoleto to this place without stopping, the illustrious Duchess and her ladies were so fatigued, that she decided to rest a day in Spoleto and another in Foligno. Therefore we shall not arrive in Urbino before next Tuesday. . . . And as we feel certain that the Duchess will stop frequently to rest, because she does not wish to be worn out when she reaches Ferrara, there is little hope of us arriving before the last of the present, or the first of next month.

A further delay seems to have been caused by Lucrezia's habit of washing her hair every few days. Her characteristically feminine excuse was that she suffered from headaches unless her head was constantly washed and tended. But a far more likely explanation was that the celebrated golden hair was in need of certain brightening rinses whose effects wore off after a short time. In that strange book of natural science and of magic lore compiled by Giovanni della Porta at the end of the fifteenth century, we find many recipes for the dyeing and bleaching of hair including one in which we read: 'To dye the hair yellow, add enough honey to soften the lees of white wine, and keep the head wet with it all night, then brew the roots of celandine and mix them with the oil of cummin seed, box-shavings and saffron, and cover the head with this for twenty-four.hours, when it should be washed off with a lye of cabbage stalks and ashes of rye straw.'

It is not surprising if Lucrezia's retinue spent many idle hours or rather days in waiting for their mistress to complete this complicated ritual, while their unfortunate host had the added expense of providing food and lodging for another day. In their anxiety to placate the Borgias, princes and communes had vied with one another in their offers of hospitality, but political considerations dictated that the Pope's daughter was to travel to her new home by way of the papal states, the duchy of Urbino and her brother's territories in the Romagna. Once she had reached Bologna she was to proceed by water along the canal which in those days linked Bologna with the Po, thereby saving her the discomfort of travelling by land and enabling her to arrive at Ferrara sufficiently rested to partake in the strenuous round of festivities prepared in her honour.

A new Lucrezia emerges on this journey, more definite, more capable of asserting her own will, as if she were conscious that what she now made of her life depended on herself rather than on Cesare. Duke Ercole was to find that the daughter-in-law who wrote him such sweet and submissive letters had suddenly developed a determined will of her own. And in writing to the Marchioness of Mantua, El Prete comments on what he calls 'the new Duchess's sagacity and wisdom', and with an enthusiasm which can hardly have pleased the vanity of his patroness he adds:

> every day the Madonna Lucrezia makes a better impression on me. She has a very fine brain, so subtle and astute that one has to be very much on the alert in conversation with her. In short she is a very intelligent woman, and this is not only my impression but reflects the general opinion.

With the departure of Cardinal Ippolyto, Lucrezia remained in sole command of her undisciplined retinue, whose quarrels and grievances were reported to her direct. For neither her cousin the old Cardinal of Cosenza, who was accompanying her as far as Gubbio, nor the young Este princes had the necessary energy and tact to deal with the divergent elements of Romans, Spaniards and Ferrarese, who many a time would have come to blows had it not been for her unfailing patience. At the same time she had her own problems to contend with, for it needed courage to face the welcome of magistrates and priors in cities she would willingly have avoided. Spoleto and Pesaro in particular evoked embarrassing and hateful memories, for though Alfonso of Bisceglie and Giovanni Sforza were names she had tried to bury in the limbo of the past, there were times when they still intruded too vividly into the present. With that extraordinary resilience she had inherited from her father, Lucrezia was ready to throw herself wholeheartedly into the new life. But on occasion the past still clung to her, as at Gubbio, when she cried on taking leave of Rodrigo's guardian, who during the past years had acted as her counsellor, confessor and loyal friend.

In a corrupt and ruthless family, Francesco Borgia, Cardinal of Cosenza, stands out as a gentle and saintly character, and it speaks for Lucrezia's common sense, that from all her cardinal cousins, she should have chosen the unworldly son of Calixtus III to act as guardian to her child. But despite her depression at her cousin's departure she appears to have recovered in time to make a radiant appearance at a ball in Urbino, where writing to his sister Isabella, Ferrante d'Este describes the new duchess as 'surpassing herself in beauty in a magnificent black velvet gown, slashed and embroidered in gold, with the Este rubies round her neck, and on her head a coif of beaten gold ornamented with an enormous diamond'. 'She has dresses such as you have never seen,' adds the susceptible young prince who was already half in love.

At Urbino and elsewhere Lucrezia was received with royal honours. Duke Guidobaldo had little reason to love the Borgias, but his fear of Cesare, who was already casting a covetous eye on his duchy, led him to humble his pride in paying homage to the Pope's daughter. All the resources of one of the most civilized courts of Europe were placed at Lucrezia's disposal; the treasure houses of the Montefeltros were thrown open to her, and both she and the Este princes were lodged in the ducal palace vacated by their host. Six months later when Duke

Guidobaldo discovered that all his efforts had been to no avail, he complained with bitterness that the entertainment of Lucrezia and her suite of a hundred and fifty ladies with two thousand mouths to feed had cost him a month's revenue. Even the proud Duchess, who was born a Gonzaga princess, had gone to the length of accepting Duke Ercole's invitation to the wedding festivities in Ferrara, in the hope that by travelling in company with Lucrezia, she might win the friendship of one 'His Holiness was supposed to love more than any other person of his blood'.

From Urbino the two Duchesses travelled together in the sumptuous litter provided by the Pope to ensure his daughter's comfort on the journey. But though her father had exhorted Lucrezia to cultivate the Este and Gonzaga princesses and to emulate their behaviour, she had little in common with the grave-eyed Elisabetta, whose love for her good duke and pity for his physical infirmities had led her to seek refuge in an intense intellectual life and the chilly comforts of platonic love. How could any Borgia sympathize with such a touching fidelity, remembering the coarse jokes at the papal court, where the subject of Duke Guidobaldo's impotence was a favourite topic of conversation. Lying side by side in the stuffy intimacy of the brocaded litter it was difficult for these two women, so dissimilar in character and upbringing, to find any point of contact. And as the road brought them ever nearer to Pesaro, Lucrezia must have sensed the fundamental aversion underlying the politeness of the Duchess of Urbino; remembering that she was not only Giovanni Sforza's former sister-in-law, but that ever since his flight from Pesaro Giovanni had been living in exile at Francesco Gonzaga's court. Whether or not Lucrezia blamed herself for the part she had played in her divorce, it can hardly have been pleasant to make her state entry into Pesaro under the coldly critical eye of the Duchess of Urbino.

The little Adriatic town was decked out in welcome. There were the same triumphal arches as of old, the same tedious orations delivered by the magistrates, while the whole population had come out into the streets to cheer her with the same demonstrations of affection. The only difference was that instead of shouting 'Sforza! Sforza!' they now shouted 'Duca! Duca!', waving the red and yellow banners which proclaimed her brother's rule. Everywhere the Borgia bull had replaced the Sforza lion, and on the steps of their former palace stood Cesare's deputy, Ramiro di Lorqua, to welcome her in her brother's name. Did Lucrezia notice the way in which the Duchess of Urbino and her ladies instinctively recoiled from the handsome Spaniard, whose reputation for sadistic cruelty had spread beyond the confines of the Romagna? Did she recall the incident of the previous year, when on a visit to the court of Urbino, Cesare had fallen to the blue eyes of one of the Duchess's maids-of-honour, who was shortly afterwards kidnapped while on her way to join her bridegroom in Venice? At the time no one had doubted that this was another of the occasions where the faithful Spanish henchman had acted on his master's orders. But whatever Lucrezia may have noticed and remembered, at twenty-one she was already far too cynical to sympathize with the delicate susceptibilities of the virginal Duchess. Circumstances had forced her to make friends with her brother's cut-throats and with her usual charming smile she accepted Don Ramiro's proferred arm to lead her over the threshold of the palace where she had ruled as a girl bride.

Nevertheless she was not entirely insensitive, for during the twenty-four hours she spent in Pesaro, she remained closeted in her room and declined to take part in the festivities. The Ferrarese councillors who appear to have deliberately ignored her past as Countess of Pesaro, ascribed this behaviour 'to her natural inclination to solitude'. But no sooner had they left the city than the Duchess regained her spirits. Having turned her back on an embarrassing past she was free to enjoy the present. El Prete gives a delightful glimpse of Lucrezia and Don Ferrante leading the dance at Rimini, while the Spanish clowns cut capers round the room, calling out to the assembled company to admire their lovely duchess, 'the peerless Borgia who dances with such lissom grace'.

At Forli the city elders escorted Lucrezia to what had formerly been Caterina Sforza's palace. Only a few months ago she had seen the formidable virago released from captivity in St. Angelo; stout, white-haired and prematurely aged; a woman from whom neither the Pope nor Cesare had anything more to fear. So they had made the magnanimous gesture calculated to please the French and let her depart for Florence, bearing a papal Bull in which His Holiness recommended his 'beloved daughter in Christ, Caterina, to the care of the Signory'.

While Lucrezia rode in triumph through her brother's dukedom, her travelling companion, the Duchess of Urbino, saw with apprehension how within less than two years, the ruthless ambition of a single-minded man had welded the petty tyrannies of the Romagna into a concerted whole. Even in Faenza, where the majority of the people still remained loyal to their former lord, the young Astorre Manfredi, who after his surrender had put his trust in Cesare, only to find himself six months later thrown into the dungeons of St. Angelo—even here there were cheering crowds shouting 'Duca!' and 'Lucrezia!'.

At Imola Lucrezia took leave of Don Ramiro di Lorqua who had escorted her across the Romagna. Six months later when Cesare suddenly turned on the monster whose brutal excesses and abuse of power were endangering his whole régime, it was rumoured that Don Ramiro was being punished not only on account of his crimes but because of a certain scandalous incident connected with Donna Lucrezia's honour said to have occurred during her journey to Ferrara. Nothing is known of this incident, nor is it likely ever to have taken place, with Lucrezia under the constant supervision of five hundred Ferrarese.

As the bridal cortège wended its way northwards across the Emilian plain, the first of the wedding guests were already arriving at Ferrara. In obedience to her father's request came the Marchioness of Mantua, leaving her husband at home to guard his dominions in the eventuality of Cesare Borgia choosing the moment of his sister's wedding for a surprise incursion into northern Italy. To use her own words, 'it was in violent anger' that Isabella consented to do the honours in her father's palace and officially to receive Lucrezia into the bosom of the family. But Duke Ercole, of whom she was the favourite child, knew her well enough to realize that whatever might be her private sentiments, she preferred to play a leading rôle as hostess in her native city rather than be relegated to the position of a visitor. Now that Beatrice Sforza was dead she was the only one of his children with whom he had anything in common. They had the same cold cerebral natures and artistic flair, and as they toured the city inspecting the decorations, discussing the musical programme with the court musicians, attending the rehearsals of the Plautine comedies, the representation of which provided Duke Ercole with the only real pleasure in a week of tedious entertainment and expense, the Duke deferred to his daughter's judgment, relying on her impeccable taste, so intolerant of the second-rate, so quick to discern the slightest vulgarity. However parsimonious by nature, in common with the princes of the Renaissance, Ercole d'Este recognised the necessity of providing his people with lavish spectacles and shows, and no expense was being spared to make the State entry of Lucrezia Borgia into the most magnificent pageant ever witnessed in Ferrara. Masons, carpenters and goldsmiths were working overtime; whole palaces were being transformed to accommodate the five thousand guests. All the poets of Duke Ercole's court were being mobilized to compose odes in honour of the bridal couple, and it is not surprising, if, working under duress, even Ariosto's genius should have descended to a dreary Latin panegyric, in which the poet condoled with Rome on having lost Lucrezia and congratulated Ferrara on having gained an incomparable jewel, going to the length of referring to the thrice-married duchess as 'pulcherrima virgo'.

The one person who appears to have taken no interest in these elaborate preparations was the bridegroom. There was no love lost between the Duke of Ferrara and his eldest son, who resented the little share he was given in the administration and governing of the state and who consoled himself for this lack of activity at home by extensive travel, studying in different countries the latest developments in modern warfare. Proud and uncompromising by nature, Alfonso d'Este had been so averse to marriage with a Borgia that till now he had left his father to conduct the negotiations and his younger brothers to do the wooing. But suddenly his curiosity appears to have been aroused. Maybe he was intrigued by the description of Lucrezia given by Don Ferrante or some chance reference made by one of his father's councillors, or maybe it was just the natural reluctance on the part of a virile and sensual man to have his first encounter with his wife under the curious eyes of his entire family. Whatever may have been his motives, on the 31st of January, when Lucrezia was journeying towards the Bentivoglio castle in the marshes of the Po, from where she was to proceed on the following day by canal and river to Ferrara, Don Alfonso, accompanied by three of his friends, left the city in disguise to keep tryst with an unsuspecting bride.

Lucrezia had hardly arrived at Bentivoglio when the arrival of Alfonso d'Este was suddenly announced, and one can picture the excitement and commotion, the bustle and flutter of her ladies. There was no time to change into one of her elaborate dresses or to deck herself with jewels, no time for ceremonial etiquette. Already he claimed the right of entry, a tall stalwart figure with a square, rather brutal face, redeemed by the fine aquiline Este nose, the slate-blue eyes, which noted her every movement. Here was a man who would subjugate her to his will and maybe this knowledge gave her a certain erotic excitement which brightened her eyes and illumined her smile.

He had seen her before as a spoiled sophisticated girl of thirteen on the eve of her engagement to Giovanni Sforza. Face and features had hardly changed, but there was now a wisdom and tolerance in her smile, and experience in her eyes, promising a sensuality which matched his own, an acceptance of life on his own terms. They stayed together for two hours, then he left as suddenly as he had come. And though little is known as to what passed between them, the chroniclers of Ferrara wrote 'that the people greatly rejoiced, as did the bride and her own followers, because His Highness had shown a desire to see her and had received her well—an indication that she would be accepted and treated still better.' Unofficial reports went even further and asserted that during these two hours Alfonso had already claimed his marital rights. Whether or not this was true, it was during these two hours that Lucrezia won her first victory. The physical magnetism she inherited from her father helped to overcome her bridegroom's aversion and to disarm his suspicions. In Lucrezia Alfonso had found a wife who combined the aspect of a virgin with the talents of a courtesan, the subtlety of a diplomat with the gaiety of a child, and who despite her outward modesty was at heart so utterly indifferent as to ask for little beyond respect, the respect which was due to a duchess of Ferrara.

XXVII

LUCREZIA BORGIA made her State entry into Ferrara on February 2nd, 1502, and though there was no lack of chroniclers and envoys to describe the wedding festivities, no one gives a more vivid picture than Isabella Este, who in her letters to her husband the Marquess of Mantua, evokes both the pageantry of the Este court, and the underlying emotion, the jealousy and vanity, suspicion and coldness, which for all their demonstrations of affection marked the relationship between the two sisters-in-law.

It was eight o'clock of a cold winter morning when the Marchioness of Mantua in company of her half-brother Don Giulio d'Este set out in a *bucantaur* to travel up the Po as far as Malalbergo, where they were to meet the bride. Neither time nor place were conducive to good humour, and the knowledge that Alfonso had secretly, and without consulting her, visited Lucrezia the previous evening must have robbed Isabella of any pleasurable anticipation of sharing in his first impressions. Only her insatiable curiosity and her indomitable vanity helped her to maintain her spirits, triumphantly beautiful in her emerald velvet tunic studded with plaques of gold, her black velvet robe lined with the finest lynx, and fastened with a fabulous diamond collar. But even her self-confidence must have failed her for a moment, as through the mist came the gilded *bucantaur* with Lucrezia standing at the helm, a gay little figure in scarlet and gold protected from the northern winter by an enormous sable cape. 'I will not describe Madonna Lucrezia's appearance as you have already seen her,' wrote Isabella to her husband. Maybe she suspected him of too warm an admiration for his new sister-in-law, remembering the cold, bald letter he had once written her from Rome, which instinctively she had recognized at the time as being too deliberately casual in its references to the Pope's daughter. But if Isabella chose to ignore Lucrezia's appearance, one of her devoted ladies-in-waiting was ready to inform the Marquis:

> the bride is not beautiful but sweet and attractive in appearance and although she had many ladies with her, and among them that illustrious Madonna, the Duchess of Urbino, who is very handsome and a worthy sister of your Excellency, yet my illustrious lady was universally pronounced both by our people and by those who came with the Duchess, to be by far the most beautiful, so much so, that if the bride had foreseen this, she would have made her entry by torchlight.

The biased opinion of a lady-in-waiting was not sufficient to reassure Isabella as she observed Lucrezia's effect not only on her brothers but also on her frigid father.

> About four o'clock we reached Torre della Fossa, [she writes] where my father was standing on the shore awaiting us. The archers in their red and white liveries, seventy-five in number, were drawn up in a row and the whole court gathered round the Duke, who took Madonna Lucrezia by the hand and kissed her after she had first insisted on kissing his hand.

Duke Ercole had every reason to be pleased with his daughter-in-law. He had already been informed of the good impression she had made upon his son, which promised well for the future, and two days ago he had welcomed the safe arrival of his beloved nuns, shepherded by one of his counsellors, who told him that had it not been for the assistance of the Duchess, he would never have persuaded them to leave Rome. 'In fact he had never known what labour was, until he had to make so many stubborn heads agree.' Other and more important considerations helped to influence the Duke. The Pope had made it clear that future favours to Ferrara depended on the welcome given to Lucrezia. In no uncertain terms he had warned the Cardinal of Modena: 'Tell the Duke to treat my daughter kindly, and we will continue to exert ourselves on her behalf.' Therefore it was not surprising if Duke Ercole was prepared to treat his daughter-in-law 'in such a way, that His Holiness would see that he regarded her as the most precious jewel he had in the world'. But even someone of his cold and calculating nature may have been capable of a spontaneous spark of feeling in response to Lucrezia's sweet and disarming smile. And Isabella observed that her father was both gayer and more animated than usual.

> We entered the Ducal bucantaur, where all the ambassadors shook hands with us, and we sat down in the following order—the bride between the French and the Venetian—myself between the Venetian and the Florentine, and the Duchess of Urbino between the Florentine and the Siennese, the Lucchese being close by. My father and Don Alfonso sat in the poop, talking and joking together, and were much amused by the Spanish clowns who paid the bride all manner of compliments. And so amid cheering and shouting and the sound of trumpets and guns we reached Casale at about five.

Here, two miles from the city gates, the river journey came to an end, and Lucrezia in company of her Spanish and Roman courtiers was escorted to the castle where she was to spend the night, before making her official entry on the following day. The rest of the party returned to Ferrara, leaving behind them a group of shivering strangers, lost and bewildered in a world of grey mists and marshy plains where the poplars cast their barren shadows against the leaden sky and the great swollen river flung its load of shingles onto a muddy shore. Wrapped in their furs the courtiers huddled round fires and braziers, while Lucrezia retired to her room to write her daily letter to the Pope recounting her triumphs in the Valencian dialect which was still their native tongue.

The following day the Duke of Ferrara, together with Don Alfonso and the various ambassadors attached to his court, rode out to fetch the bride. And in the early afternoon the cavalcade of princes, diplomats and prelates, preceded by trumpeters and archers and followed by twelve chariots full of ladies-in-waiting, and seventy mules laden with the bride's trousseau entered into the city. All the consummate artistry of the Estes had manifested itself in a procession worthy of the brush of a Tura or an Ercole Roberti. But all that survives are written descriptions, monotonous in their insistence on the value of every suit of brocade and golden necklace. The main object of these processions was to impress the onlooker with the wealth and magnificence of the ruling house. No people were more money-conscious than the fifteenth-century Italians, and both in the diaries of Marino Sanudo and in the chronicles of Zambotto, we read of how 'no less than seventy gentlemen of Ferrara wore golden chains some of which were worth up to twelve hundred ducats', while Isabella writes to her husband with pride of how none of the Spanish gentlemen in the bride's suite 'had necklaces equal to those worn by our own Mantuan gentlemen'. In describing her brother riding at the head of the procession, she dwells not so much on the magnificence of his appearance, as on the fact that 'his grey velvet suit covered in scales of beaten gold was worth six thousand ducats'. Only once does she give way to sentiment—a sentiment based on a profound resentment to see Lucrezia wearing the diamonds and rubies, which had formerly belonged to her mother, 'the Madonna of Ferrara of blessed memory'.

It must have been galling to Isabella to watch the Spanish adventuress being acclaimed in the streets of her native town, for there was no doubting the enthusiasm of the people. Lucrezia captured their hearts from the moment when, in crossing the river bridge, her horse took fright at the sound of the guns and stumbled. Badly thrown and shaken, she merely laughed at her discomfiture and proceeded on a mule amidst a frenzied burst of cheering. Years later Ariosto was to sing of:

> "Lucretia Borgia di cui d'Noza *in Noza*.
> La Belta, la virtu, la fama honesta
> e la fortuna crecera nomeno
> Che giovin pianta in morbido terreho'
> > Ariosto.

But before Lucrezia had taken root in Ferrara, before her impeccable conduct as their Duchess had vindicated her reputation, her charm and gaiety alone sufficed to conquer her future subjects, whom according to Zambotto 'she pleased so greatly that they were perfectly satisfied with her and already looked to her for protection and good judgment.'

Proudly she rode into the city, surrounded by a characteristic

Borgia entourage of Spanish captains, prelates and buffoons, and from the windows of the Customs House, the Marchioness of Mantua, who with her natural curiosity had insisted on watching the parade before proceeding to the ducal palace, described her arrival:

> Then came the bride's suite, [she writes] twenty of whom were Spaniards clad in black velvet and gold. . . . These were followed by the bishops of Adria, Comacchio and Cervia and two others sent by the Pope. Then came the ambassadors, walking two abreast—last of all the four Roman ones in long cloth-of-gold mantles lined in crimson satin. Behind them were six drummers and two Spanish jesters in brocades of variegated colours. Then the bride riding under a crimson baldaquin mounted on a roan mule with velvet trappings covered in gold lace, and wearing a cloth-of-gold gown with purple satin stripes, cut with flowing sleeves in the French fashion and a mantle of wrought gold open at the side and lined with ermine.

Isabella noted that for once Lucrezia had deserted her Spanish fashions in favour of the French, a gesture which was no doubt intended as a compliment to the King of France, who had been so largely instrumental to her marriage.

Behind the bride rode the Duke of Ferrara in company of the Duchess of Urbino, and it must have seemed strange for Ercole d'Este to see the day he had done all in his power to postpone being hailed by his subjects as the glorious climax of his reign. Nevertheless he must have observed with pleasure the grace with which Lucrezia acquitted herself as the central figure in his pageant. In his daughter-in-law he had found a consummate actress worthy of his staging—a woman too subtle and intelligent ever to endanger her position as the future Duchess of Ferrara, the future mother of the Estes. But there was someone who had even greater reason to take pride in Lucrezia's performance, and this was her former governess, Adriana Mila. As widow to an Orsini and a kinswoman of the Pope, Adriana had a prominent place in the procession, and it speaks for the robust Spanish stock of the Borgias, that she and Lucrezia's two cousins, Girolama Borgia married to Fabio

Orsini and her beautiful fifteen year-old-sister Angela, were the only women to ride horseback in the procession.

It was evening when the vast cortège reached the cathedral square, coming to a halt outside the ducal palace, where in the marble courtyard illuminated by torches, the Marchioness of Mantua waited to receive the bride. As Lucrezia passed under the archway flanked by the statues of former dukes, pipers and trumpeters burst into a fanfare of welcome, the prison doors swung open to release the inmates, and from the lighted tower of the Rigobello two rope-walkers dropped down at the bride's feet to deliver laudatory addresses. Too weary to pay attention to the orations of the poets, too weary to do anything more than smile her eternally radiant smile, the young bride passed across the threshold of the Este palace. But even now there was no respite. For next morning Duke Ercole was already informing his ambassador in Rome, in a letter intended for the Pope's consumption, 'Last night our illustrious son Don Alfonso went to bed with his wife Donna Lucrezia, and from all accounts it appears that they were well satisfied with one another.'

Nevertheless in the opinion of the Marchioness of Mantua 'It was a very cold wedding', so much so, that neither she nor her younger brothers ventured to indulge in the customary wedding pranks, by which members of the family would burst into the privacy of the bedchamber and subject the bridal couple to every kind of ribald joke. Lucrezia's attitude did not encourage such intimacy. However amenable or forthcoming she might show herself in her relations with her husband, she persisted in maintaining a cold and polite reserve towards his family, particularly towards his sister, the Marchioness of Mantua. From the very first she sensed in Isabella the same underlying hostility as in the Duchess of Urbino. The two were the closest friends and they lost no opportunity of emphasizing their intellectual superiority. Lucrezia's intelligence was eminently practical. She had no use for the literary conceits and affectations in vogue at the humanistic courts, and her first contact with the Este and Gonzaga princesses left her both irritated and suspicious. At twenty-two, experience had taught her that to love one's husband was the gravest and cruellest of errors, and it was surprising to find the two most intellectual women in Italy were faithful and adoring wives; still more surprising to discover that Isabella d'Este, of whose political acumen even her brother spoke with ill-concealed respect, was so beset by feminine vanity as to go to the lengths of bribing the Spanish clowns to sing her praises.

The rivalry of Marchioness and Duchess was the focal point of interest during a week of otherwise dreary festivities. If Isabella judged the wedding to be cold, the elaborate entertainments organized by her father were still colder. Forced to spend twenty-five thousand ducats on the entertainment of his five thousand guests, Duke Ercole was determined they should be made to appreciate his favourite classical comedies. His passion for the drama amounted to an obsession, and however careful in his personal expenditure, there was always money to spare for a new production of Plautus. But it is doubtful whether his guests shared his enthusiasm. Even his cultured daughter complained of the inordinate length of these comedies, while one of them, the celebrated *Casina*, was considered by her 'to be lascivious and immoral', so that she refused to allow her maids of honour to attend. Characteristic of Lucrezia, it appears to have been the only performance she really enjoyed, laughing heartily at the situations and innuendoes her sister-in-law decried. But on the whole she must have been bored by those interminable comedies and fêtes. For once carnival had lasted far too long. At her father's orders it had already started in Rome, and the same decorated floats and mythological allegories had greeted her in every city on her journey north. For the past months she had had a surfeit of compliments and entertainments, and even a stronger constitution than her own would have wilted under the strain. It is not surprising if she spent the greater part of the day relaxing in the company of Adriana and her Spanish ladies, refusing to admit visitors to the privacy of her apartments, so that before long the Ferrarese ladies were complaining to the sympathetic ears of the Marchioness of Mantua 'of being neglected by the new Duchess who had no use for anyone but her Spanish relatives'.

'All the ladies come and visit me in the morning,' wrote Isabella to her husband, 'for Donna Lucrezia is not to be seen

218

until she appears in the *sala*.' As a postscript she added, 'I must tell you to my credit that I am always the first to be dressed.' Somewhat maliciously she attributes her sister-in-law's unpunctuality to the fact that 'Madonna Lucrezia chooses to spend all these hours in dressing, so that she may outshine the Duchess of Urbino and myself in the eyes of the world'. No doubt Isabella was right for it was not in the nature of a Borgia to take second place. Conscious of her intellectual inferiority, Lucrezia must have made all the more effort to exploit her physical assets, and even Isabella paid tribute to her grace on the occasion when, dressed in a gown of mulberry brocade with a jewelled coronet on her flowing hair, she danced French country dances with infinite charm and spirit.

'Sparkling, animated, for ever laughing,' the ambassadors used the very words they employed in describing her father. It was as if the Borgias alone possessed the secret of eternal youth, overcoming boredom and fatigue by their triumphant vitality, their insatiable zest for life. But though Lucrezia might appear in public to be radiant and expansive, in private she continued to be both reticent and cold, and throughout the week Isabella was accorded no more than a formal politeness. When the Lenten sermons finally put an end to the festivities and the wedding guests prepared to depart, it must have been with mutual relief that Isabella and Lucrezia said goodbye. Jealousy and distrust on the one hand, and defensive pride on the other, had prevented the maturing of any friendship or understanding. But Lucrezia did not expect either friendship or understanding from the Estes. So long as her husband shared her bed at night and honoured her in public she was content to remain a stranger in their midst.

XXVIII

EANWHILE THE POPE was being kept informed of every detail of Lucrezia's reception in Ferrara. Costabili, the new Ferrarese envoy, was always at his side, and it seemed as if he would never tire of hearing his daughter's praises sung. Nothing pleased him so much as the news that Don Alfonso slept every night with his wife. 'As for his days, let him do as he pleases. He is young and is free to take his pleasure where he finds it.' The Borgia Pope was hardly likely to expect fidelity of his son-in-law. But he continued to miss his daughter, and even the prostitutes provided by Cesare failed to compensate him for her absence. Such was his longing for feminine companionship that he summoned the turbulent Sanchia and her husband back to Rome, presenting them with a splendid palace in the Borgo, and bolstering the pride of the neglected Joffré by giving him the condotta of a hundred men. Though it was not in the nature of a princess of Aragon either to forget or to forgive, Sanchia seems to have found it preferable to accept life in Rome on the old terms, rather than to live on in exile in the corkwoods of Squillace, and before long she was once more living on terms of intimacy with her brother's murderer.

A new addition to the Borgia family circle was Ippolyto d'Este, whose position at the Vatican was in reality that of a hostage to Lucrezia's fortunes. On more than one occasion we hear of him carrying out her commissions in Rome, giving her news of her little son. And the young Cardinal, who at heart was the cruellest and most unscrupulous of all the Estes, and fully a match for his new relatives, writes with the tenderness of a woman describing a visit to the baby *duchetto*, whom he found sleeping peacefully in his cot 'as healthy and as beautiful as ever'.

Meanwhile the foreign ambassadors in Rome were waiting on Cesare Borgia's next move. Throughout the winter and the early spring, he continued to make his headquarters in the Vatican, surrounding himself with the usual atmosphere of secrecy, refusing to give audience, but nevertheless being present at every interview granted by the Pope, as if he feared lest his garrulous father might commit some indiscretion as to his future plans.

There was no longer any trace of the modesty and high spirits which had rendered Cesare so attractive in his youth. In his journal, Branca de Talini describes him as 'the haughtiest man he had ever met', while his temper was so ungoverned that on occasion he even lost control in presence of his father. A Mantuan agent relates

> how one day in front of His Holiness and members of his court, the Lord Valentino, seized by a violent anger, made passes with a dagger at one of the cardinals, and on being severely reproved by the Pope merely replied by threatening him that if he did not hold his peace, he would do the same to him.

But apart from a few official excuses, an occasional complaint to one of his ambassadors, Alexander appears to have made little attempt to curb the excesses of his son. Cesare's spies policed the city and anyone who in a tavern dared to speak against the Borgias was in danger of having his tongue cut out by order of the Duke. Left to himself the Pope would have been indifferent to these slanders. When the most defamatory of all the libels ever circulated against the Borgias appeared in the form of a letter addressed to Silvio Savelli, one of the dispossessed Roman barons living in exile at Maximilian's court, Alexander VI insisted on having the document read out to him. And though it contained all the most outrageous charges ever brought against a Pope, naming him as the anti-Christ and calling on Savelli to rouse the Emperor to take up arms against him, he made no attempt to discover the author or to prohibit the circulation. Cesare's attitude was very different, and his father deplored his vindictiveness, telling the Ferrarese ambassador:

> the Duke is good-hearted, but he cannot bear an insult. I have often told him that Rome is a free city, where a man

may say and write what he will but he only answers that if that is their custom, then he will teach the people to change their ways. For my part I have always been forgiving. Witness the cardinals who plotted against me when Charles VIII invaded Italy. I might have rid myself many times of Ascanio Sforza and Giuliano della Rovere, but I did not do so.

Alexander was speaking the truth, for, judged by the standards of the secular princes, he was both tolerant and forgiving. It was the schizophrenic slant to his character which rendered him so inhuman as a Pope, even to a generation inured to the scandals of a Sixtus IV, the nepotism of an Innocent VIII. This schizophrenia became ever more marked in his old age; so that his actions as Cesare's father had no relation to his position as the head of Christendom, while the duties of his sacred office afforded no restraint to the ruthless pursuing of family interest, the frenzied haste to found a Borgia dynasty in the few short years which remained to him. While Cesare appears to have become completely indifferent to the young duchess he had left behind in France, his father kept writing to Charlotte d'Albret to join her husband in Italy and settle down to 'the business of breeding sons'. But gossip and rumour appear to have been sufficiently scandalous to disillusion Charlotte from her first transports of youthful passion, and Italy never saw the Duchess of Valentinois. No dynasty of young Borgias grew up in the palace of Cesena, the town chosen by Cesare as his capital of the Romagna. There was only an ugly little girl in France, who within a year of her birth was already betrothed to the heir of the Gonzagas—negotiations conducted by Cesare Borgia and Isabella d'Este with all the cunning and mutual distrust which characterized their relations, for after criticizing her father for receiving Lucrezia Borgia into the family, Isabella was now ready to fawn on Il Valentino, begging him to act as godfather to her son, accepting in the most flattering terms his offer of a matrimonial alliance.

The fantastic luck of the Borgias persisted throughout the year. Circumstances combined to favour their plans. France and Spain were already quarrelling over their respective boundaries in the Neapolitan Regno, and each was anxious to have the Pope as ally.

The energies of Venice were absorbed in fighting the Turks, and all the rich provinces of central Italy lay at the mercy of Il Valentino and his condottieri. Where would he strike next? Some talked of Florence, with whom his ablest captains, the Orsini and the Vitelli, had an old grudge to settle. And when in the month of June both Pisa and Arezzo rose in rebellion in favour of the exiled Medicis, with Vitellozzo Vitelli and Paolo Orsini openly fighting on the side of the insurgents, it was generally believed that Cesare Borgia had incited the revolt. But at the time when all eyes were turned towards the Florentine frontiers and the panic-stricken Signoria was imploring the help of France, came the news of the invasion of Urbino. Swiftly and suddenly Cesare Borgia had struck, disregarding the fact that Guidobaldo of Montefeltro had always acted as a loyal condottiere to the Church, and that the duchy of Urbino had never been included among the proscribed vicariates. The attack was as dastardly as it was brilliant: to the very last Cesare had kept his plans a secret, and though in the past year Guidobaldo had lived in fear of Borgia ambitions, the invasion came at the moment when he least expected it. Only a few days previously Cesare had assured him 'that he loved him as a brother'. Now within the space of a few hours the man 'who loved him as a brother' had taken Guidobaldo's fortresses by storm. And, disguised as a peasant, the wretched duke had barely time to flee before'the invader was at the gates of his town.

The spectacle of a Montefeltro being hounded out of his Duchy shocked even the most cynical of princes. And coinciding with the rape of Urbino came the news of the murder of the young Manfredi of Faenza, who after the surrender of his town had entrusted himself to his conqueror, and whose body was now found drowned in the Tiber—an innocent boy guilty of no other crime than of being too well loved by his people. No one felt safe—not even those who had bought the alliance of the Borgias. And when it became known that the King of France was about to return to Italy to organize his defences against Spain, a concerted league of Italian princes, both those who were ruling and those who had been dispossessed, made plans to travel to Milan to make King Louis aware of the growing danger of supporting 'one who would be content to be nothing less than King of Italy'.

In Ferrara Lucrezia was beginning to discover that life at the Este court was fraught with difficulties. It was only in the intimacy of her Spanish entourage that she allowed herself to relax. And the number of these Spaniards was dwindling day by day, for ever since their arrival in Ferrara, her father-in-law had been viewing with a jaundiced eye, 'the band of arrogant foreigners, whose presence involved him in unnecessary expense and whose general unpopularity did little good either to His Holiness or the Duchess'. On the pretext of economizing in her household, Duke Ercole was sending back to Rome all those whom he suspected of being Cesare Borgia's spies, but now for the first time he found that Lucrezia was not as amenable as he had hoped. Deprived of her favourite Spaniards, she retaliated by ostracizing the Ferrarese ladies attached to her service. And before long Duke Ercole was being beset by weeping women and indignant courtiers complaining of the cold treatment accorded them by the new Duchess. When his ambassador, Costabili, warned him that the returning Spaniards were complaining to the Pope and embittering his good relations with His Holiness, Duke Ercole deemed it wiser to allow his daughter-in-law to retain a nucleus of her foreign court.

But there was another and more serious difference between Lucrezia and her father-in-law, which concerned the question of her allowance. Duke Ercole categorically refused to give her the 12,000 ducats demanded by the Pope, declaring that 10,000 ducats was more than sufficient for her needs. But when it came to money the Borgias were as hard-headed as the Estes. Alexander VI had allowed himself to be fleeced in order to buy his daughter a ducal crown, but he was determined 'that mean old tradesman of an Ercole d'Este' should treat Lucrezia with a consideration due to one 'who had brought a dowry of nearly 200,000 ducats into the family'. As for Lucrezia, she had no intention of economizing. Since her earliest childhood she had had her most extravagant whims gratified at the expense of the papal treasury. And it was characteristic of her attitude in regarding the Church as an inexhaustible source of supply, that in writing to her father, complaining of 'being so hard up that she had been forced to pawn some of her jewels', she asked him as if it were the most natural thing in the world to grant her the yearly revenue of the Archbishopric of Ferrara. Meanwhile she ordered velvets and brocades on credit from the Venetian merchants, and short of having an open quarrel with the Pope, Duke Ercole had no means of checking his daughter-in-law's extravagance.

Alfonso d'Este seems wisely to have kept out of these domestic quarrels. His relations with his wife were almost entirely confined to the bed-chamber. By day he left her to preside with his father at court, while he spent his time between the arsenal and the tavern, experimenting with some new type of cannon or drinking in company of the rough and bawdy soldiers whose company he preferred to the effeminate and perfumed poets of his father's circle. In public Duke Ercole continued to treat his daughter-in-law with every mark of deference and in his frigid fashion he seems to have had a certain admiration for her spirit, for hardly a day passed when he did not call for her in his *caretta*, a kind of open chariot he used for making excursions in the neighbourhood. But Duke Ercole's idea of a pleasant afternoon, spent in visiting his beloved Sister Lucia in her new convent, or in watching his court painters at work on the frescoes of the castle of Belfiore, was not calculated to enliven a young woman suffering from the first effects of a difficult pregnancy. Nor was the atmosphere of the 'Castel Vecchio' which he had handed over as a home to the young couple, likely to dissipate the pangs of loneliness and melancholy.

To this day the grim castle of the Estes, with its rust-coloured bastions overlooking a sunless moat, remains one of the gloomiest and most desolate of Italian palaces, haunted as it was already in Lucrezia's time by the most tragic of all the Este ghosts, the lovely ill-fated Parisina, murdered by her husband when he caught her in adultery with his own son. The proximity of Parisina's dungeon may have served as a salutary reminder to one of Lucrezia's temperament, warning her that in the matter of family relationships the Estes were by no means as tolerant as the Borgias. And any budding intimacy there may have been between her and her young brothers-in-law withered in this knowledge.

Lucrezia had barely been married four months when Cesare Borgia marched into Urbino, and for once even her loyalty to her brother could not prevent her from expressing her horror and disgust. In the privacy of her apartments she confided to her intimates that 'she would have given 50,000 ducats never to have known the Duchess of Urbino or to have accepted Duke Guidobaldo's hospitality'. And as usual Isabella's spies were there to overhear and to repeat, though it is doubtful whether Isabella believed in the sincerity of her sister-in-law's assertion. The women of the Renaissance were not given to sentiment, and despite her genuine affection for the Duchess of Urbino, the warm welcome she had given the exiles at her court, Isabella was already intriguing with the conqueror, hoping to secure for her famous *grotto* two masterpieces she coveted in the Montefeltro collection. Barely a week after the Duke of Romagna, clad in golden armour, had made his state entry into Urbino, Isabella was already negotiating for her share of the spoils. With cold-blooded effrontery she writes to Cardinal Ippolyto in Rome, begging him to interest himself on her behalf, to secure her a certain Venus and a little Cupid she had set her heart on, 'for she herself was not on sufficiently intimate terms with the Duke to ask such a favour at his hands'. Never is one more conscious of the self-centred ruthlessness of the Estes, than when without a trace of shame Isabella writes:

> since I am very anxious to collect antiques for the decoration of my studio, I desire exceedingly to possess these statues, which does not seem to me impossible as I hear that His Excellency has little taste for antiquities and would accordingly be more ready to oblige.

The Cupid Isabella believed to be an antique was in reality an early work of the young sculptor Michelangelo Buonarotti, which Cesare had himself presented to Duke Guidobaldo. And though willing to comply with the wishes of one whom he calls his 'Honoured Godmother' and 'Dearest sister', Cesare reminded Isabella that if she were so anxious to remain on friendly terms with the Borgias it would be as well for her to persuade her husband not to harbour within his territory so many enemies of the Church.

Unfortunately for Isabella, Francesco Gonzaga had none of the Este caution, and when he travelled to Milan to persuade King Louis to throw out the 'Priest's bastard' who was destroying Italy, his loving wife had every reason to fear for his safety. On the very day when she received from Cesare the coveted Cupid, she was warning her husband to take precautions against the possibility of Borgia poison.

> There is a report that Your Excellency has spoken angry words against Il Valentino before the most Christian king and the Pope's servants. And whether this be true or not, it will doubtless reach the ears of Valentino, who having already shown that he does not scruple to conspire against those of his own blood, will I am certain not hesitate to plot against your person . . . it will be perfectly easy for anyone to poison Your Excellency since you have neither guards nor proper servants. I pray and implore you therefore to be more careful both for my sake and for that of our little son.

So writes Isabella of the man from whom she was ready to accept both presents and favours. And four months later, when Guidobaldo made an abortive attempt to regain his Duchy, only to be expelled once more by Borgia arms, his sister-in-law was among the first to congratulate the victor on his conquest, sending him the gift of a hundred masks 'with which to find some rest and recreation from the exertions of his glorious undertakings'.

But while Isabella was negotiating with Il Valentino, and Duke Ercole was advising his son 'not to commit himself regarding the conquest of Urbino, but to speak about it in such a way as not to offend his most Christian Majesty or the illustrious Duke of Romagna', Cesare's sister, acting on her own accord, was writing to her father begging him to assist the unfortunate Duchess of Urbino. It was not Lucrezia's fault if the Pope's offer of assistance was couched in such a way as to outrage the proud Gonzaga princess. Openly referring to Guidobaldo's physical infirmities, Alexander VI had no other suggestion to make than that the Duchess's marriage should be annulled, and that a Cardinal's hat should compensate the Duke for the loss of both his Duchy and his wife.

XXIX

THE DUCHESS OF FERRARA was ill and there was alarm and consternation at the court. It was not so much concern for Lucrezia as fear at the possible repercussions lest her illness should prove fatal. At first it had seemed to be no more than a slight attack of fever, which during the summer months was prevalent in the Po valley. But then complications set in, aggravated by her difficult pregnancy, and both the Pope and Il Valentino were informed of the gravity of the situation. However much against his will, Duke Ercole had now to submit to a constant come and go of papal emissaries. To have opposed the Pope and his son from sending their own physicians to consult with the doctors of his court would have been tantamount to admitting the possibility of poison. The Ferrarese envoys were already sending unpleasant reports from Rome of how His Holiness had hinted that his daughter's illness was brought about not so much by physical as by moral causes, namely her distress at the niggardly way in which the Duke was behaving over the matter of her dowry. His Holiness had gone so far as to imply that 'should the Duchess die, the Estes might have even greater reason to mourn her than the Borgias'—a thinly-veiled threat that Ferrara's future security depended on the fragile life of the young Duchess.

It was imperative for the Estes to give the impression of cherishing the Pope's daughter, and Don Alfonso was hastily summoned from Milan to play the rôle of a devoted husband by his wife's sickbed. But for once there was no need for diplomatic play-acting. In her illness Lucrezia seems to have succeeded in touching a softer chord in her husband's rugged nature. Till now he had regarded her as a mistress rather than as a wife. But in this new mood of protective tenderness, Don Alfonso showed genuine anxiety at his wife's condition, solemnly vowing that should she recover he would make a pilgrimage of thanksgiving to the·Madonna of Loreto.

Another and even greater egotist than Alfonso d'Este appears to have been moved by the news of Lucrezia's malady, and barely a day passed without a messenger from Cesare arriving in Ferrara. Only a few of his letters survive and these strike us as cold and self-centred, giving but little insight into the true nature of the relationship between brother and sister. When Cesare blandly assumes that 'nothing could be better medicine for Lucrezia than to hear of his victory at Camerino', adding, 'we trust that on receiving this news your condition will improve and that you will inform us at once of it, for your indisposition prevents us from taking pleasure in either this or any other victory', he might just as well be writing to Duke Ercole as to the sister whom 'he loves better than he loves himself'. For in his strange perverse fashion Cesare was genuinely devoted to Lucrezia. Why should he otherwise have left King Louis's court to hurry to Ferrara the moment he heard her illness had taken a graver turn, insisting on staying with her till the doctors assured him she was out of danger? And again a few weeks later, after Lucrezia had given birth to a stillborn child and was reported to be dying, we hear of Il Valentino suddenly arriving at night 'with his brother-in-law the Cardinal d'Albret and thirteen gentlemen of his following', all of whom the Estes were forced to entertain. While the doctors attempted to alleviate Lucrezia's fever by the application of leeches, Cesare remained at his sister's bedside, holding her foot during all the operation and distracting her attention with ribald stories.

If Cesare's feelings towards his sister are difficult to understand, Lucrezia's attitude is even more incomprehensible. For whatever she had suffered from her brother in the past, or still feared in the future, she nevertheless loved him so blindly that his very presence was sufficient to infuse her with a new life and vitality. In their own palace the Estes had to submit to having secrets whispered in Spanish behind closed doors and not even Alfonso was admitted to share the intimacy between brother and sister. Il Valentino had only to appear upon the scene and the Duchess of Ferrara became once more Lucrezia

Borgia to whom the future of her husband's state was incidental to her brother's ambitions.

In Milan Cesare had triumphed over his enemies. Those who had sought to discredit him in the eyes of the King of France saw him received with royal honours. He was lodged in the castle, in rooms adjoining the King; he ate at the King's table, served with all his favourite dishes; the royal wardrobe and stables were put at his disposal. 'In short', as one of the Ferrarese envoys remarked, 'the King could not have done more for him, had he been his brother or his son'.

So overweening was Cesare's arrogance that when the Duke of Ferrara came to Milan, he never even troubled to return his visit. Ercole d'Este had little difficulty in tracing this deliberate insolence to the fact that Lucrezia had been complaining about her treatment at the Este court. The matter of her allowance was still unsettled. 'But if God himself intervened in favour of his daughter-in-law', Duke Ercole was determined not to part with a ducat more than the 10,000 already promised. It was unfortunate that Lucrezia's illness should have coincided with the visit of the French king, which brought her brother to the North of Italy and enabled him to make his unexpected, and from the Estes' point of view, totally unwarranted visits to his sister's bedside. Troche and Michel Remolino, two of the most sinister of the Borgia agents, were constantly carrying messages between them, but the Duke of Ferrara was powerless to intervene so long as Louis XII continued to treat Cesare Borgia as the favourite of the hour.

Meanwhile Lucrezia's fever persisted in varying degrees throughout the summer. The doctors gave conflicting diagnoses, but Duke Ercole's personal physician was nearest to the truth when he affirmed that there could be little improvement till after the confinement. Unfortunately the confinement itself was so exhausting that when she finally gave birth to a dead baby in the first days of September, she had so little resistance left that her own life was despaired of and a priest was summoned to administer the last sacrament. It was during these days when she was believed to be on her death-bed that she insisted on adding a codicil to her will, leaving a further legacy to her son Rodrigo.

The little Aragonese prince whom she had deserted so light-heartedly in her first enthusiasm at becoming Duchess of Ferrara, seems now to have been constantly in her thoughts. Religious in her primitive fashion, she may well have looked upon her abortive pregnancy as a punishment for having deserted her child. And as her health began to improve, the effect of her illness began to show itself in a cold indifference to both Ferrara and the Ferrarese. For the time being her father-in-law's exquisite courtesy, and her husband's genuine solicitude left her equally unmoved.

It was all-important for the Estes to have an heir, and Lucrezia knew that the only consolation they derived from her failure was that the dead baby had been a girl. Also in Rome her father was railing against the cruel fate which denied him any more grandchildren. The Pope's anxiety was justifiable. He was seventy-three and wanted to see his children firmly established before his death. He fully realised that the Estes would be capable of divorcing Lucrezia if she failed to produce a son. Without the protection of the Papacy even Cesare's kingdom would be in danger of disintegration unless secured by a Borgia dynasty. But with Charlotte d'Albret refusing to come to Italy there was little likelihood of Cesare producing any more legitimate heirs. As for Joffré and Sanchia, their loathing of one another was the common talk of Rome. And the Pope had to console himself with the two children who were already living in the Vatican—one of them the baby 'Duchetto', the other, the five-year-old *Infante Romano*. When Cesare's latest conquest of Camerino was bestowed on this nameless child, some said the Pope had acted in direct opposition to his son; others affirmed that Cesare had promised at his sister's sickbed to provide for the little boy. Even the ambassadors were now silent as to the origin of the new Duke of Nepi and of Camerino.

Fear of Cesare paralysed men's tongues. Sudden and mysterious deaths in the Sacred College; the acts of brutal aggression against defenceless neighbours, were tolerated and accepted as the order of the day. The same month which saw the rape of Urbino saw the death of the wealthy Cardinal of Modena, who had acted as intermediary in negotiating with the Estes. His death alone brought the Borgias 50,000 ducats, for he was not yet buried before the Pope had seized his possessions and distributed his benefices. This 50,000 ducats went towards helping Cesare to pay the fantastic salaries which led soldiers of fortune to enrol under his banner rather than enlist in the armies of France or Spain. But it was not only the soldiers of fortune who entered his service. The greatest brains of Italy were now ready to follow the Borgia star. In this year of 1502 Leonardo da Vinci became architect and engineer-general to the Duke, making surveys for roads and fortifications in the Romagna. To the men of the Renaissance personality was more important than ethics, and the fascination of Cesare Borgia's personality can best be summed up in the words of the celebrated Florentine, Niccolo Machiavelli, who met him for the first time four days after the capture of Urbino, when as secretary of the Signoria he accompanied Francesco Soderino on a mission to the Borgia court.

> This Duke is so enterprising [he writes] that nothing is too great to daunt him. And for the sake of glory and the extension of his dominions, he deprives himself of rest, yielding neither to fatigue nor danger. He arrives at one place before one hears that he has left the other. He gains the goodwill of his soldiers. He has got hold of the best men in Italy and has constant good luck, all of which things make him victorious and formidable.

This was the moment when Cesare saw himself holding the balance of power in Italy. The Spanish general, Gonsalo of Cordoba, had already invaded French territory in the Regno, and in order to prevent the pre-eminently Spanish Pope from succumbing to the overtures of Spain, Louis XII had to make further concessions to Borgia ambitions. It was now the turn of Bologna to be sacrificed to secure Il Valentino's active co-operation in the war with Spain. But just as his ambitions were about to be realized, Cesare was to pay for his own ruthlessness. For the price of Bologna he had waived his claims on Florence, and his condottieri were ordered to evacuate Arezzo. Vitellozzo Vitelli, who was thirsting to revenge his brother's execution by the Florentines, the Orsinis, who were plotting to restore the

233

Medicis, and the Baglionis, who were hoping to enrich themselves at the expense of Florence, saw themselves treated as no more than puppets to be used at will and cast aside if necessary. However divergent their interests, terror and indignation now combined to unite them, and in the first days of autumn the disaffected condottieri met in one of the Orsini castles on the shores of Lake Thrasymene to plot the overthrow of Borgia rule.

Cesare now faced the most serious opposition he had encountered in his hitherto meteoric career, and he confronted it in such a way as to earn the admiration of Machiavelli, who, observing him at work in his headquarters at Imola, marvelled at the quiet strength, the rapid adjustment to circumstances, with which he dealt with the emergency. With the utmost calm he accepted the inevitable setbacks, such as the revolt of Urbino and the return of Guidobaldo, followed by the loss of Camerino. At a time when his whole kingdom seemed in danger of disintegration, he appeared to have no more pressing occupation than to design new uniforms for his militia, or to discuss with Leonardo the plans for the Palace of Justice in Cesena. The disaffection of his ablest captains had depleted his forces, but he knew them to be incapable of concerted action. Mutual distrust hampered their movements and he was content to wait until jealousy and intrigue had done their work.

Meanwhile French aid was on its way, fresh funds had arrived from Rome to finance the levying of Swiss and Gascon troops in Lombardy. Even Lucrezia raised money from her already strained exchequer. But still he waited and this deliberate inaction spread panic among the insurgents, who each in turn suspected the other of having made a separate peace.

In Rome the old Pope used all his diplomatic wiles to ensnare the Orsinis to effect a reconciliation, and gradually one by one his enemies walked into the trap, double-crossing one another, leaving Guidobaldo to be chased once more from his dominions, while they came crawling for forgiveness, accepting the proferred hand, the welcoming smile, lured to Senigallia, where on the shores of the Adriatic, treachery was repaid by treachery. And on New Year's Eve of 1503 was enacted the drama which Machiavelli hails as 'the superb betrayal of Senigallia'. None of the four captains who travelled to Senigallia ever emerged alive. Those who had been wise enough to evade the invitation fled for their lives. The rebellion had failed and Cesare emerged as master of Central Italy, receiving messages of congratulation from the very princes who had prayed for his defeat. Estes and Gonzagas, who had been equally evasive in their offers of help, now outvied with one another in rejoicing over his victory. But though there are the letters of Duke Ercole and of Isabella, there are none of Lucrezia's. Her actions, however, speak for themselves, for she was barely out of the sickroom before she was negotiating for the pawning of her jewels to provide her brother with the money the Estes had refused. And the man who acted as her agent in this transaction was none other than her father-in-law's favourite courtier, the charming poet and dandy, Ercole Strozzi, who not only was responsible for reconciling Lucrezia to Ferrara and the Ferrarese but for introducing into her life the disturbing, fascinating presence of Pietro Bembo.

XXX

AFTER MONTHS of illness, Lucrezia had recovered her old zest for life. From the time she returned from the convent, where she had spent her convalescence, she gave the impression of being delighted both with Ferrara and the Ferrarese. Gone was her cold indifference, the haughty reticence with which she had treated her ladies. All were now included in her smiles. And even her apartments in the gloomy castle seemed to please her, since her father-in-law had decorated them according to her taste. The old Duke had also made amends regarding her allowance, which was finally settled by the ducal purveyor provisioning her household and the treasury paying her a revenue of six thousand ducats for her personal expenses.

Alfonso left for Loreto to fulfil his vows and give thanks for his wife's recovery. And Lucrezia took her place on the throne beside her father-in-law, presiding at those endless theatrical entertainments, with which Duke Ercole celebrated her return to health. But for all the Duke's attentions the prospect of a northern winter might have been very dismal, had she not found a new friend and companion in Ercole Strozzi.

A poet and the son of a poet, Ercole belonged to a collateral branch of the Florentine Strozzis, who had settled in Ferrara at the beginning of the thirteenth century. His father, Tito Vespasiano Strozzi, was one of the most accomplished Latinists of the day, and Duke Ercole's greatest friend. By virtue of this friendship, his son, beautiful, talented, but born lame—an infirmity which only rendered him the more appealing to women—had since his earliest youth been the cherished companion of the Este princesses. Poet and courtier at the same time, a natural confidant and a born intriguer, Ercole Strozzi was eminently fitted to introduce Lucrezia Borgia into the realm of humanists and scholars—the realm of passionate friendship and platonic love.

There had been no lack of poets and artists in the papal entourage, but they had only interested her father in so far as they contributed to the glory of his family. Except for one or two musicians—and, like the Pope, music was the only art of which Lucrezia had any real understanding—few artists could boast of having enjoyed her patronage. A catalogue of the books she brought with her to Ferrara makes pathetic reading when compared with the vast library of an Isabella d'Este, for it comprises little beyond a copy of Dante and of Petrarch, a collection of Spanish songs and proverbs and a few religious works also written in Spanish. In her short, tempestuous life, Lucrezia had had neither time nor opportunity to delve into the teachings of the humanists, till Ercole Strozzi introduced her into the charmed circle of poets and scholars whom his father attracted to his palace in Ferrara and to his villa at Ostellato. And it was here in the late autumn of 1502 that Lucrezia first encountered Pietro Bembo.

He was thirty-two at the time of their meeting and already recognized as one of the greatest living masters of Italian prose. Born the son of a Venetian patrician, educated partly in Venice, partly in Messina under the celebrated Greek scholar Lascaris, Bembo was more at home in the humanistic courts of Ferrara and Urbino than in his own native republic. Pride had led him to seek his fortunes abroad, for in a rich and selfish oligarchy like Venice, position was largely dependent on wealth. And political setbacks coupled with financial reverses had deprived his family of much of their former influence.

In Ferrara Pietro Bembo was assured not only of Duke Ercole's patronage, but of the unfailing friendship and generosity of the Strozzis. Their villa at Ostellato became his second home, and no place could have been more suited for quiet study than this turreted villa built on a floating piece of land among the lagoons of Comacchio, a perfect place for peace and meditation up to the day when the young Duchess of Ferrara paid her first visit to Ostellato. Then the heavy tomes of Aristotle were laid aside and poetic fancies chased philosophy away. Scholars became once more courtiers, whose erudition was designed to fascinate rather than to instruct. The legends of the troubadours mingled with the myths of ancient Rome,

Roland's paladins took their place next to the knights of the Round Table and Petrarch's Laura met with Lancelot's Guinevere. From her slender stock of knowledge Lucrezia contributed her Spanish songs, which doubtless had an added charm when sung to the lute in her soft and lilting voice. And though in maturer years Bembo might write of the corrupting influence of the Castilian tongue, he was only too willing to translate the Spanish verses transcribed in the fine slanting hand of the Duchess of Ferrara.

It is open to question as to whether Strozzi's devotion and Bembo's love for Lucrezia were calculated or sincere. It was a cynical age and even the most romantic of poets was in need of patronage. Lucrezia was not only Duchess of Ferrara, but the Pope's daughter, and at the very beginning of their friendship Ercole Strozzi was already confiding to her his ambition to become a cardinal. But neither the 5,000 ducats he was willing to pay (for no one was any longer under the illusion that a cardinal's hat could be had on merit alone), nor the warmest of recommendations written in Lucrezia's own hand, were sufficient to win him a seat in the Sacred College. Cesare Borgia's pressing need of money had raised the entrance fee to an exorbitant figure. And Ercole Strozzi had to resign himself to the rôle of Lucrezia's general factotum, running her errands, travelling to Venice to choose with his exquisite taste the rare brocades and patterned velvets which, despite her father-in-law, she continued to buy on credit. And maybe the hold he established over Lucrezia was all the stronger because he never aspired to be more than a friend, willing to be eclipsed by Bembo's more brilliant star.

His own relationship with the young Venetian appears to have been based on mutual admiration for each other's talents. But there is little doubt, particularly in the case of Strozzi, that other and more questionable emotions intruded themselves. Nurtured in the Greek tradition it is more than likely that their friendship followed in the classical pattern. Nevertheless it was Strozzi who not only brought his friend to Lucrezia's notice, but who from the very first encouraged a relationship which probably neither Lucrezia nor Bembo himself envisaged as going beyond the limits of platonic dalliance.

But Pietro Bembo was not only an enchanting personality, one of those natures which becomes ever more fascinating the more one explores them; he was also the exact opposite to everything which had dominated Lucrezia in her youth. There is no trace of sensuality in the handsome, ascetic face, which in old age was immortalized by Titian. His emotions seem always to have been under control, even when he allowed himself to write passionate and in certain cases highly indiscreet love letters. What greater contrast to the lust and violence of Lucrezia's Roman past, than this scholar who laid his verses at her feet and treated her as some exquisite nymph escaped from an arcadian glade. Even her father-in-law favoured their friendship, for Bembo's presence lent lustre to his court. So the young Venetian stayed on at Ostellato, making ever more frequent journeys to Ferrara, leaving his studies to take part in the masquerades which celebrated carnival, advising Duke Ercole on the presentation of his comedies, and according to the rules of platonic courtship proclaiming himself the Duchess's devoted servant, so that even old Tito Strozzi addressed his Latin verses '*ad Bembum di Lucretia*'.

Meanwhile Alfonso d'Este had returned from Loreto. But apart from his nightly visits to her room, he seems to have played little part in Lucrezia's life. His appearances at court continued to be few and far between and Pietro Bembo was included in his general dislike of his father's favourites. But so long as her husband remained at Ferrara, there was no danger of Lucrezia's romantic fancies leading her into more dangerous channels. Physically Alfonso d'Este appears to have been capable of satisfying even a Borgia. And it was only when he set out on his travels in the spring that Lucrezia began to interpret Bembo's verses in a more equivocal fashion.

One day at Ostellato there arrived a letter written by Strozzi but addressed in Lucrezia's hand. Maybe it was no more than a teasing gesture but it was sufficient to encourage a poet who was already half in love. Bembo had nothing to lose in court-ing the Duchess of Ferrara. Where an Ercole Strozzi might have been afraid of incurring the vengeance of the Estes, he, as

239

a foreigner, ran no greater risk than banishment. But Lucrezia lived in constant view of the dungeon where Parisina Malatesta had expiated the crime of having betrayed an Este, and she was fully aware of the necessity for secrecy and caution. As her court poet, Bembo could be publicly as amorous as he pleased, but when it came to making secret assignations and sending notes by her maids-of-honour, then it was necessary to revert to the devices she had already practised in the days of her banishment to Nepi. Once more we find her writing the letters in cipher to which we have no key. Names become initials. 'FF is what I stand for,' she writes, and though biographers have tried to read different meanings into these initials, they still remain unsolved—a secret lovers' code. For there can be little doubt that Bembo and Lucrezia were lovers. Otherwise he would never have dared to write those impassioned letters, most of them anonymous and addressed to a third person, which are to be found in his collected works side by side with those openly written to the illustrious Duchess of Ferrara. The former speak with the language of the heart, the others contain nothing but courtly phrases.

Dissimulation was necessary, but in the art of dissimulation Lucrezia was a past master. There was not only the devoted Ercole Strozzi to serve as a go-between, there was also her young cousin Angela, who as a true Borgia was already fully versed in carrying on both her own and her mistress's intrigues. Was it to this sixteen-year-old maid-of-honour that Bembo addressed a letter referring to her as 'angel' in the masculine sense? 'They say that everyone has a good angel who prays for him. I pray that angel, who can pray for me, that he prays to F.F. for what he knows I need. If I myself were an angel, I would be seized with pity for anyone who loves, the way I love.' The letter breaks off, and it is as a lover speaking direct to the object of his passion that he adds, 'With my heart do I now kiss that hand of yours, which soon I shall kiss with lips that ever have your name engraved upon them'. Was it likely that a woman of Lucrezia's temperament would turn a deaf ear to such a plea? And into her letters, so careful and circumspect, there creeps an involuntary note of tenderness. 'Messer Pietro Bembo mio!'—the tone is both caressing and possessive, and

19. Lucrezia Borgia in her prime, an impression by the engraver von Balen, probably mid-seventeenth century.

what she dares not write herself she borrows from the poets, transcribing the words of an old Castilian song:

> *Yo pienso si me muriesce*
> *Y commis males finase*
> > *desear*
> *Tan grande amor finesciese*
> *Que todo el mundo guedase*
> > *sin amor.*

'I feel that if you die, the whole world would remain without love.' And for the moment Lucrezia envisaged Bembo's world as her own. But though they might write of their twin souls, 'their hearts beating in unison', this world transformed by a poet's imagination was a place where she might be tempted to linger, but where no Borgia could ever stay. The ghosts of Cesare's latest victims were beginning to intrude even into the gardens of Ostellato. And not a day passed without some fresh report of another arrest or assassination.

The revolt of the condottieri had had vast repercussions throughout Italy. And some of Cesare's closest associates were involved. One day the people of Cesena woke to find the body of Cesare's dreaded governor, the blue-eyed Spaniard Ramiro di Lorqua, suspended from a gibbet outside his own palace. Even Bembo's beloved Duchess was not spared in the rumours which circulated round Ramiro's death. For in confidential despatches we read of 'how Il Valentino had never forgiven his lieutenant for his dishonourable behaviour to the Duchess of Ferrara, on the occasion of her journey through the Romagna'. Next it was the turn of Troche, the most sinister of all the Borgia agents, who was suddenly arrested when on his way to Genoa, accused of betraying his master's secrets to the French. Loyal servants or treacherous agents, old enemies or former friends—their fate seemed to be the same. Whether it was the Pope's devoted compatriot, Cardinal Lopez, who suddenly died in mysterious circumstances, 'suspected of being poisoned, because the great Gonfaloniere was known to be unfriendly to him', or the young Duke of Gravina, one of Lucrezia's former suitors, who, together with his cousin

Paolo Orsini, had been captured at Senigallia—they were equally victims to the Borgia terror. The dispatches of the ambassadors describe the atmosphere of fear and uncertainty prevailing in Rome, with no one knowing who was to be the next victim.

For once it was the Pope rather than his son, who indulged in an orgy of blood lust. The part taken by the Orsinis in the revolt of the condottieri had aroused all Alexander's former animosity. And while Cesare counselled prudence and moderation, recognizing the Orsinis as the allies of France, his father was bent on exterminating the whole family. The Pope's bitterness towards the Orsinis—a bitterness which had prevailed even when circumstances forced him to come to terms with them, gave rise to the question as to whether he held them responsible for the murder of the Duke of Gandia. And in contrast to the Pope's intransigence was Cesare's curiously forgiving attitude, so that whereas he would have been ready to murder a Vitellozzo Vitelli with his own hands, he was prepared to pardon the Orsinis their part in the conspiracy, even to the length of quarrelling with his father, who according to the Venetian ambassador, Giustinian, threatened in a fit of rage to excommunicate 'this bastard son of a whore' unless he hurried back to Rome to subdue the last Orsini strongholds in the Campagna.

And while Cesare deliberately procrastinated, receiving the submission of Perugia and Citta di Castello, waiting to see which way the wind was blowing in the Regno, where the French were suffering a series of defeats at the hands of Gonsalvo of Cordoba, the Pope launched out on his exterminating campaign against the Orsinis. Those who were unwise enough to remain in the capital were placed under arrest. No one was spared, not even the vain and foolish cardinal whose castle on Thrasymene had been the headquarters of the rebellion, and who, believing himself to be reconciled with the Borgias, had been rash enough to boast 'that all his differences with the Pope had always ended to his own advantage'. Only two days after he had celebrated Mass in the presence of His Holiness, he was flung into a dungeon of St. Angelo, and neither the tears of his eighty-year-old mother nor the intervention of his fellow cardinals could prevent Borgian justice from running its full course. In the last days of February the Venetian ambassador wrote in one of his secret dispatches 'that the Cardinal Orsini was dying, having already partaken of the fatal draught'.

No one felt safe, whether from incursions outside the city or assassination from within. Not even the Pope's assurance to the city magistrates 'that he had made all the arrests that were necessary, and that from now on the Romans could live in peace and enjoy the coming carnival' could put the people's minds at rest. More and more cardinals were beginning to absent themselves on indefinite leave from Rome. Giuliano della Rovere hurriedly left for France after discovering a plot to kidnap him from his castle of Ostia, and in the early spring the popular young Cardinal d'Este suddenly decided that a change of air would be beneficial to his health. His departure coincided with a fresh scandal in the Borgia family circle—the imprisonment of the Princess Sanchia in the fortress of St. Angelo. Some said she was accused of being in league with the Orsinis, others declared her to be in the pay of Spain. Some said the great Gonfalonier was tired of her, others that he was jealous of her intrigue with Ippolyto d'Este. And the fact that the Ferrarese cardinal chose this moment to absent himself from Rome lent colour to the tale. Even as a prisoner, Sanchia's treatment appears to have been sufficiently lenient to enable her to continue in her career as a trouble-maker. For one of the principal sights of Rome was to see the beautiful princess of Aragon haranguing the crowds from her prison balcony and openly inveighing against her father-in-law, the Pope, to any casual passer-by.

Meanwhile Ippolyto d'Este returned to Ferrara, though his departure was too carefully planned to be called a flight. Not only did he take affectionate leave both of the Pope and Lucrezia's son, the little duchetto, but he even stopped off on his way north to visit Cesare in Umbria. Nevertheless once he was back in Ferrara he seemed strangely reluctant to return to Rome. And this sudden arrival of her brother-in-law broke with a violent impact into Lucrezia's idyllic world, destroying her illusions of happiness, recalling memories from which there was no escape.

XXXI

SUMMER CAME early and with a tropical intensity in this year of 1503, bringing fever to the cities and a general flight to the country. Only in Ferrara the young duchess, who had half a dozen summer residences to choose from, was suddenly so attached to her gloomy castle that she could hardly be prevailed upon to leave the city. The reason was not hard to find. Pietro Bembo was lying ill in the Strozzi Palace, and Lucrezia was anxious for news. It was a princess's privilege to show solicitude for the health of her court poet, and even the Estes had no objection when she carried condescension to the length of visiting Bembo's sick-bed, accompanied by her favourite maids-of-honour. At the beginning of their courtship, Bembo may have looked upon Lucrezia as no more than a useful stepping-stone to his career, but now he was helplessly and irrevocably in love, lamenting in one of the finest of his lyrics '*Avessi Io almen di un bel cristallo il core*', as if he sensed that to love a Borgia could bring him nothing but unhappiness in the end. Lucrezia's feelings towards him were far simpler and more primitive, and within a year she would have forgotten him as easily as she had forgotten in the past. But for the moment she knew a re-flowering of the young romantic love she had felt for Alfonso of Aragon, and she treasured it jealously and secretly as if she were treasuring the last moments of her youth.

No sooner was he recovered from his illness, than Bembo returned to Ostellato, and Lucrezia moved her court to Medelana, one of the ducal villas in the neighbourhood. Here she was free to resume her summer idyll, safe from the prying eyes of the Cardinal Ippolyto, whose return from Rome had been singularly unwelcome to her, not only on account of the ugly stories he circulated round the Este court, but because like his sister Isabella, he was both observant and perspicacious, and knew her well enough to suspect that her relationship with

Bembo was hardly likely to be platonic. But no Este intruded into the rose gardens and heronries of Medelana—a villa built in the middle of the marshes by some solitude-loving ancestor. And during those long hot summer days, when Alfonso was still on his travels, Lucrezia and Pietro Bembo drifted into an ever closer intimacy fostered and encouraged by Ercole Strozzi. But while the laurel walks of Medelana and of Ostellato re-echoed to the recital of Petrarchan stanzas and the refrains of Spanish love songs, the world beyond the gardens and lagoons fell once more into the throes of war.

In the blazing summer heat, French troops were marched across Italy to reinforce their hard-pressed armies in the Regno, where Gonsalvo of Cordoba had made himself master of Naples. And in the wake of war came pestilence, decimating the ranks both of conqueror and conquered, taking its toll from princes and peasants alike. By August the plague carts had made their appearance in almost every city, and nowhere was the epidemic so virulent as in Rome. One of the first to succumb was the Pope's favourite nephew, the Cardinal of Monreale. But according to the gossip of the ambassadors, no one any longer died from natural causes, and the Venetian envoy, Giustinian, did not hesitate to write: 'The Cardinal of Monreale is said to have been dispatched in the same way as all the others, once they are properly fattened up'. In this particular case the term 'fattening up' was singularly appropriate, for Juan Borgia was even more corpulent than his uncle. But contrary to the implications of Giustinian, his nephew's death appears to have had a depressing effect on the Pope, who was overheard to remark with an air of gloomy foreboding, that 'it was a bad month for fat men'. Eye-witnesses recount that when the funeral procession passed beneath the windows of the Vatican, a bird flew in at a balcony and fell dead at the Pope's feet, a presage of ill-omen to all who were present.

Though half the members of his court were reported to be sick, Alexander stayed on in Rome, giving the impression of being as young and vigorous as ever, busily intriguing both with France and Spain, secretly assuring the Venetian that though he was a Spaniard by birth, 'he was Italian both in sentiment and upbringing, and it was the duty of all good Italians to unite in driving the foreigners from their country'.

Meanwhile Cesare had returned to the city, and after bringing the campaign against the Orsinis to a successful conclusion, had retired from public view, leaving his lieutenants to raise fresh troops, though no one, not even his own father, knew whether these troops were to be used in King Louis's service or for his own purposes in central Italy. As usual his comings and goings were cloaked in such impenetrable secrecy as to give rise to the wildest rumours. Some said he was no longer willing to restrict his ambitions to central Italy, and was preparing to strike in open defiance both of the Pope and of the King of France. Those to whom he had refused to give audience revenged themselves by asserting that all this uncertainty and secrecy was due to the fact that he was once more suffering from an acute attack of '*morbo gallicum*' (a story which gained credence in view of later events). But whatever may have been the rumours, both the Duke of Romagna and the Pope appear to have been in the best of health and spirits, when on the evening of August 6th, 1503, they attended an alfresco supper party, held in Cardinal Corneto's villa on the slopes of Monte Mario.

It was the Pope's habit to sup with one or the other of his cardinals in the cool of their vineyards outside the city, and Adriano Corneto, who had formerly been his private secretary, was the most recent and most favoured of these cardinals. At seventy-three Alexander Borgia was still as gay and convivial as in his youth, and against the advice of his physicians, he continued to venture out after nightfall, exposing himself to 'the pestilence-ridden air', partaking of highly-seasoned foods, which in the excessive heat can rarely have been fresh, and carousing in gardens, where a thousand venomous insects hovered round the laden tables. It was not surprising if within a few days of Cardinal Corneto's alfresco banquet, every one of the guests, including the Pope, had been taken ill. On August 11th, the anniversary of his accession, the Venetian ambassador noted that 'His Holiness appeared to be downcast and preoccupied and not at all his usual self'.

The following morning both the Pope and the Duke were

reported to be sick, and though at first the gravity of their malady was kept from the public, it gradually transpired that they were suffering from acute fever and continual vomiting. For a time it seemed as if the vigorous Borgia constitution would assert itself in the fight for life, but by the fourth day it was generally known that His Holiness had little hope of recovery. Apoplexy, 'the curse of all fat men', had attacked him in his last struggle and by the evening of August 18th he was reported to be dying.

Those who attended Alexander VI in the last hours of his life describe him as cheerful and serene, summoning his confessor and receiving the sacraments, as if even now he were sure of his ultimate salvation. Popular superstition, however, refused to believe that Rodrigo Borgia had died a natural death, and the story of how the devil appeared at his bedside and called upon him to deliver up his soul, as the price of a pact he had made in purchasing the Papacy, is only one of many legends. No sooner was he dead than there were rumours of his having been killed by poison. Gucciardini writes of how the Pope and Il Valentino had connived to kill the wealthy Cardinal Corneto at his own supper table, but that owing to an error on the part of their cup-bearer, they themselves had drunk of the fatal draught. This story was all the more readily believed owing to the repellent aspect of the Pope's body, which in the abnormal heat decomposed so rapidly that within a few hours it had 'become hideously black and swollen, of scarcely human shape'.

But whatever legends gathered after Pope Alexander's death, he appears to have passed away as peacefully as if he were still the elect of God, immune from any punishment in after life. And strangely enough his attendants assert that during his illness he never once mentioned his children. No word was said of Cesare, who was too sick to leave his bed, even when he knew his father to be dying. And even if it were true that the Pope and his son were in conflict at the time, and that their public appearances were only dictated by political necessity, it is curious he should have made no reference either to the two little Dukes or to the daughter whom 'he loved in such a superlative degree' that only a few days previously he had granted her request in handing over to her the two years' revenue of the rich bishopric of Ferrara. Maybe in those moments of lucidity which precede death, he found at last the strength he had been lacking all his life, and that in divesting himself of his human frailties, he recognized his love for his children to have been both his curse and his undoing.

Racked with fever, at the mercy of circumstances, Cesare remained confined to his apartments in the Borgia tower. The treatment the physicians had not dared to give his father on account of his age, was applied to him with terrifying results. This drastic method of reducing fever appears to have consisted in wrapping the affected parts of the body in the still quivering entrails of a freshly disembowelled mule, and then plunging the patient into a bath of ice. However successful as a cure, it left its permanent marks, for when Cesare rose from his sickbed there was no longer any trace of the beauty which till now had survived the scars of his ever-recurrent illness. It was not only in body but in mind, that Cesare disintegrated. Later he was to confess to Machiavelli that 'he had prepared against every eventuality in the case of his father's death, but he had never faced up to the fact that at the time he might himself be incapable of action'.

With what agony of mind he must have watched the hours go by, while his secretary Agapito brought him the last reports from his father's sickroom. Too ill to move, he left his captain Michelotto to carry out his orders. And the last act of Borgia terror was when Cesare's henchman forced his way into the Pope's bedroom, and at the point of his sword forced the terrified chamberlain to deliver the keys of the papal treasury. Michelotto was only the first of a horde of scavengers and looters, who before the Pope had breathed his last were already invading his apartments, pillaging and destroying in their wake, while the cardinals fled in terror and the papal guards stood by powerless or unwilling to intervene. Only Burchard, calm and meticulous as ever, persisted in carrying on his duties in the midst of chaos and the Pope who had loved too freely and too well was now left to the care of this cold-blooded German bureaucrat, who recorded his last moments as laconically as he had recorded his triumphs and his crimes.

Before long the news of the Pope's death had spread like wild-fire through the city, unleashing pent-up hatreds, fanning the desire for vengeance, and from his room in the Borgia tower Cesare could hear the ominous cries in the courtyard below, 'Down with the hated Catalan', 'Death to the dog of a Marrano'. With prophetic vision, the Venetian envoy Capello had prognosticated that Il Valentino would lose his power within a few days of his father's death. And Alexander VI had barely been dead four hours before the almighty Duke of the Romagna was dragging himself from his sickbed to seek refuge in the Fortress of St. Angelo.

Lucrezia was still at Medelana when the news of the Pope's death reached Ferrara, and it fell to the lot of the Cardinal Ippolyto to break her the news. To his daughter, Alexander had always represented the life force, from which she derived her own vitality and strength, and when her brother-in-law brought her the tidings, she afterwards confessed 'that it left her with no other wish than to die herself'. Of all the Pope's children, she was the one who was the nearest to him. His human frailties had only made him the more lovable, his tyrannies the easier to forgive. They had shared so much together, even to their love and fear of Cesare. And it was probably the thought of Cesare, sick and helpless and for the first time in his life in need of her, which gave Lucrezia the strength to dominate her grief.

Bembo has left a touching description of Lucrezia Borgia mourning for her father. In one of the simplest and most human of his letters, he writes of how he called on her,

> partly for the purpose of telling her how great was his sorrow on her account, and partly to endeavour to console her and to urge her to compose herself.

But he adds:

> I was able to do neither the one, nor the other, for as soon as I saw you in that dark room, in your black gown, lying weep-ing, I was so overcome by my feelings that I stood still, unable to speak, not knowing what to say. Instead of giving

sympathy, I myself was in need of it, so I departed completely overcome by the sad sight, fumbling and speechless. . . . Perhaps this happened to me because you had need neither of my sympathy nor of my condolence.

With a poet's perception, Bembo realized that in this family tragedy, even the tenderest of lovers could be no more than an intruder. The whole of Lucrezia's future was at stake, and even her tears were open to misinterpretation. Wisely he warned her, not to give cause to anyone to think 'that you grieve less on account of the shock, than you do on account of any anxiety as to your future position'.

Bembo had every reason to be apprehensive. Before Lucrezia had recovered from the first transports of her grief, Duke Ercole was already writing to his ambassador in Milan, a letter intended to be handed on to the French governor, Chaumont, which shows that he was under no illusion as to King Louis's intentions in regard to Cesare Borgia.

Knowing that many will ask you [he wrote] how we are affected by the Pope's death, we wish to inform you that it was in no way displeasing to us . . . there was never a Pope from whom we received fewer favours than from this one, even after concluding an alliance with him. In fact it was only with the greatest difficulty that we secured from him what he had promised, but beyond this he never did anything for us, for which we hold the Duke of Romagna responsible. He was never frank with us, he never confided his plans to us, although we always informed him of ours. Finally as he inclined to Spain, and we remained good Frenchmen, we had little to look for, either from the Pope or from his Highness.

Cesare's secret negotiations with Spain had been betrayed to France by one of his own agents. But when it came to treachery and deceit, Louis XII was on a level with the Borgias. He had always intended to repudiate Il Valentino, once the Pope was no longer there to facilitate his plans. At the time of the Este marriage he had consoled Don Alfonso by telling him that 'as soon as Alexander VI was dead, there would be no necessity to recognize the lady he had married'. So now he informed the

Ferrarese envoy 'he was well aware, that the Estes had never been pleased with the Borgia alliance, and therefore the Court of France did not regard Madonna Lucrezia as Don Alfonso's real wife.'

Ominous words for Lucrezia's future, had not Duke Ercole been both too cautious and too proud to act on the advice of France. His daughter-in-law may as yet have failed to produce an heir, but Cesare Borgia was still lord of the Romagna and in control of the Spanish votes in the next papal election. Despite the cynicism of fifteenth-century politics, Lucrezia's own personal charm may also have played a part in influencing Duke Ercole's decisions. His people were devoted to their young duchess. In the past year his courtiers had grown to idolize her, and, strangest of all, the son who had been coerced into marrying her, now acted as a loyal and loving husband.

Don Alfonso's kindness to Lucrezia in the weeks which followed her father's death served as another barrier to her relations with Pietro Bembo. No sooner had he heard the news of her father's death than he hurried back to Ferrara and the autumn saw him for the first time as a guest at Ostellato, where he could combine the pleasures of the chase with visits to his wife at Medelana. Delighted to give hospitality to a prince with whom they were rarely in favour, the Strozzis suggested to Pietro Bembo that for the moment it would be wiser for him to return to Venice. Alfonso d'Este was of a jealous nature and likely to suspect his wife's platonic relationships. But this autumn Lucrezia appeared to be equally indifferent to the consolations of either husband or of lover. All her thoughts and energies were devoted to helping Cesare, who after a slow and painful recovery was making a last desperate attempt to retain his heritage. Protected by the cannon of St. Angelo, he staked his remaining hopes on the coming papal elections.

XXXII

BARELY A FORTNIGHT after his father's death, Cesare's kingdom had already begun to disintegrate. The Montefeltri returned in triumph to Urbino, Giovanni Sforza was acclaimed at Pesaro, the Baglionis were back in Perugia and the Varanos were reinstated at Camerino. Only the Romagna remained loyal to its 'duca' and despite their hatred of Il Valentino, certain neighbouring states preferred to see a Borgia in control, rather than have the Romagna swallowed up by Venice. Both the Estes and the Gonzagas were of this opinion, and in the month which followed on the Pope's death, the Duke of Ferrara and the Marquis of Mantua continued to correspond with Cesare Borgia and to lend a sympathetic ear to Lucrezia's pathetic appeals to help in preserving her brother's kingdom. Dominated by his fear of Venice, Duke Ercole raised no objection when, despite her extravagance and debts, Lucrezia managed to find the money to raise a company of fifteen hundred men to serve under her brother's orders.

Backed by the loyalty of the Romagna, the devotion of his captains and the support of the Spanish cardinals, Cesare was still in a position where, had he been in full possession of his faculties, he might have emerged as master of the situation. But he who was usually so cold and clear now committed mistake after mistake. And in seeking to isolate his enemies he only ended in isolating himself. Rome was crowded with his former victims; the Orsinis retook possession of their castles in the Campagna; Prospero Colonna arrived from Naples; Silvio Savelli was back in his palace, and to add to the general confusion, the prisons were now opened, letting out a horde of desperate men, venting their vengeance on anyone of Spanish blood. Yet still the Spaniards held their own. Don Michelotto's troops patrolled the Borgo, for in the first days of chaos the Sacred College had no alternative but to confirm

Cesare's privileges as Gonfalonier of the Church, and to charge him with the keeping of public order. With his brother still confined to his sick-bed, Joffré Borgia took command, displaying in adversity an audacity and courage worthy of his name. As effeminately beautiful as ever, he could be seen riding across the St. Angelo Bridge at the head of his company of soldiers defying the Orsinis to cross the river. Cesare's apartments were still the centre of Vatican intrigue, but for the first time in his life he vacillated. The disease from which he had been suffering at intermittent periods during the past six years, coupled with the malignant effects of his fever, appears to have affected his brain, and there is no surer proof of his failing powers than that he, who had never trusted anyone before, now believed in the promises of his former enemies. He made peace with the Colonnas and with characteristic unscrupulousness used his sister's child as a means to bargain. For a projected alliance between Rodrigo of Bisceglie and a little Colonna girl was the price of the agreement. But when the King of France, in fear lest Cesare might now join up with Gonsalo's armies, came forward to offer him his protection and guarantee his estates in return for his support of a French Pope, Cesare veered round to the cause of France, forgetful of the fact that when Spain and France made peace, he would be equally mistrusted and as easily deceived by one as by the other.

Meanwhile the College of Cardinals, anxious to avoid a clash between the various armed parties and wishing to rid themselves of their dreaded captain-general, ordered all troops to evacuate the city before the opening of the conclave. For the first time Cesare had no choice but to obey, and though he was still too weak to stand, he set out for Nepi on September 2nd, 1503. With him went the whole of the Borgia clan—his mother, Vanozza, now a massive sixty-year-old matron, but still young and vigorous enough to ride on horseback rather than in a litter; his brother Joffré, and the two little dukes with their tutors and governors. Only Sanchia was absent. Released from St. Angelo, she had preferred to place herself under the protection of Prospero Colonna, who, beguiled by her blue eyes, was escorting her back to her beloved Naples.

Thin and shrunken, the ghost of his former self, carried by

twelve halberdiers on a crimson velvet stretcher, Il Valentino still retained his unfailing theatrical instinct. And the Romans saw the last of the great Borgia processions as his hundred wagons stamped with the papal arms, and his superbly mounted cavalry filed out of the city. There were the characteristic Borgia touches, a richly caparisoned war-horse led by a beautiful young page—a mysterious masked prisoner riding on a mule—and the inevitable concourse of ambassadors who, so long as Cesare commanded eleven votes in the coming Conclave, still deemed it worth their while to accompany him to the city gates.

With Cesare Borgia safely out of Rome and the Orsinis retired to their castles, the cardinals went into conclave. But the eleven votes of the Spanish cardinals still dominated the elections, checkmating the ambitions of della Rovere, the pretensions of the French cardinal Amboise, so that at the end of the eighth day the aged and infirm Cardinal Piccolomini, who represented no particular party and was supported by no particular power, was elected to St. Peter's chair under the name of Pius III.

For the moment Cesare believed himself to be safe and, trusting to the protection of the King of France, returned to Rome. The beginning of October saw him back in the Borgo and according to Giustinian 'not so ill as he makes himself out to be, and behaving with all his former arrogance'. The Venetian ambassador also noted that he was living in Ippolyto d'Este's palace, thereby proving that the Estes were still ready to support Cesare Borgia's claims on the Romagna. But what was interpreted as Duke Ercole's diplomatic cunning may have been no more than a gesture on the part of the young Cardinal to please the sister-in-law who would one day be reigning duchess. Alfonso had publicly declared his loyalty to his Borgia wife and Ippolyto d'Este may already have envisaged the day when Lucrezia would rule as regent in her husband's absence. Therefore the conciliatory gestures—the palace lent to Cesare, the continued attentions to the little Duke of Bisceglie—whom Lucrezia hoped to welcome to Ferrara. But though Duke Ercole was willing to shut his eyes to intrigues which redounded to his own advantage, he had no intention of giving

a home to the little Aragonese prince, and Lucrezia's letters to
the old Cardinal of Cosenza make pathetic reading. On the one
hand is a loving, anxious mother, frightened for her son's
future. On the other hand is Cesare Borgia's sister, not daring
to commit the slightest action which might endanger his
success. It was not the moment to press the claims of Rodrigo
of Bisceglie, when Duke Ercole's goodwill might be needed
in settling the future of the Romagna. It was better to placate
and temporize, to suggest what no maternal nature would ever
have suggested—that the little prince of Aragon should be
dispatched to Spain—a solution welcomed by Duke Ercole,
who in a somewhat unctuous letter praises the wisdom of his
daughter-in-law's decision.

But in the end it was the Princess Sanchia who took pity on
her brother's child, and her new lover, Prospero Colonna,
brought Rodrigo down to Naples, to grow up under the care
of his Aragonese aunts. And though his mother continued to
send him presents she was never to see him again, for he died
at the age of fifteen while living at Bari at the court of his aunt,
the widowed duchess of Milan.

Rodrigo of Bisceglie was not the only one to be sacrificed to
Lucrezia's anxiety for her brother during the months which
followed on the Pope's death. With tender sympathy and
understanding, Pietro Bembo attempted to prolong a relationship, of which the end was now inevitable. Gratitude had sup-
planted passion, till there came the day when Lucrezia received
from Bembo's hands the first copy of 'Gli Asolani', those
poems and treatises on love dedicated to the memory of their
summer idyll. In verses, which served as his last refuge, Bembo
reverted to the times of their first courtship, the days of platonic
dalliance, of amorous friendship, when the Duchess of Ferrara
was still a patroness, not yet a mistress. And on these terms
they parted, lovers who had not had time to tire of one another,
nor feel the first cold breath of disillusion.

Even in Lucrezia's gratitude, Bembo had only second place.
Foremost was Alfonso d'Este whose loyalty now served as a
protection for Cesare. While Ferrara remained loyal to its
Borgia duchess, the Romagna remained loyal to its Borgia
duke. But the news from Rome was grave, and despite the

favour of the aged Pope, Cesare was to suffer for having attempted to double-cross both France and Spain. While King Louis had no troops to spare for a distrusted ally, Gonsalo of Cordoba denounced as traitors all Spaniards who continued to serve under the orders of the Duke of Romagna, so that within a few days of his return to Rome, two thousand of Cesare's finest troops deserted, leaving him only a mixed company of Italian and German mercenaries, and a handful of devoted Spaniards, who had dared to disobey the orders of El Gran Capitan. Seeing him so weak and abandoned, his enemies gathered round, claiming the right to try him for his crimes, menacing him if he so much as dared to venture out of his barricaded palace. Before long he was in such mortal peril that the Spanish cardinals who still remained faithful to his father's memory conveyed him in disguise to the fortress of St. Angelo. Here he was ostensibly under papal protection. But in reality he was little more than a prisoner, and maybe the sense of his own helplessness contributed towards his making what he afterwards recognized as the crowning mistake of his career.

Pius III died after a reign of only twenty-seven days—an interregnum sufficiently long for Giuliano della Rovere to consolidate his position and bribe his way to power—sufficiently long for a sick and desperate man to reach a point, when he was ready to come to terms with his father's enemy and delude himself in the belief that della Rovere would be willing to reinstate the son of Alexander VI as Gonfalonier of the Church. Ambassadors and chroniclers were at a loss to explain Cesare Borgia's action when, on October 31st, 1503, Giuliano della Rovere was unanimously elected Pope, after the eleven votes of the Borgia faction had been cast in his favour.

Did Cesare really believe that, as Pope Julius II, della Rovere would forgive or forget the years of exile and the numberless betrayals he had suffered at the hands of the 'hated Marranos'? Or did that curious megalomania, which appears to have been characteristic of his malady, warp his judgment to an extent that in his own eyes he was still the omnipotent Duke of the Romagna, whom Popes were forced to humour and pay court to? Whatever may have been his motives, he believed in the promises of della Rovere, and signed an agreement, which according to the Venetian envoy 'might as well have been a death warrant'. For if the new Pope continued to flatter Cesare Borgia's vanity and foster his illusions, it was only because he still possessed the keys of the Romagna fortresses. Over half a century had passed since the first of the della Rovere Popes had descended into the political arena, to establish the temporal power of the Papacy. But Sixtus IV had died too soon to achieve his ambition, and it had remained for Alexander VI and his half-Spanish, half-Italian son, to weld the scattered vicariates of the Church into a single state. Now it was the turn of Pope Sixtus's nephew to claim his uncle's inheritance and put an end to Borgia rule in the confines of the papal state.

Cesare was lodged in the Vatican, but within a week of Pope Julius's election, favours had degenerated into threats, promises had become ultimatums. And when with all his former arrogance the duke refused to surrender up the fortresses, he found himself a prisoner of the Pope. But Julius II had still to reckon with the loyalty of the Borgia captains in the Romagna, the attachment of the Romagnuoli to their Duke, and the fact that a Borgia was still the Duchess of Ferrara.

Throughout the autumn Lucrezia was working secretly in defence of her brother's duchy. For though the Estes continued to tolerate the presence of Cesare's captains at her court, all form of assistance had to be unofficial, so as not to give offence to either Venice or the Vatican. It was only later it transpired that the fifteen hundred soldiers who had repulsed a Venetian attack on Cesena had been raised and equipped at her own expense, and that she had given a purse of gold in reward to the Spanish commander of Forli, when in reply to the order of surrender he had seized the papal envoy and impaled him on the castle battlements. Outwardly she gave the impression of having no other thought than of her duties towards Ferrara and the Estes. No ceremony was too tedious, no courtier too ponderous to receive her attention, but night and day her secretaries were at work transcribing the letters in which she sought assistance from every court in Europe—letters to Isabella d'Este warmer and more affectionate than of old, but not likely to delude the cool-headed Isabella, who was already contemplating repudiating her son's betrothal to Cesare's daughter; letters to her sister-in-law in France, begging Charlotte d'Albret to intercede with the French king, so that Cesare could retire to his duchy of Valence; a letter to King Louis himself, written not as Lucrezia Borgia, but as Duchess of Ferrara, a letter to which the King replied in flattering terms with perfidious promises. But they were promises she can hardly have believed in, as proved by her letters to her brother Joffré, who had joined the Spanish forces on the Garigliano in the hopes of persuading Gonsalo to forgive the Borgia treachery. And most secret of all were her letters to the Vatican, to the Spanish cardinals, who had been her father's friends, and which on more than one occasion included messages to be smuggled to the prisoner in the Borgia tower.

Whether by coincidence or intention, Cesare Borgia was now lodged in the room where Alfonso Bisceglie had been strangled at his orders. Yet no pangs of conscience appear to have disturbed his nights, for we hear of his sleeping peacefully, his sword at his side, eating well and insisting on being served with all his usual luxury. Visitors to his prison, like Niccolo Machiavelli, newly-appointed Florentine envoy to the Vatican, who came not because Florence was any longer afraid of Il Valentino, but to observe with a frigid detachment his reactions to adversity, noted that he was dressed with all his former elegance, and that 'though step by step he was nearing his end' he still maintained his spirits, passing his time in gambling with his guards or lying motionless on his bed, watching with that cold concentration, which was characteristic of him, two of his gentlemen playing a game of chess. Now that he was beginning to recover from the effects of his illness, he would discuss the situation with lucidity and calm, recognizing his mistakes, scornful of his enemies, praising the few friends who remained loyal to him, and though knowing himself to be at the Pope's mercy, still persistent in his refusal to sign the order of surrender.

But, at the moment when his fortunes were at their lowest ebb, and France had finally withdrawn her support, when it seemed as if nothing could save him, came the news of the Spanish victory on the Garigliano—the total rout of the French forces in the Neapolitan Regno, and the triumph of the Spanish party in the Vatican. On January 5th, only two days after the result of the battle was known in Rome, Gonsalo of Cordoba, acting on the instances of Joffré and the Spanish cardinals, formally intervened on behalf of a man whom a few months previously he had denounced as a traitor. Both Cesare and the Pope now consented to negotiate, and at the end of a three months' imprisonment, the Duke of Romagna renounced his claims to his fortresses in return for his freedom and the enjoyment of his property and his belongings. Neither of the two signatories to the agreement had any intention of abiding by the clauses. The Pope's plan was for his prisoner to remain immured in the della Rovere fortress at Ostia, waiting for a papal galley to convey him to freedom—a galley which was never to arrive. But this time Cesare was not so easily deceived, and on April 28th, 1504, his enemies learned in consternation that Il Valentino had escaped from Ostia and had landed at Naples with a safe-conduct from 'El Gran Capitan'.

XXXIII

IN FERRARA the Estes received the news of Cesare Borgia's escape with caution and reserve, but Lucrezia made no secret of her joy and her courtiers shared her happiness. Foreign envoys commented on the revival of the Duchess's looks and spirits. It was as if she were born again, and even her heavy Spanish mourning only served to accentuate her ever-youthful beauty. Other reasons may have contributed to the gaiety of her mood. The Marquess and Marchioness of Mantua were on a state visit to the Este court and in the rôle of sister-in-law, Lucrezia welcomed Francesco Gonzaga to Ferrara, displaying all her powers of fascination to win him as an ally, and in defiance of Isabella's watchful eye exploiting their family tie to establish a tender and intimate relationship.

Ten years had passed since Francesco Gonzaga had seen her in Rome after the victory of Fornovo, and there is no greater tribute to Lucrezia's charm, than to have made a conquest of a man to whom the very name of Borgia was anathema, who even in the days when his wife and his ambassadors were wooing Il Valentino's favour persisted in his dislike to the extent of challenging the Pope's son to open combat in Milan —a quarrel which was only settled through the mediation of the King of France. As the brother of Elisabetta Montefeltro, the brother-in-law of Giovanni Sforza, he had been fed on every scandal and libel associated with her name. And yet within a few days of their re-meeting he was already embarking on the first stage of a romantic and highly imprudent love affair; an affair which would never have begun had Alfonso d'Este been at home. But following his usual custom in the spring, the prince had set out on his travels, which this time were to take him as far abroad as Spain and England. And in his absence Lucrezia presided with Duke Ercole at the festivities in honour of the Gonzaga visit.

However great her physical attractions, however versed in all the arts of love, Lucrezia must have possessed some secret formula which enabled her to work her will on two such hard-headed soldiers and experienced sensualists as Alfonso d'Este and Francesco Gonzaga. It was a time when recipes for love potions and aphrodisiacs had a place in every book of house-hold lore. What more natural, than that the Borgias, who were credited with the use of mysterious poisons known to the Spanish Moors, should also have had the secret of some magic potion to smooth the way for love? Whatever arts Lucrezia may have resorted to, they were employed with good effect, for within a week of his arrival the Marquis of Mantua was so completely subjugated as to espouse Cesare Borgia's cause. But this time Lucrezia was caught in her own wiles, falling to that vitality and charm which despite Franscesco Gonzaga's reputed ugliness rendered him irresistible to women. All unsuspectingly their relationship, grafted on the one dominat-ing emotion of her life, her passion for Cesare, gradually drifted into what was to be the last of all her love affairs—a romance which persisted through the years, fed on no more than a few stolen meetings—a few surreptitious letters, yet curiously enough more binding, and on her side more genuine than her romantic interlude with Pietro Bembo. Echoes of that courtship still prevailed in messages from Venice. Bembo's love, like that of so many poets, flourished in absence, rekindled by the breath of his own words. But to Lucrezia, who was once more living in the cold world of power politics and fighting for her family's survival, there was more comfort to be derived from the monosyllabic phrases of a condottiero, than the tender outpourings of a poet.

The Gonzaga visit to Ferrara coincided with the news of Cesare Borgia's arrival in Naples. And while the Marchioness Isabella viewed the event with the customary Este caution, her husband allowed his feelings for Lucrezia to influence him to the extent of writing a letter to Il Valentino to congratulate him on his escape. For the moment it seemed as if Cesare's star was once more in the ascendant. The papal thunders sounded in vain and the rage of Julius II, now vented on the Spanish cardinals, had no other effect than to send two of the remaining

Borgia cardinals and Cesare's old friend and mentor, Francesco Remolino, to seek refuge in Naples. Gonsalo of Cordoba
was a magnanimous conqueror and Naples basked in an
atmosphere of general amnesties and pardons. Former differences were forgotten, and the princes and princesses of the
dispossessed House of Aragon lived in their palaces in royal
splendour. Also Cesare Borgia appeared to be forgiven for the
mistakes he had committed in the past, and together with his
brother Joffré he was a constant guest at the Castel-Nuovo,
where Gonsalo ruled as Spanish viceroy surrounded by the
poets and beauties of the former Aragonese court. Lodged in
the palace of one of his cardinal cousins, Cesare soon regained
his former confidence and pride, parading the streets with an
armed escort and filling the Florentine and Venetian ambassadors with such nervous apprehension, that they were ready
to believe the rumour that Gonsalo had now given Il Valentino
permission to raise troops on Neapolitan soil in preparation for
an expedition to Pisa from where he was to harry the Florentines and force a passage through to the Romagna.

Travelling by way of the Adriatic coast, so as to avoid
passing through the papal states, trusted servants carried
messages between Naples and Ferrara. Lucrezia was the first to
hear of Cesare's arrival, of his welcome by Gonsalo, his
reunion with Joffré and meeting with Sanchia. And at the
mention of Sanchia, Lucrezia may have felt vaguely alarmed
lest Cesare might not be over-confident in thinking that their
sister-in-law would be ready to forgive him all the wrongs the
Borgias had done her in the past. Cesare had need of Sanchia
who was now virtually the Queen of Naples, having exchanged
the protection of Prospero Colonna for one who was still more
powerful, no less a man than the great Gonsalo himself. Confident of his powers of fascination, his magnetism for women,
Cesare expected Sanchia to forget the months of imprisonment
in St. Angelo, the insults and the injuries. But ravaged by his
illness, with bloodshot eyes and lacerated skin, Cesare was no
longer the all-conquering lover and Sanchia was now filled
with such loathing and repulsion for the Borgias that despite the instances of 'El Gran Capitan', she refused to have
Joffré living in her palace, and if she consented to meet her

262

brother-in-law under the Viceroy's roof, it was only in order to gloat over the reversal of his fortunes.

There is no trace of the correspondence between Lucrezia and Cesare, but her letters to the Cardinal of Cosenza show her to have been uncertain of her brother's future. There were too many relatives of Borgia victims living in Naples, too many loyal servants of the House of Aragon, too many witnesses of former crimes, no witness more eloquent than Sanchia who could divulge the truth of so many unsolved mysteries. But Sanchia was not the only princess married to a Borgia who had a past grievance to atone. During these weeks there appeared at Queen Isabella's court in Spain the hitherto neglected figure of the widowed Duchess of Gandia. After years of silence and frustration, Pope Alexander's Spanish daughter-in-law came forward to claim justice for her murdered husband, openly naming the Duke of Romagna as his brother's assassin. Her petition fell on sympathetic ears. The Spanish monarchs had always regarded Cesare as his father's evil genius in dictating the pro-French policy of Alexander VI's later years. And coupled with this distrust of Cesare, was King Ferdinand's growing jealousy of Gonsalo of Cordoba. As Viceroy of Naples, the servant was becoming too powerful to please the master and the rumour of his giving military aid to Il Valentino was hardly calculated to allay suspicion. Whether he was dominated by his hatred of the Borgias or his distrust for Gonsalo, or merely acting with a view to winning the favour of the new Pope, King Ferdinand ended by signing the order which forced the most chivalrous of all his generals to break his word.

Cesare Borgia was confidently planning his expedition against Pisa and drilling his new recruits in full view of the foreign envoys, when on May 25th, barely a month after he had arrived in Naples, he was summoned at night to the Castel-Nuovo. All unsuspectingly he went to what appeared to be a friendly assignation. Gonsalo gave him his usual cordial welcome, entertaining him at supper and discussing questions of military strategy. But on leaving the castle he was arrested in the courtyard by the officer on guard. In later years, when he in turn had been betrayed by his King, Gonsalo is said to have confessed to having three things on his conscience, one of which was the betrayal of Cesare Borgia.

As a prisoner of Spain, Cesare was now conveyed to the island of Ischia, and there was jubilation at the court of Julius II, jubilation among the Roman barons and the petty tyrants of the Romagna and the Marches, who had not yet realized that the Borgia menace had only been exchanged for that of della Rovere. But in Ferrara the Estes greeted the news of Cesare's arrest with the same reserve with which they had heard of his escape, and only the stricken face of the young Duchess bespoke a grief too deep for tears. Spanish by upbringing and sympathy, Lucrezia had never envisaged the possibility of being betrayed by Spain. Whatever may have been the vacillations of her father's politics, she had always looked upon Spain as her native land, to whose glory the Borgias had contributed as the first of the Spanish Popes. But now even Cesare's friends had failed him and having failed him, could do nothing more. In the whole of Europe hers was the only voice to cry out in protest, and even her voice was suffocated in the oppressive reserve of the Este court. With unfailing courtesy Duke Ercole expressed perfunctory regret, in beautifully-worded phrases the Marchioness of Mantua and the Cardinal Ippolyto assured her of their sympathy, while with sanguine optimism Francesco Gonzaga boasted of his influence with the Pope, his good relations with both the Emperor and the King of France, promising to leave no stone unturned to procure her brother's release. But the great powers of Europe were now leagued together in bringing about Cesare Borgia's downfall and the generosity of a Francesco Gonzaga was no more than a quixotic gesture.

After two months' incarceration on Ischia, Cesare finally gave the order for the surrender of the Romagna fortresses. In one of the few letters written in his own hand, addressed to his Spanish captains, he who until now had never admitted defeat confessed to failure: 'decidedly fortune is let loose against us'. And August 11th saw the last of Il Valentino's garrisons march out of the citadel of Forli, still wearing the red and yellow colours of their Duca, still cheering for 'Borgia' and 'Valenza'.

Nine days later, under the guard of Prospero Colonna and attended by only one page, the ex-Duke of Romagna embarked on a Spanish galleon bound for the same port of Valencia from where his great-uncle Alfonso Borja had set sail for Italy over half a century before, to raise a family dynasty on the foundations of the Church.

EPILOGUE

IT WAS SNOWING in Ferrara on the morning of January 25th, 1505, but undaunted by the weather, the people lined the streets to show their loyalty to the Este dynasty. During the last weeks of Duke Ercole's illness, before Alfonso had returned from England, Lucrezia, assisted by the Cardinal Ippolyto, had administered the state. And today she attended her husband's coronation, enthroned on the palace balcony, facing the cathedral, defying the elements in her gold and crimson gown and ermine mantle, with the snowflakes falling on her hair and face—the face which tragedy and crime had left unmarked, still that of the little girl who, twelve years ago, had watched from a balcony in St. Peter's Square the Roman crowds acclaiming her father as the head of Christendom. Twelve years had passed—twelve years on the perilous crest of an adventure in search of a Borgia crown—an adventure which had required so many sacrifices, so many tears, only to end in the grim fortress of Medina del Campo.

Eight months had elapsed since Cesare Borgia had been brought as a prisoner back to Spain, a pawn in the hands of King Ferdinand in bargaining with Pope and Emperor. And immured in a high tower, surrounded by the windswept, snowbound emptiness of the Castillian plain, he was facing for the first time the inevitability of the end. Even if he succeeded in escaping, even if in pity for the father of her child, Charlotte d'Albret persuaded her brother, the King of Navarre, to give him refuge, life in a provincial court would be no more than a living death for one whose ambitions had known no frontiers, who had once dreamt of a united Italy under a Borgia crown. Already the hatred of his enemies was giving way to silence and indifference, and only Lucrezia's voice was still heard in protest, refusing to be silenced or to accept defeat.

The Borgia reign in Italy was over. But side by side with the Este eagle the banner of the Golden Bull still fluttered above the rooftops of Ferrara, reminding the world that a Borgia still wore a crown, and that Borgia blood would pass into the royal houses of Europe. Enthroned on the balcony, Lucrezia sat secure and unassailable, carrying in her womb a future Este prince, but powerless to help the brother who had placed her on the throne.

With a fanfare of silver trumpets, the doors of the cathedral opened and, preceded by the elders of the city, followed by the Este princes, Alfonso came out into the Square; a handsome impressive figure in his white brocaded doublet and ducal crown, silhouetted against the Romanesque portals of the church, flanked by the great stone lions upholding the twisted columns. Slowly he advanced towards the palace, hemmed in by the cheering crowds, and at his approach Lucrezia descended from the balcony to make her first public act of obeisance. Gallantly he raised her to her feet, proclaiming her to his people as his duchess and his wife. Then, taking her by the hand, he led her into the palace, while all the bells of Ferrara rang out a *Te Deum* and a thousand voices shouted 'Long live Alfonso and Lucrezia d'Este', 'Long live the Duke and Duchess of Ferrara'.

HISTORICAL APPENDIX

1440	Alfonso II of Aragon claims throne of Naples; Alfonso Borja (b. 1385) accompanies him to Italy as his private secretary.
1441	Birth of Don Francisco de Borgia, Alfonso's bastard son, at Valencia.
1442	Birth of Vanozza dei Catanei, Lucrezia's mother.
1445	Alfonso now at Rome, having left service of Alfonso of Aragon, with rank of Cardinal Presbyter as reward for diplomacy in negotiations between Alfonso of Aragon and Pope.
1446	
1450	Rodrigo (de Lanzol) Borgia, aged 18, nephew of Alfonso and canon of Valencia, newly arrived in Italy; start of his personal influence and great wealth at the side of his uncle.
1451	
1452	
1453	

POLITICAL EVENTS IN EUROPE	ARTS, RELIGION AND COMMERCE
Frederick III (Hapsburg) succeeds Albert II as Holy Roman Emperor (Empire consists of Upper and Lower Bavaria, Brandenburg, and Mecklenburg).	Fra Angelico paints altarpiece of St. Mark's, Florence.
	Death of Jan van Eyck, originator of oil painting.
Alfonso of Aragon becomes King of Naples.	
	Birth of Sandro Botticelli, most famous for his *Birth of Venus* and *Primavera*. Birth of Perugino, painter (c.1445).
Corinth falls to Ottoman Turks.	Death of Brunelleschi, architect.
Sforza dynasty established in Milan. Rebellion in England led by Jack Cade.	Birth of Hieronymus Bosch (painter of *The Seven Deadly Sins*) and of Luca Signorelli, painter. Gutenberg invents printing.
Ottoman Empire firmly established in Anatolia and Balkans; death of Sultan Murad II, succeeded by Muhammad II.	Birth of Christopher Columbus. Extraction of silver from argentiferous copper discovered. Beginning of mining boom in S. Germany, Tyrol and Hungary, centred on Nürnberg and Augsburg.
Frederick III crowned Holy Roman Emperor at Rome.	Birth of Leonardo da Vinci. Piero della Francesca starts the Arezzo frescoes.
Byzantine Empire ends with fall of Constantinople to Muhammad II. End of the Hundred Years War. Florence, ruled by Medicis and with Pisa as her outlet, begins to rival Venetian trade.	Constantinople, hitherto a Greek cultural centre, becomes part of Ottoman (Islamic) Empire.

1454	
1455	Following death of Nicholas V, Alfonso Borgia succeeds to Holy See as Calixtus III; his nephew Rodrigo is made notary of Holy See and Juan Luis (de Mila) Borgia, also nephew of Alfonso, is made governor of Bologna.
1456	Calixtus secretly makes his nephews Cardinals; Rodrigo officially Cardinal of Valencia in following year, and his brother Pedro Luis Gonfalonier of Papal forces and Prefect of Rome.
1458	Death of Calixtus III; Rodrigo and Pedro Luis attempt reconciliation with Alfonso of Aragon (Calixtus refused to recognize Ferrante as heir of Naples); death of Pedro Luis, Rodrigo's brother. Juan Luis retires for rest of his life to Lerida.
1459	Rodrigo ingratiates himself with newly crowned Pius II.
1460	Rodrigo severely reproved by Pius II for orgy in Siena.

POLITICAL EVENTS IN EUROPE	ARTS, RELIGION AND COMMERCE
Peace of Lodi ends long period of Italian wars between Milan, Venice, Florence, Naples and Papal States.	The first Gutenberg Bibles printed.
Italian League: theoretical solidarity of Italian states against Ottoman threat; in fact, Milan, Florence and Naples form triple alliance against Venice and Papal States.	Death of Nicholas V, founder of Vatican Library. Calixtus III orders review of trial of Joan of Arc. Death of Fra Angelico. Birth of Johan Reuchlin, distinguished German Hebraist.
Hunyadi leads Hungarian Crusade against Turks.	Paolo Uccello paints *Battle of San Romano*; one of first painters to use perspective. François Villon: *Le Petit Testament*.
Death of Alfonso of Aragon; succeeded by King Ferrante. Accession of Mathias Corvinus to throne of Hungary; under his leadership Hungary briefly becomes most powerful country in Central Europe.	Pius II becomes Pope.
Turks complete conquest of Serbia.	Failure of Congress of Mantua, called by Pius II to organize European Crusade against Turks. Mantegna completes *Madonna and Saints* at Verona.
French sovereignty over Naples under Jean d'Anjou.	Death of Henry the Navigator (Portuguese). Portugal colonizes Madeiras and Azores.

1461	Birth of Pedro Luis, bastard son of Rodrigo, mother unknown. Rodrigo astounds Rome with display of wealth at Festival of Corpus Christi.
1462	Plague in Rome. Rodrigo superintends new building in Pienza for Pius II, and outshines all other Cardinals in wealth on occasion of Papal procession at Viterbo.
1463	
1464	Rodrigo accompanies Pius II to Adriatic coast whence it was intended to launch new Crusade; death of Pius II; Rodrigo stricken with fever, unable to return to Rome for crowning of Paul II.
1465	Rodrigo strengthens his position under Paul II.
1466	
1467	Birth of a daughter to Rodrigo, Girolama (mother unknown).

POLITICAL EVENTS IN EUROPE	ARTS, RELIGION AND COMMERCE
England: fall of the House of Lancaster; Edward IV ousts Henry VI. France: death of Charles VII, accession of Louis XI. Italy: the Sforzas drive Jean d'Anjou out of Genoa; collapse of French sovereignty.	François Villon: *Le Grand Testament* (exiled in 1643, unheard of after that date).
Russia: death of Basil II (the Blind), accession of Ivan III (the Great) d. 1505; rise of Muscovite Russia.	
Bosnia in Turkish hands. Venice at war with Turks (until 1479); her presence on Black Sea on Aegean forfeited.	
	Death of Pius II; succeeded by Pope Paul II. Death of Rogier van der Weyden, father of Flemish painting.
France: civil war; League of the Common Weal (Anjou, Orléans, Burgundy and Bourbon, led by Charles the Bold) against King Louis XI. Genoa under Sforzas.	Printing introduced into Italy.
Galeazzo Maria Sforza succeeds Francesco Sforza in Genoa. Pitti and Medici families rivals in Florence.	Birth of Erasmus (1466 or 1469) the humanist. Birth of John Colet, English ascetic, mystic, author of *Devotio Moderna*.
	Louis XI introduces silk industry, formerly Italian monopoly, into France.

1468	Son, Pedro Luis, the eldest of Lucrezia's brothers, born to Rodrigo (by Vanozza Catanei?).
1469	Rodrigo honoured at Viterbo by German Emperor on state visit to Pope.
1470	
1471	Rodrigo sent to Spain to preach crusade against Muslim Infidels; on his return takes initiative in Papal elections, supporting della Rovere; he is rewarded with the abbey of Subiaco.
1474	Birth of Juan, son of Vanozza and Rodrigo Borgia.
1475	Birth of Cesare Borgia, Rodrigo's third son by Vanozza dei Catanei.
1476	Plague again in Rome: Rodrigo moves to Viterbo to avoid infection.
1477	

POLITICAL EVENTS IN EUROPE	ARTS, RELIGION AND COMMERCE
Turks raid Dalmatia and invade Croatia.	
Lorenzo de' Medici, " Il Magnifico, " becomes lord of Florence on death of Piero de' Medici. Union of Aragon and Castile under joint reign of Ferdinand and Isabella.	Death of Fra Filippo Lippi. Birth of Machiavelli and Vasco da Gama.
Turks take Negroponte from Venetians. Mathias Corvinus proclaimed King of Bohemia.	Birth of Pietro Bembo; made Tuscan the literary language of Italy.
Ercole d'Este becomes Duke of Ferrara.	Birth of Dürer. Death of Thomas à Kempis. Paul II succeeded by Sixtus IV (della Rovere).
Sixtus IV quarrels with Medicis; Pazzi become Papal bankers.	Ficino: *Theologica Platonica.* Building of Sistine Chapel. Birth of Fra Bartolomeo, and Ariosto, author of *Orlando Furioso.*
	Birth of Michelangelo Buonarotti. Sixtus IV opens Vatican library to public. Birth of Cardinal Wolsey.
Assassination of Galeazzo Sforza; succeeded by Ludovico Sforza, father of Lucrezia's first husband.	
Louis XI defeats Charles the Bold at Nancy; Mary of Burgundy marries Maximilian, heir to Holy Roman Empire; House of Hapsburg gains Netherlands, Luxemburg, and Franche-Comté.	Birth of Giorgione. University of Uppsala founded in Sweden.

1478	
1479	
1480	Birth of Lucrezia Borgia in Subiaco. Vanozza makes respectable marriage to Giorgio di Croce, Apostolic clerk and Venetian scholar.
1481	Lucrezia and her brothers living in Suburra district of Rome; a very gay household.
1482	Birth of Joffre Borgia, Lucrezia's younger brother, by Rodrigo or di Croce? Girolama marries Gianandrea Cesarini. End of Rodrigo's liaison with Vanozza Catanei.
1483	Isabella, illegitimate daughter of Rodrigo, marries Matuzzi, a Roman noble (her date of birth unknown).

POLITICAL EVENTS IN EUROPE	ARTS, RELIGION AND COMMERCE
Medici and Pazzi are rival banking-houses in Florence: Pazzi conspiracy (with Papal consent) to assassinate Lorenzo and Giuliano de' Medici is bungled; Lorenzo escapes, and is even more popular with the people.	Start of the Spanish Inquisition, sanctioned by Sixtus IV's Papal Bull. Birth of Castiglione, author of *The Courtier* (1528).
Florence menaced by Naples and Papal States; peace restored in 1480. Peace of Constantinople: end of Venetian-Ottoman War.	University of Copenhagen founded by Christian I (of Oldenburg).
Turks seize Otranto. Siege of Rhodes, last Christian outpost in Eastern Mediterranean; the Knights of St. John hold out for a year.	Savonarola, fiery Dominican friar, begins to preach in Florence. Birth of Lotto and Grünewald, painters.
Death of Muhammad II; succeeded by Sultan Bajazet II. (Ottoman Empire established in Aegean, on Adriatic coast, and in Otranto in South Italy.)	Botticelli begins Sistine frescoes. Death of Fouquet, official French court painter.
End of the War of the Common Weal in France marked by Treaty of Arras: Louis XI gains Burgundy, Picardy, and Somme. Italy: Venice and Papal States opposed by triple alliance of Florence, Milan, and Naples.	Leonardo da Vinci working in Milan. Ficino completes translation of complete works of Plato.
England: death of Edward IV of York, accession of Richard III of Gloucester. France: accession of Charles VIII on death of Louis XI; Venice appeals to Charles VIII for aid.	Birth of Martin Luther, leader of the Reformation. Birth of Raphael.

1484	Rodrigo withdraws from public life to strengthen his position as candidate for Papal crown.
1485	
1486	Death of Lucrezia's stepfather, Giorgio di Croce; Vanozza remarried to Carlo Canale, protégé of Gonzaga family. Lucrezia's brother, Juan, sent to join elder brother Pedro Luis at Spanish court.
1487	Cesare and Lucrezia living with Adriana Mila (second cousin to Rodrigo, and married to Orsini) at the grim Orsini palace.
1488	
1489	Cesare goes to Perugia University to study theology; a more intense relationship develops between him and Lucrezia.
1490	Julia Farnese comes to Orsini Palace as wife of Adriana's son, Orsino Orsini; her brother Alexander Farnese, is made Bishop when Julia becomes Rodrigo Borgia's mistress.
1491	Death of Pedro Luis Borgia, Lucrezia's eldest brother; his Dukedom of Gandia inherited by her elder brother Juan, much to Cesare's chagrin.

POLITICAL EVENTS IN EUROPE	ARTS, RELIGION AND COMMERCE
End of war between Venice and Ferrara (started 1481).	Death of Luigi Pulci, precursor of Rabelais, author of *Morgante*. Death of Sixtus IV, succeeded by Innocent VIII who orders witchhunts to be increased.
England: Richard III killed at Battle of Bosworth Field by Stanley and Richmond; fall of the House of York and end of the Wars of the Roses; accession of Henry Tudor as Henry VII. Naples: revolt against King Ferrante supported by Pope.	*Bourse* at Antwerp opened; city becomes financial capital of Europe in place of Bruges. Death of Agricola (German) scholar, musician, artist and humanist.
Maximilian (III) becomes Holy Roman Emperor elect; beginning of creation of Hapsburg empire.	Birth of Andrea del Sarto.
England: the battle of Stoke; pretender Earl of Warwick (Lambert Simnel) defeated by Henry VII.	Birth of Tiziano Vecelli (Titian).
England: repeated attempts by Perkin Warbeck (claiming to be Duke of York) to overthrow Tudor rule.	Bartholomew Diaz rounds the Cape of Good Hope.
	Pope condemns Mirandola. Leonardo da Vinci paints *The Virgin of the Rocks*.
Venetians occupy Cyprus. Djem, brother of Sultan Bajazet, takes refuge at Papal court.	Birth of Correggio. Mirandola: *Heptaplus*. Start of Portuguese influence in Congo.
Charles VIII of France acquires Brittany by marrying Anne of Brittany; consolidation of France almost complete, having secured neutrality of England, Spain, and Holy Roman Empire.	Building of the Belvedere in the Vatican.

1492	Lucrezia is betrothed to Don Cherubino de Centelles, then to Count of Aversa. Her father becomes Pope Alexander VI, her engagement broken off. Giovanni Sforza visits Rome. Cesare returns to Rome and is made Cardinal of Valencia; his brother Juan appointed Cardinal. Lucrezia's engagement to Giovanni Sforza, Lord of Pesaro.
1493	Marriage of Lucrezia and Giovanni Sforza. Marriage contract between Joffre and Sanchia of Aragon. Juan marries Maria Enriquez of Gandia.
1494	Lucrezia visits her husband's state of Pesaro. Birth of Juan II, son of Lucrezia's brother, Juan, Duke of Gandia. French army enters Rome.
1495	Lucrezia leaves Pesaro for Perugia.
1496	Lucrezia returns to Rome. Arrival of Sanchia of Aragon. Pope Alexander VI (Rodrigo) launches campaign against Orsini.

POLITICAL EVENTS IN EUROPE	ARTS, RELIGION AND COMMERCE
Conquest of Muslim Emirate of Granada completed by Ferdinand and Isabella. Death of Lorenzo de' Medici (Il Magnifico).	Death of Pope Innocent VIII, succeeded by Alexander VI. Death of Piero della Francesca. Start of Columbus' voyage to West Indies. Pinturicchio's frescoes in the Borgia apartments.
Maximilian succeeds Frederick III as Holy Roman Emperor.	Return of Columbus, having charted Caribbean from Florida to Brazil; way open for Spanish conquest of Central America under Cortes.
First French invasion of Italy; Charles VIII claims throne of Naples, leaving behind an army of occupation. The Medicis surrender Pisa to French; popular uprising expels Medici from Florence; fall of the Medici Bank, their property confiscated.	Death of Giovanni Santi, Raphael's father. Death of Angelo Poliziano, internationally famous for his Greek and Latin scholarship. Venetian printing works founded. Birth of François Rabelais. Publication in France of Ficino's translation of the *Hermetic Books*, repositories of occult wisdom of Ancient Egypt.
Charles VIII driven out of Naples by Italian League.	Death of Giovanni Pico, humanist and founder of Hebrew and Cabalistic studies in Italy. The Papal court in exile at Orvieto (due to French invasion).
Reconquest of Naples by Spanish troops stationed in Sicily; King Ferrante restored to throne. Warbeck and James IV of Scotland invade England in another effort to overthrow Henry VII, but are repelled.	Copernicus visits Italy and studies there for ten years.

1497	Lucrezia and Giovanni still childless; Giovanni causes scandal by accusing Lucrezia of incest with father; divorce follows, Lucrezia retiring to convent of St. Sixtus. Juan, Duke of Gandia murdered, his body thrown into Tiber.
1498	Cesare suspected of murder of brother, Juan. Pedro Calderon, Pope's chamberlain, becomes Lucrezia's lover, and is murdered. Lucrezia gives birth to a son (by Calderon or Cesare?) Lucrezia marries Alfonso of Aragon, Duke of Bisceglie. Cesare, released from Cardinal's vows, becomes Duke of Valence, known as Il Valentino.
1499	Cesare Borgia marries Charlotte d'Albret of Navarre. Lucrezia gives birth to stillborn child. Her husband, in fear of Pope and Cesare, flees to Colonna. Lucrezia appointed regent of Spoleto, then reunited with husband. She gives birth to a son, Rodrigo of Aragon. Daughter born to Charlotte d'Albret. Cesare campaigns in the Romagna, captures Imola.
1500	Cesare defeats Caterina Sforza's plot against Pope, his father, and becomes Duke of Romagna. Death of Cardinal Juan Borgia, the younger. Cesare murders Lucrezia's husband, Alfonso of Aragon; she flees to Nepi, is reconciled with Cesare and returns to Rome.
1501	Lucrezia is regent of Vatican while Pope tours Papal States. She is married to Alfonso d'Este.

POLITICAL EVENTS IN EUROPE	ARTS, RELIGION AND COMMERCE
	Excommunication of Savonarola. Leonardo: *The Last Supper*. John Cabot sails to Newfoundland. Vasco da Gama rounds Cape of Good Hope and sails up the east coast of Africa.
Death of Charles VIII of France, accession of Louis XII (d. 1515). First treaty between France and Spain, agreeing upon partition of Naples.	Vasco da Gama lands on Malabar coast of India. Savonarola hung and burnt as heretic in Florence. Fra Bartolomeo: frescoes of Sta. Maria Novella and *The Last Judgement*. Birth of Hans Holbein (the younger). Dürer: *The Apocalypse*. Third voyage of Columbus.
Venice and Ottomans again at war (until 1503); Morea under Ottoman rule. Second invasion of Italy by France; Louis XII conquers Milan (fall of Sforzas); Ludovico Sforza prisoner in France.	Cardinal Ximenes expels all Muslims and Jews from Spain. Michelangelo: *Pietà*. Death of Ficino, pioneer of Neo-Platonism. Signorelli completes Orvieto frescoes. Amerigo Vespucci and Alonso de Ojeda discover mouth of Amazon.
Birth of Charles V, future Holy Roman Emperor (accession 1519). Second Franco-Spanish treaty for partition of Naples.	Leonardo starts the *Mona Lisa*. Lotto: *St. Jerome in the Desert*. Cabral, sailing via Cape Verde Islands, reaches Brazil and claims it for Portugal; Portuguese threaten Arab trade monopoly in East Indies, opening way for colonization.
France and Aragon re-invade Naples.	Giovanni's finest portrait: *The Doge Loredano*. Gaspar de Corte Real voyages to Greenland and Labrador.

1502	Lucrezia settles in Ferrara, the state of the Este family; she is ill throughout the summer; her first meeting with the poet, Pietro Bembo.
1503	Death of Pope Alexander VI, Rodrigo Borgia, after attack of apoplexy. Cesare Borgia seriously ill with syphilis; his kingdom begins to disintegrate, only Romagna remaining loyal to him; he is aided by Spain and Lucrezia. Montefeltri regain Urbino in Papal States, Giovanni Sforza acclaimed at Pesaro. College of Cardinals excludes Borgias, who flee to Nepi. On election of Julius II as Pope, Cesare returns to Vatican, hoping for favours; taken prisoner by Julius II, he escapes and flees to Naples.
1504	Liaison between Lucrezia and Francesco Gonzaga of Mantua. Duchess of Gandia, at Spanish court, denounces Cesare as her husband's murderer. Spain takes Cesare prisoner and escorts him back to Valencia. On death of Duke Ercole d'Este, Alfonso and Lucrezia become Duke and Duchess of Ferrara. Lucrezia lives exemplary life as patroness of the arts at Ferrara until her death in 1519.

POLITICAL EVENTS IN EUROPE	ARTS, RELIGION AND COMMERCE
War between France and Aragon in Naples.	Leonardo da Vinci appointed engineer in the service of Cesare Borgia. Fourth voyage of Colombus. Second voyage of Vespucci along coast of Brazil.
Crown of Naples added to that of Castile, Aragon and Sicily. Failure of French invasion of Spain.	Pope Alexander VI succeeded by Pius III, who only lived for 27 days. Julius II becomes Pope. Michelangelo: *The Holy Family*. Raphael: *The Knight's Dream*. Leonardo: *La Giaconda*. Erasmus: *Enchyridion*, or practical guide to piety. First large shipment of pepper and spices from East Indies reaches Lisbon.
Death of Isabella, Queen of Castile. Margaret of England marries James IV of Scotland.	Fra Bartolomeo: *The Virgin appearing to St. Bernard*. Michelangelo completes statue of *David*. Pietro Bembo dedicates his *Asolani* to Lucrezia Borgia.

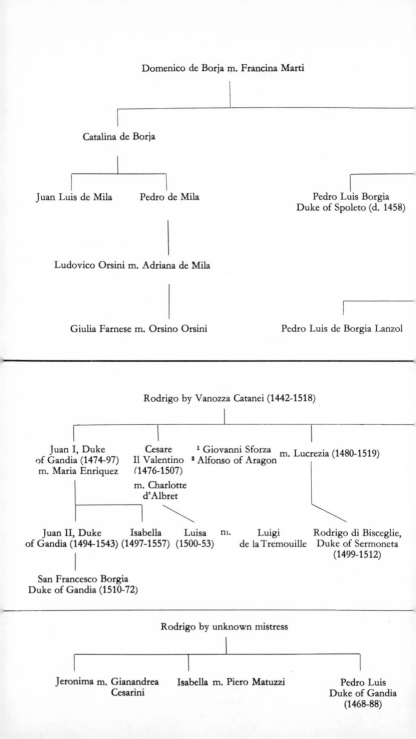

Domenico de Borja m. Francina Marti

Catalina de Borja

Juan Luis de Mila   Pedro de Mila

Pedro Luis Borgia
Duke of Spoleto (d. 1458)

Ludovico Orsini m. Adriana de Mila

Giulia Farnese m. Orsino Orsini

Pedro Luis de Borgia Lanzol

Rodrigo by Vanozza Catanei (1442-1518)

Juan I, Duke
of Gandia (1474-97)
m. Maria Enriquez

Cesare
Il Valentino
(1476-1507)
m. Charlotte
d'Albret

¹ Giovanni Sforza
² Alfonso of Aragon   m. Lucrezia (1480-1519)

Juan II, Duke   Isabella   Luisa   m.   Luigi   Rodrigo di Bisceglie,
of Gandia (1494-1543) (1497-1557)   (1500-53)   de la Tremouille Duke of Sermoneta
                                                                               (1499-1512)

San Francesco Borgia
Duke of Gandia (1510-72)

Rodrigo by unknown mistress

Jeronima m. Gianandrea
Cesarini

Isabella m. Piero Matuzzi

Pedro Luis
Duke of Gandia
(1468-88)

THE BORGIA FAMILY

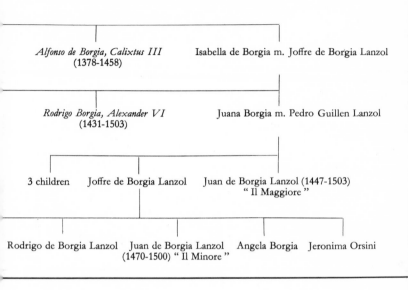

Alfonso de Borgia, Calixtus III (1378-1458) — Isabella de Borgia m. Joffre de Borgia Lanzol

Rodrigo Borgia, Alexander VI (1431-1503) — Juana Borgia m. Pedro Guillen Lanzol

3 children — Joffre de Borgia Lanzol — Juan de Borgia Lanzol (1447-1503) "Il Maggiore"

Rodrigo de Borgia Lanzol — Juan de Borgia Lanzol (1470-1500) "Il Minore" — Angela Borgia — Jeronima Orsini

DESCENDANTS OF RODRIGO BORGIA, POPE ALEXANDER VI

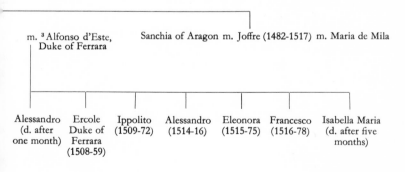

m. ³Alfonso d'Este, Duke of Ferrara — Sanchia of Aragon m. Joffre (1482-1517) m. Maria de Mila

Alessandro (d. after one month) — Ercole Duke of Ferrara (1508-59) — Ippolito (1509-72) — Alessandro (1514-16) — Eleonora (1515-75) — Francesco (1516-78) — Isabella Maria (d. after five months)

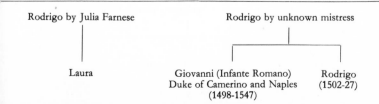

Rodrigo by Julia Farnese — Rodrigo by unknown mistress

Laura — Giovanni (Infante Romano) Duke of Camerino and Naples (1498-1547) — Rodrigo (1502-27)

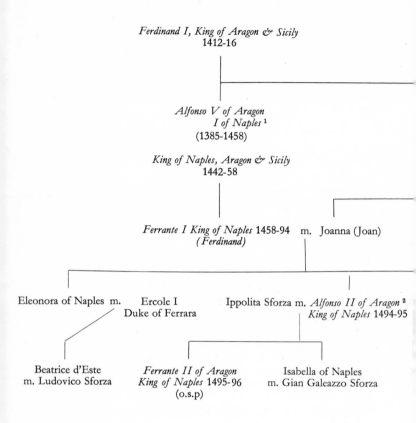

Ferdinand I, King of Aragon & Sicily
1412-16

Alfonso V of Aragon
I of Naples [1]
(1385-1458)

King of Naples, Aragon & Sicily
1442-58

Ferrante I King of Naples 1458-94   m.   Joanna (Joan)
(Ferdinand)

Eleonora of Naples m.   Ercole I   Ippolita Sforza m. Alfonso II of Aragon [2]
                            Duke of Ferrara   King of Naples 1494-95

Beatrice d'Este   Ferrante II of Aragon   Isabella of Naples
m. Ludovico Sforza   King of Naples 1495-96   m. Gian Galeazzo Sforza
                               (o.s.p)

[1] Called Alfonso II in the text.
[2] Called Alfonso III in the text.

HOUSE OF ARAGON IN SPAIN, NAPLES AND SICILY

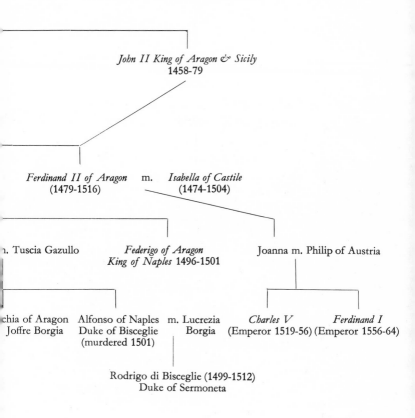

John II King of Aragon & Sicily
1458-79

Ferdinand II of Aragon   m.   *Isabella of Castile*
(1479-1516)   (1474-1504)

1. Tuscia Gazullo   *Federigo of Aragon*   Joanna m. Philip of Austria
                           King of Naples 1496-1501

chia of Aragon   Alfonso of Naples   m. Lucrezia   *Charles V*   *Ferdinand I*
  Joffre Borgia   Duke of Bisceglie   Borgia   (Emperor 1519-56) (Emperor 1556-64)
                   (murdered 1501)

                   Rodrigo di Bisceglie (1499-1512)
                   Duke of Sermoneta

NOTE ON THE CLOSING YEARS
OF LUCREZIA BORGIA'S LIFE

With Pope Alexander's death in 1503, Lucrezia Borgia ceased to be used as a pawn in her family's intrigues and under her the court of Ferrara became a centre for poets, painters and humanists, including Ariosto, Titian, Dosso Dossi, Pietro Bembo, and Aldus Manutius. Apart from the murder of the poet Ercole Strozzi in 1505 – allegedly ordered by the Duke in jealousy of Strozzi's attentions to Lucrezia – the rest of her life was tranquil, being devoted to patronage of the arts, charitable works, and the education of her children.

Cesare Borgia was killed in 1507, during the siege of Pamplona. He had led a charge so recklessly that the circumstances of his death seemed almost suicidal. Although he was mourned by his mother Vanozza, by Joffre – now established in the principality of Squillace with his second wife Maria de Mila – and also doubtless by various captains and soldiers who admired his outstanding mastery of their craft, in Italy and beyond people generally heaved a sigh of relief. Included among these were Pope Julius II, who had dreaded the possibility of Cesare fighting against him under the Venetian flag, the King of France, and, finally, the members of the Este family who no longer had to negotiate a careful policy between their own interests and those of Lucrezia's family. It was Lucrezia who gathered together the remnants of her brother's following, giving refuge to the page who had brought the news of his death to Ferrara, and to the Spanish priest who had helped Cesare in his flight from Medina and was now homeless. She summoned an illegitimate daughter of Cesare's from Rome – also called Lucrezia – clothed her in satin, velvet and fur and gave her over to Angela Borgia.

In 1512 Rodrigo di Bisceglie, Lucrezia's son by her second marriage, died, while in the same year her husband distinguished himself in the Battle of Ravenna fighting the Venetian and Papal forces. War over the duchy of Ferrara formed the background to the remaining years of Lucrezia's life. She herself seems to have been pregnant more often than not. She had seven children by Alfonso of Ferrara – Alessandro, who lived only from September to October 1505, Ercole, the future Duke of Ferrara (1508-59), Ippolito (1509-72), Alessandro (1514-16), Leonora (1515-75), Francesco (1516-78) and Isabella Maria (June to November 1519). Vanozza Catanei, mother of Lucrezia, died in 1518, and Lucrezia herself on the 24th of June the following year. To the very last she maintained a tenacious hold on life, unable to resign herself to the idea of death until she lost consciousness, then holding on for several days at the edge of death. " The poor woman is having great difficulty in departing, " said the courtiers. But the end came peacefully.

THE RENAISSANCE

It was only natural that Italy should have been the cradle of the Renaissance; her classical tradition was unbroken, her greatest poets were still Vergil and Ovid. Petrarch and Boccacio, whose major works, both in Latin and the vernacular, appeared between 1350 and 1375, perpetuated and invigorated this classical heritage, and as founders of the Renaissance their influence spanned the fifteenth and sixteenth centuries and even beyond. Of all the aspects of the Renaissance, the literary is the most easily defined, the most obvious and, in the final analysis, the most influential.

Yet before going into further detail about the rebirth of arts and letters, one question must be answered: what were the causes of the " Rinascimento "? – the word was first used in the 1550's to describe the preceding one-and-a-half centuries.

Byzantium fell in 1453. But Italy, and to some extent the rest of Europe, had felt the influence of Byzantine culture – a direct inheritance from the classical world – since the beginning of the thirteenth century. Even before that there had been close contact between the Crusaders and Islamic culture, which again had absorbed much of the classical learning. More, too, of the ancient learning, preserved and interpreted by Arab scholars, had filtered into Europe from Moorish Spain. In 1204 the Venetians and their crusading allies sacked Constantinople, looting and desecrating the city as no Goths or Vandals had ever done, and much of the precious loot found its way back to Venice. To Venice too came Greek refugees fleeing from the advancing Ottoman Turks, for, half a century before Constantinople fell, the Ottoman Empire, surging around and beyond that seemingly impregnable stronghold, had reached into the Peloponnese and Balkans. Had it not been for Tamerlane, last of the great Mongol conquerors, who diverted the Turks from their westward surge, Constantinople would probably have fallen half a century earlier. The situation was so desperate in 1399 that Manuel II Palaeologus visited Venice, Paris and even London to seek aid against the Turks; but in vain, for the crusading spirit of medieval Europe was fast dying. The last influx of

Greeks into Italy, bringing with them their Greco-Byzantine culture, coincided with the collapse of Constantinople.

The acquisitive Venetians and their Arab rivals were the trading people of the Mediterranean. Venetian galleys sailed the length and breadth of the Mediterranean, touching Alexandria, Jaffa, Rhodes, Crete, Trebizond and the Black Sea ports. Inevitably remnants of the old learning trickled back to Italy. The tide of the Arab conquests had ebbed from Spain, Malta and Sicily long before the fifteenth century, but it left behind its legends, its graceful Moorish architecture, and the stimulus of its great philosophers and alchemists, such as Averroes and Avicenna.

Yet this vast store of learning and other acquisitions would have remained dormant but for two factors: the invention of printing and the social conditions of early fifteenth century Italy. Many dates have been put forward as the year the modern world was born. Perhaps 1450, when Johann Gutenberg printed the first imperfect books on his newly constructed press comes closest, although he could hardly have realized the world-shattering importance of his invention. First, of course, had to come the art of paper-making, accomplished first by the Chinese, then by the Arabs, who learnt it from craftsmen taken prisoner during a ninth century Chinese attack on Muslim Samarkand. Paper was not manufactured in Italy until the thirteenth century, and in Germany not until the fourteenth. With the advent of printing dazzling possibilities arose: knowledge was no longer to be restricted to those few scholars to whom precious manuscript books were accessible; men of reasonable means could now constitute a new " reading public ." The endless potential of the printed word excited scholars and litterateurs, who hastened to satisfy the awakened curiosity of the public and the new demand for books.

Bibles were naturally enough the first books to be printed in quantity; next came new and legible editions of the classics, for Latin was understood by all educated men and women. A craving for first-hand knowledge gave impetus to Greek and Hebrew scholarship, to new translations of Plato, Homer, Aristotle and the Hebrew Cabala, and even of the Hermetic Books, repositories of Ancient Egypt's occult wisdom. And from translations it was only one step to the adaptation of classical themes, written both in Latin and in the vernacular. Following the adaptations came finally the original creations of a Pulci, an Ariosto, of a Bembo and Castiglione.

In Italy the new Renaissance culture germinated in the hectic political and capitalistic climate of her city states, both despotic and republican, in which nobility and plutocracy, flocking to the cities the better to assert their commercial and political independence, had fruitfully mingled. Italy's feudal nobility, struggling vainly against changing values, had long since disappeared. To a large extent status had become a matter of accumulating enough wealth to launch individual enterprises, and much surplus capital was widely invested to give ballast to precarious fortunes. Records of transactions, credit terms, bills of exchange became necessary as more and more business was conducted on paper – and a fair amount of education was necessary to keep these records. Lay culture and education began to develop as nobles and merchants accumulated sufficient capital to enable them to devote their leisure hours to cultivating their particular interests. The door was wide open to those whose claims were intellectual and esthetic.

The terms Early and High Renaissance must be used with some care. In Italy the term " Early " Renaissance can be used to define the period from 1420 to about 1500, with the " High " Renaissance extending a mere thirty years into the sixteenth century. In other countries, however, the span of the Renaissance had different beginnings and endings. Each country, differing in social structure from the next, developed its own " home-grown " version of Renaissance culture, with its own highlights, its own rate of development. France, for instance, brought into violent contact with Italy during the invasions at the turn of the century, began to catch up with Italy towards 1530. Ronsard, Du Bellay and especially Rabelais imprinted Italian humanism with their own Gallic genius, asserting, against tradition, the excellence of French as a literary language. But the Renaissance in France was cut short by the bloody wars of Protestant and Catholic; humanism and the Reformation did not mix. In Holland the Renaissance can be said to have begun with Jan van Eyck, whose best-known works began to appear in the 1430's;

even compared with the Italians van Eyck was a master in the technique of oil painting. Again the intense economic life of northern Europe, linked as it was with Venetian trade and centred around Bruges and Antwerp, provided scope for artists such as Dieryck Bouts, the Master of Flémalle, Massys, Hieronymus Bosch, and Rogier van der Weyden. In Germany the growth of the metal industry in the south during the second half of the fifteenth century created the wealth that was necessary for the encouragement of a Dürer or a Grünewald. England, however, had to wait until the age of Marlowe and Shakespeare for her Renaissance flowering, since Chaucer, although influenced by Boccacio and Petrarch, more properly belonged to the Middle Ages. By 1500 all Europe had relinquished for good the concept of chivalry and courtly love; replacing it was a new and intense awareness of the dignity of man.

Nevertheless, the visual splendour of the Renaissance remains its most powerful and evocative expression. Looking back over the complex and fantastic tapestry of the fifteenth and early sixteenth centuries, artistic genius seems to have been an everyday commodity. The terrors of Hell and the bliss of Heaven were equally portrayed with faultless, meticulous technique. In painting and sculpture more stress was laid on fluidity and movement; the immobility and eternal fixedness of Gothic art yielded to finer textures, to a sensuousness that flowed into both the sacred and profane. The writhing Gothic demons and the convulsions of the damned were a long time dying, but gradually a powerful serenity and confidence took their place. Nowhere is the richness, power and humanity of this age more perfectly portrayed than on the ceiling of the Sistine Chapel in Michelangelo's *Birth of Adam*.

Although epochs are brought to life most vividly through the visual arts, currents of thought, more subtle, tend to combine in one the past, the spirit of the times, and the future. Thus Humanism, an aspect of the Renaissance, led directly into the Reformation; for both Erasmus and Calvin, and Luther to a lesser degree, were exponents of the rich Humanism of the north. While in Italy Humanism, in general terms, meant a rediscovery of the vitality of man through the

Greek and Roman classics, in the north its emphasis was rather upon a rediscovery of the Church fathers, the Greek New Testament, and the literature of the Hebrews, leading to a new appreciation of the simplicity and directness of the early Christian ethos. The northern Humanists also discovered for themselves an astonishing similarity between Christianity and the philosophy of Platonism. Already the Great Schism, which lasted from 1378 to 1417 and produced two, and sometimes three Popes at a time, had greatly weakened the prestige of the Papacy. Did not the Church's pomp and worldliness, her ostentatious wealth, her warrior Popes, her entanglement in politics, her theological wranglings deny the very spirit of Christ's message? Thus the purist elements of Humanistic thinking brought on a hardening which burst into open revolt against the Church of Rome.

Politically speaking, the fifteenth century was an age of consolidation, when the different countries of Europe began to assume the shape and size they still generally hold today. Spain had to wait until the last of her Moorish invaders were crushed before becoming, for a brief period, one of the world's richest and most powerful of seafaring nations. The year 1492 not only saw the conquest of the last Moorish kingdom of Granada, but also the launching of Columbus' voyage by Ferdinand and Isabella, which was soon to unlock the fabulous wealth of Central and South America. And the gold of the Americas in turn was to accelerate the already burgeoning economy of Renaissance Europe.

Both in France and England a period of internal strife followed the conclusion of the Hundred Years' War in 1453. France's troubles ended with the victories of Louis XI; and with the acquisition of Brittany in 1491 its consolidation was complete. In England the breakdown of the medieval policy during the Wars of the Roses was succeeded, once Henry Tudor had gained the throne in 1485, by the formidable stability of the Elizabethan period, while on the continent the foundations of the Hapsburg Empire, which by 1800 was to dominate more than half of Europe, were laid by Frederick III and his two successors, Maximilian and Charles V. Russia, another giant of the new age, also began its sure and steady development in the fifteenth century. After the final shaking off of the Mongol yoke in 1480, the shape of a greater Russia began to emerge as Ivan the Great extended his rule to Novgorod, Tver, Smolensk, Polotsk and Chernigov. Although the crumbling of Tamerlane's Empire had been followed by the precipitous decline of Mongol power, in Russia as elsewhere, the fifteenth century witnessed a new upheaval in Asia as the Turkish Ottoman Empire moved into the gap and at its height extended from the walls of Vienna to the Persian Gulf. The lifetimes of the great Ottoman Sultans, Murad II, Muhammad II, Selim I and Suleiman the Magnificent, spanning the years between 1450 and 1560, coincided with those of Italy's greatest Renaissance artists, Botticelli, Leonardo da Vinci, Michelangelo and Titian.

Not only was this the age of new empires and old ones crumbling; it was also an age of infinite new perspectives. The Old World discovered the New; half a world was there for the taking. The discoveries of Columbus, Diaz, Cabot, Magellan and Cabral can be seen as a practical demonstration of one of the main tenets of Humanism: Seek and ye shall find; for as long as the spirit of human enquiry endures there will always be knowledge worth the finding.

THE PAPACY IN THE FIFTEENTH CENTURY

The Council of Pisa met in 1409, hoping to end the Great Schism and to inaugurate religious reforms. It was a failure. Reforms were postponed, and both the Roman and the rival Pope of Avignon refused to resign. The next attempt to break this deadlock, on which the heresy of John Hus and Jerome of Prague thrived, was made at the Council of Constance, held from 1414 to 1417. Again no reforming measures were achieved, but two important decrees were voted: first, that general councils should meet at regular intervals, and secondly, that the voice of these councils should outweigh the single will of the Pope. Both Gregory XII of Rome and Benedict XIII of Avignon were tried and deposed, and Martin V, a member of the Colonna family, was elected Pope. The Great Schism was over. It had been a full one hundred and twelve years since Rome had had a Pope in sole control of all Christendom. But the prestige of the Papacy had sunk to a low level.

In order to regain even part of her former political power the Church of Rome would be forced to make adjustments to fit the new political and intellectual realities. In 1431 therefore the Council of Basle was called by Eugenius IV to face five principal problems: the old question of whether the Pope should obey the will of the Council, or the Council the will of the Pope; the increasing sting of heresies and of intellectual criticism; whether the menace of the militant Ottoman Turks, bringing with them the teaching of Islam, should be contained by reunion with the Eastern Church; the policy of the Church vis-à-vis the revival of classical scholarship and the growing currents of Humanism; and last and in the long run, most pressing, ecclesiastical reform.

Unfortunately the Council of Basle merely demonstrated on a small scale the fundamental disunity within the Roman Church. A strong anti-papal faction, ignoring Eugenius' dismissal of the Council, forced through a decree demanding the attendance of the Pope and his cardinals while the Council was in session. Even after a second summons the Pope failed to attend, and with his supporters left for Ferrara, where yet another council was held (1438-1439) and yet more words

303

wasted in futile discussion. Meanwhile in 1439 the Council of Basle had elected Felix V as anti-Pope, and continued in dwindling numbers to propose anti-papal reforms. Finally in 1449 Felix abdicated, and the Council of Basle was dissolved. But the movement to reconcile Papal supremacy with some measure of reform bore bitter fruit for Rome. In 1438 France ceased to pay tribute to Rome after Charles VII had accepted the Pragmatic Sanction of Bourges, which embodied most of the anti-papal decrees of the Council of Basle.

The question of union with the Greek Church was resolved of itself in 1453 when Constantinople fell. The question of reform had once more been pushed aside. As for the threat of Islam, the aged Calixtus III's efforts to gain support for a full-scale crusade were a dismal failure. This Borgia Pope's militant nature, which had won him the Papal election, was ineffective against the dissensions amongst the German and Hungarian crusading forces, which had raised the Turkish siege of Belgrade in 1456. No sooner was this victory for Christendom won than the crusaders began to quarrel and Belgrade once again fell into Turkish hands. After Calixtus' death in 1458 the war against the Turks became solely the concern of Venice, and hardly for religious reasons.

Calixtus' predecessor, Nicholas V, had done much to update the image of the Church by making Rome itself, temporarily at least, a centre of Humanism. Nicholas, who had once served Cosimo de' Medici as librarian, collected many manuscripts which furnished the first shelves of the Vatican library. Moreover the militant atmosphere of Calixtus' reign was markedly tempered by his successor, Pius II, distinguished as the only Pope to write, amongst many essays and orations, an autobiography.

Having thus gradually and partially come to terms with the age in which it found itself, the Vatican began to play the Renaissance game: acquisition of wealth, nepotist politics, and the extension of her own territory. In his ambition to consolidate the Papal States, the intransigent Sixtus IV followed in the tracks of his predecessor, Paul II, who had notably been a strong advocate of centralizing Papal power, but also a fastidious collector of carvings and precious stones. The ostentatious wealth of Rodrigo Borgia as Pope Alexander

VI during the last decade of the fifteenth century was nothing new – neither was his open immorality; for the same scandalous behaviour had been displayed by his immediate predecessor, the indolent Innocent VIII, who supped publicly in female company and made no secret of having fathered several children.

After the first French invasion of Italy in 1494 the Popes were, more than ever, obliged to become military rather than religious leaders, for the strong foreign presence precipitated a reshuffle of political allegiances. Alexander took advantage of the partnership of the French to attack Naples, and in return France helped Cesare Borgia to put down a revolt in Senigallia. However Julius II, elected Pope in 1503, changed sides. Having regained the Romagna from Venice, his main aim was to expel the French from Italy. And by the time the triple crown rested on the head of Leo X, the son of Lorenzo de' Medici, the persistent worldliness of the Papacy and its failure to bring about reform had done its work. Martin Luther was at the height of his powers, and the Reformation was in full flood. Leo's excommunication of the German reform leader in 1521 was but a poor solution to a situation which had existed ever since the martyrdom of John Hus, executed at the Council of Constance a hundred and six years before.

Girolamo Savonarola's eloquent denunciations of the corruption of the Papacy and the state were cut short in 1498. He was hung and burnt as a heretic. But the same expedient was useless against the distant Luther and his followers; from the north came the *coup de grâce* for the Church of Rome.

THE FRENCH INVASIONS OF ITALY

The Italian Wars cover the period from 1494 to 1559, but after the Treaty of Noyon (13th August 1516) they become part of the rivalry between Hapsburg and Valois kings, which from the time of the accession of the Emperor Charles V in 1519 included the whole European field. The earlier stage of these wars was confined to Italy – in the late fifteenth century that country held undisputed supremacy as intellectual and artistic leader in Europe, but was so divided politically that she fell an easy victim to the strong monarchies then arising in the West, all of which coveted her wealth.

There were at that time five major Italian states: Venice, strongest of all, deriving her wealth and influence from her eastern possessions and her extensive oriental trade; Milan, ruled by Ludovico Sforza; Florence under Lorenzo the Magnificent; the Papal States, carved from the central part of the peninsula and in process of expansion in the late fifteenth century, and the Kingdom of Naples, ruled by a branch of the Spanish house of Aragon. These states maintained a precarious balance among themselves but were all so imperialistic that they constantly attempted to victimize each other and would often resort to the expedient of calling in the foreigner. Thus Italy became the "cockpit of Europe" – the prey of French, German, and Spanish ambitions.

Charles VIII's first French invasion of Italy was poorly planned and carelessly executed, but had much importance in dramatizing the international nature of the Italian problem, as well as in disseminating Italian Renaissance learning and art throughout western Europe. The second French invasion, which followed in 1499 under Louis XII, forced Ludovico Sforza to flee from Milan to Germany. Milan thus became French.

By 1502 a combined Franco-Spanish force had occupied Naples, with the approval of Pope Alexander VI, who had declared Frederick of Naples deposed. This alliance of the Borgia Pope with the French can be partly explained on the grounds that the King of Naples had refused to allow his daughter to marry Cesare. Moreover French help was invaluable to Alexander in gaining the Romagna for Cesare. It must be said in extenuation of his policy that he gained much land and therefore power, for the Church, and succeeded in imposing some measure of order on a Rome constantly laid waste by feudal quarrels.

Two Spanish victories in the years 1502 and 1503 completed the Spanish conquest of Naples, for it was too much to hope to have the two great nations rule it together. Spain, already holding Sicily, now controlled southern Italy, as France held Milan and the north.

In 1508 a further stage of the Italian Wars began with the organization of the League of Cambrai against Venice. Under this agreement the Emperor Maximilian promised Louis XII the investiture of Milan in return for his support. Ferdinand of Aragon and Pope Julius II joined the coalition, which defeated the Venetians at Agnadello in 1509. In 1510 Julius II deserted the League of Cambrai and joined Venice against the French. When the French captured Bologna in 1511, both Ferdinand and Henry VIII of England joined the " Holy League " against Louis XII; when France won a further victory at Ravenna, even the Emperor and the Swiss cantons turned against her. The Swiss were principally responsible for the expulsion of the French from Milan and Lombardy, completed by 1513.

The accession of Francis I, who was as deeply interested in Italian politics as his two predecessors had been, led to a spectacular French victory at Marignano on 13 September, 1515. In 1516 Charles V of Spain, confronted with serious problems in his own country and in Germany and eager to secure European cooperation against the Turks, concluded with Francis the Treaty of Noyon whereby the French retained Milan, but relinquished their claim to Naples. In 1522 the first of the Hapsburg-Valois wars, many of which used Italy as a battlefield, began. Not until the Treaty of Cateau-Cambrésis in 1559 (after the abdication of the Emperor Charles V) was a relatively permanent solution arrived at. This involved the abandonment of all French possessions in Italy except Turin, Saluzzo, and Pignerolo, and the surrender of her supremacy in Italy to Spain.

THE KINGDOM OF NAPLES

Alfonso V of Aragon (Alfonso I of Naples) was adopted as heir by Joan II, Angevin Queen of Naples, but did not succeed in claiming his inheritance until 1435, being recognized as king by the Pope in 1442. A lover of Renaissance Italy, Alfonso made Naples the centre of his kingdom and became a patron of the arts. His predecessors had, from 1409, united the crowns of Aragon and Sicily, but in 1443 he had decided that whereas Aragon and Sicily would pass to his brother John, the Neapolitan succession should go to his bastard son, Don Ferrante, or Ferdinand I. Alfonso's policy of war and expenditure in Italy was designed to strengthen his son's position but in fact aggravated the instability of the kingdom. Succeeding Alfonso in 1458, Ferdinand I (Ferrante) was faced with a baronial revolt in favour of René of Anjou and his son John of Calabria, rival Angevin claimants to the throne, and in 1485-87 with a further revolt to put his own young son, Frederick (Federigo) on the throne. He was, however, able to maintain his position as ruler by trickery and ruthlessness.

Charles VIII of France had meanwhile inherited the Angevin claim to Naples and in 1494 invaded Italy to make it good. Although Alfonso II, Ferdinand's elder son and successor, abdicated in favour of his own son Ferdinand II (Ferrantino) in 1495, the kingdom, torn by faction, could not withstand the French and Charles VIII, victorious, had himself crowned King of Naples. The formation of the Holy League obliged Charles to withdraw, and Ferdinand II was restored to his throne a few months before he died. The crown then passed to Frederick (Federigo), brother of Alfonso II, under whom the kingdom enjoyed a few years of security. Finally by the Treaty of Granada (1500), Louis XII of France and Ferdinand II of Aragon agreed to divide the kingdom of Naples on the pretext of forestalling a Turkish occupation. Frederick gave himself up to Louis XII in 1501 and was pensioned off in France where he died in 1504. The French and Spaniards soon came to blows over the partition and Gonzalvo de Cordoba's victory at Cerignola and again on the Garigliano River (1504) decided the issue for Spain, which for many years thereafter ruled Naples through viceroys.

DEVELOPMENT OF THE ITALIAN LANGUAGE IN THE LATE FIFTEENTH CENTURY

Lucrezia Borgia must have been especially involved in this most absorbing of contemporary topics, the " new " Italian language, by reason of her great friendship with Pietro Bembo, ten years older than herself and a true artist with words. Her influence might even have encouraged him to break away from the classical preoccupations of his scholarly contemporaries.

The spread of Florentine trade and culture carried with it the Tuscan dialect, and gradually all Italy adopted the language of Tuscany, much in the same way as the French spoken in the Île de France became the French of today. Dante, Petrarch, and Boccacio were the earliest writers to win a measure of recognition for the Tuscan language. But like many great works, Dante's *Divina Commedia* was not fully appreciated during his lifetime. National recognition of the language used by Dante to portray the terrors of the Inferno only came when scholars began to turn away from the Latin classics in order to give the hitherto unfashionable vulgar tongue the credit it deserved.

Alberti, in 1441, was the first to reckon the vulgar tongue worthy of conveying serious thought. The sheer volume and quality of Tuscan writing, combined with its wide propagation, justified his claims. Lorenzo de' Medici enthusiastically set out to popularize the Tuscan language, his most notable contribution being a Tuscan anthology under the title of *Raccolta Aragonese* which included the masterpieces of Arezzo, Cavalcanti, Dante, Cino and Petrarch – with some of his own poetry as an epilogue.

Bembo's *Prose della volgar lingua*, written in praise of common Italian as an artistic medium, received wide recognition, for the *volgar lingua* had by that time been appropriated by the writers of Milan, Ferrara, Venice and Rome.

The tendency towards linguistic unification was hastened by the invention of printing, introduced into Italy in the 1460's. After that date the diffusion of the Tuscan language was accomplished with great rapidity and thoroughness.

THE ORSINI

This ancient Roman family, almost as ancient as its traditional enemy the Colonna, was from early times closely involved in the history and fortunes of Rome and its neighbouring states, providing a long series of soldiers, statesmen, and a number of Popes to the Church. The family dated from the time of Matteo Orsini, who in 1241 had taken the side of Pope Gregory IX against the Emperor Frederick II – allied with the Colonna – in that interminable Guelph-against-Ghibelline quarrel which so disturbed the Middle Ages. In 1297 Boniface VIII, of the Caetani family, one of the most militant of medieval Popes, declared war on the Colonna, and the Orsini, for the Papal forces, captured Nepi from their rivals. The granting of Nepi to the Orsini as a Papal fief did little to alleviate the bad feeling between the two families. On the death of Benedict XI in 1304 Cardinal Napoleone Orsini led the French supporters in a quarrel over the succession which resulted in a fierce civil war. Further feuds between Colonna, Caetani and Orsini continued to lay waste the Campagna, still a highly feudalized area in the fifteenth century, and kept Rome itself in a state of anarchy.

In 1435 Francesco Orsini was appointed Prefect of Rome and was given the title of Duke of Gravina. War broke out again in 1484 between the Orsini and the Colonna and this time, under the leadership of Virginio Orsini, the Orsini held the upper hand. Apart from an interval of Borgia rule when the Orsini were dispossessed of their castles and three of them done to death, the family retained its dominant place among the Roman aristocracy for many centuries.

THE SFORZA

Sforza, meaning " strength, " was a nickname bestowed upon Muzio Attendolo (1369-1424) of Colignola in the Romagna, a soldier of fortune. Two of Muzio's sons, Francesco (1401-1466) and Alessandro (1409-1473), *condottieri* like their father, first achieved the status of princes. In 1445 Alessandro acquired Pesaro in the Papal states, of which he was subsequently made Vicar by the Pope. His descendants retained the city till 1512, when they were expelled by Julius II.

After his father's death Francesco entered the service of the last Visconti of Milan, Duke Filippo Maria, a suspicious, morose and unpredictable prince, and for over twenty years fought now with him, now against him. In 1441 he married Filippo's illegitimate daughter, Bianca Maria, receiving at the same time a vague promise of succession to the duchy itself. Nevertheless he became Duke of Milan in 1450 by right of conquest rather than of legitimate succession.

Francesco Sforza's son, Galeazzo Maria Sforza (1466-1476), a strong ruler despite his dissipated and evil life, was assassinated in 1476. Gian Galeazzo Sforza (1469-1494) succeeded his father as a minor, ruling under the regency of his mother, who was eventually ousted from power by his uncle Ludovico (1469-1494) called " Il Moro, " husband of the beautiful and brilliant Beatrice d'Este. From 1480 Ludovico Sforza was the real ruler of Milan. Ill-famed, perhaps unjustly, for encouraging the French in their invasion of Italy, he was in 1499 expelled by Louis XII of France, imprisoned after an unsuccessful attempt to regain his duchy, and in 1508 died a prisoner in the castle of Loches. After recovering Milan, the Sforzas ruled it until 1535. Ludovico, with his equally ambitious wife, held a brilliant court at Milan as friends and patrons of the greatest of Renaissance artists, particularly of Leonardo da Vinci and Bramante.

THE ESTE

This family of Italian princes ruled in Ferrara from the thirteenth to the late sixteenth centuries, and in Modena and Reggio from the later Middle Ages to the end of the eighteenth century. They were of Lombard descent – a branch of the tenth century dynasty founded by the Marchese Oberto, who was granted the fief of Este by the Emperor Otto I. They took their name from the township and castle of Este, seventeen miles southwest of Padua. In 1070 Welf IV was created Duke of Bavaria, beginning a long-standing connection between the German princes of Brunswick and Hanover and a line of Italian dukes.

The first Este to hold power in Ferrara was Azzo VI (1193-1212) who won fame by leading the Guelfs to victory against the Ghibellines. His exploits in the area laid the foundations for the power of Obizzo II, who annexed Modena and Reggio to the family domains. Niccolo III (1393-1441) profited by the political collapse of the Visconti to seize and to hold, for a time, the Duchy of Parma. He later became an ally of the Visconti and in 1441 was nominated governor of Milan, but he died the same year, probably from poison. He was celebrated for his profusion of illegitimate children, one of whom, Leonello (1407-1450), he chose as his successor.

By the fourteenth century the Este family was famed not only for its warriors but for its men of letters and statesmen as well. Niccolo's sons became renowned patrons of the arts. Leonello, after an excellent education by Guarino da Verona, became a Humanist of note, and from the middle of the fifteenth century Ferrara flourished as a centre of Italian life and culture, a city of dukes and poets with one of the most brilliant courts in Europe. Leonello's brother and successor, Borso (1413-1471), was named Duke of Ferrara by Pope Paul II in 1471. Their half brother, Ercole I (1431-1505), succeeded to the duchy in a difficult period. He had early to face a hostile coalition of Venice and Pope Sixtus IV, and the marriage of his son Alfonso with Lucrezia Borgia was intended to protect his possessions from her father, Pope Alexander VI, and her brother Cesare. He continued his dynasty's patronage of the arts, taking the poet Boiardo as his minister and extending his favour and support to Ariosto. Ippolito d'Este (1479-1520), cardinal from 1493, was his third son and was a close friend of Ariosto.

Even more famous as patrons of the greatest of Italian artists were Ercole's daughters, Isabella (1474-1539) and Beatrice (1475-1497), the former married to Francesco Gonzaga, Marquis of Mantua, the latter to Ludovico Sforza, "Il Moro," regent and later Duke of Milan. Both were exceptionally beautiful, endowed with taste and intelligence, and carefully educated in letters and the arts. Mantegna and Leonardo da Vinci, Raphael and Bramante, Titian and Giulio Romano, Baldassare Castiglione, Matteo Bandello and many others all enjoyed their patronage and the advantages of life at one of the foremost courts in Europe. By all accounts Beatrice was the more amiable and open-handed of the two sisters, but her life was cut short in childbirth in 1497. By contrast, Isabella, as Marchioness of Mantua, guided the policies of Mantua for over thirty years, through a most difficult period, receiving at her court the deposed Duke and Duchess of Urbino and showing herself especially skilled in diplomatic dealings with the dreaded Cesare Borgia.

Alfonso I (1476-1534), Duke of Ferrara, the last husband of Lucrezia Borgia, who succeeded his father Ercole I in 1505, was an accomplished prince, famous for his skill in mechanics and artillery design. His army was one of the best equipped in Europe, and as Duke of Ferrara he commanded the Papal troops for Julius II's League of Cambrai against Venice. Threatened by Papal territorial ambitions in Emilia, Alfonso consistently adhered to the French interest in Italy, therefore coming into conflict with Pope Julius II, who deprived him of Modena in 1510 and of Reggio in 1512 – although he first managed to inflict several defeats on the Papal forces. At the Battle of Ravenna in 1512 he fought on the French side to gain a somewhat useless victory. With the French withdrawal from Italy after the Treaty of Noyon, Alfonso sought an alliance with the Papacy but did not succeed in regaining Reggio and Modena until after the death of Leo X, when Clement VII became occupied with other problems. He died in 1534, after regaining Reggio in 1523 and Modena in 1527.

Alfonso I was succeeded by his son, Ercole II (1508-1559), his second child by Lucrezia Borgia, who married Renée, daughter of Louis XII of France. Both Ercole and his brother Ippolito (1509-1572), cardinal from 1539, were active patrons of literature and the arts. The magnificent Villa d'Este at Tivoli was built by Ippolito. Alfonso II (1533-1597) was the fifth and last Duke of Ferrara, remembered for his patronage of Tasso. With him the main branch of the family ended – despite three marriages he had no issue – and although at his death he bequeathed the duchy to his cousin, Cesare (1562-1628), Pope Clement VIII refused to recognize this settlement, declaring Cesare to be illegitimate. By the Treaty of Faenza with Alfonso's sister, Lucrezia (1536-1598), he finally established direct Papal rule in Ferrara (1598).

THE MEDICI

This great Italian family, whose name for over three centuries was linked with the history of Florence and Tuscany, first appeared in Florence in the early thirteenth century, but up to the end of the fourteenth century the record is confused. The Medici accumulated an enormous fortune through trade and money-lending and played an ever-increasing part in politics, ready at any time to resort to violence in the interests of the Florentine *popolani* against the *grandi*. Salvestro de' Medici was elected Gonfalonier in 1351, emerging as a popular champion against the Guelph Party, but his reign of terror ended in a sentence of exile which much reduced the family fortunes. The most illustrious of Medici branches sprang from the sons of Giovanni de' Medici (1360-1429). Cosimo the Elder (1389-1464), later called *pater patriae*, became after 1434 virtual lord of Florence, a republic keenly jealous of its liberty, by using a policy of progressive taxation to ruin all in the way of his absolute power, while at the same time favouring the lower classes as well as his supporters. Allied towards the end of his life with the Sforza of Milan against Venice and Naples, he was moderately successful in achieving his aim of keeping a balance of power in Italy. He spent vast sums on the arts and public works, encouraging architects, painters, sculptors, and humanists. Brunelleschi, Michelozzi, Lorenzo Ghiberti, Lucca della Robbia, Leon Battista Alberti, Fra Angelico, Paolo Uccello all worked in Florence during his rule. He sponsored the first public library in Florence, protected Marsilio Ficino's Platonic Academy, and promoted the teaching of Greek.

Cosimo's son, Piero the Gouty (1416-1469), inherited his position, but his rule was completely eclipsed by that of his son, Lorenzo the Magnificent (1449-1492), who was invited by all leading Florentine citizens to undertake the government of the city-state. Lorenzo added enlightened ambitions, high ideals, and personal charm to the popular support which enabled him to suppress obsolete republican institutions, and to dissolve the Guelf Party. During the Pazzi conspiracy of 1478 Lorenzo himself was badly wounded and his brother Giuliano murdered during Mass in the cathedral. This outrage was avenged with such bloodshed that the Pope saw fit to excommunicate Lorenzo, place Florence under an interdict, and induce Ferrante of Naples to declare war on the city. But Lorenzo quickly secured the alliance of Ferrante against the French, and tightened his control over the republic by creating a new Council of Seventy responsible to himself alone. In 1489 his thirteen-year-old son, Giovanni, the future Leo X, was created a cardinal.

Although the Medici and Florence were less prosperous under Lorenzo than under Cosimo, Lorenzo's rule marked the most splendid period of the city's Renaissance. Himself a poet, Lorenzo patronized and befriended writers, artists, and scientists. Pico della Mirandola, Botticelli, Antonio and Piero del Pollaiuolo, Mino da Fiesole, Verrocchio, Benedetto di Maiano and Donatello adorned the city or were in regular attendance at Lorenzo's palaces and villas. The pleasures and pagan atmosphere of Lorenzo's Florence were denounced by the austere Dominican preacher, Savonarola, who also criticized the absolute political power which, while encouraging this licence, had suppressed the former republican freedom. Even so, Lorenzo admired Savonarola, whose blessing he received before dying at Careggi in 1492.

From 1494 to 1531 the Medici were twice exiled and restored. In 1494 the Medici palace was sacked and the republic restored by Charles VIII; thereafter Florence remained faithful to the French alliance until 1512, when Cardinal Giovanni prompted Pope Julius II to demand that Florence should enter the Holy League against Louis XII, dismiss Piero Soderini (elected Gonfalonier for life in 1502), and allow the exiled Medici to return. Thus in 1513 Lorenzo the Magnificent's constitution was restored.

While Imperial forces sacked Rome in 1527 revolution broke out in Florence. The ruling Medici were again exiled, but restored by Charles V in 1530. Alessandro, bastard grandson of Lorenzo the Magnificent's brother, Giuliano, was nominated head of state for Florence, and returned to the city in 1531. Michelangelo's greatest work for the Medici in Florence belongs to the twelve years following 1522.

315

THE COLONNA

One of the oldest of Roman families, and first in importance, this great clan of brilliant marauders, constantly at war with their arch enemies, the Orsini, helped to make a battleground of Renaissance Rome and the Campagna.

Styled Counts of Tusculum in the twelfth century, the Colonna were renowned for their lawlessness, and their power was measurable by the turbulence they created. All neighbouring states could expect attack, no traveller was safe, nor was the Papacy in any position to withstand them. In 1297 Pope Boniface VIII attempted to break their dominance through excommunication and the confiscation of their lands, but a quick revenge followed when the bold Sciarra Colonna led an armed attack on Boniface at Anagni in 1303 and humiliated him by slapping his face. By 1347, partly owing to the flagrant nepotism of the Colonna Pope, Martin V, their strength was such that they were virtually an independent power.

Nevertheless their fortunes fluctuated greatly. In 1431 their power was effectively challenged by Pope Eugenius IV, and was finally broken by the Borgia Pope, Alexander VI, a defeat which did not, of course, end their influence and importance in Italian politics. From the later years of the sixteenth century the family lived in unbroken peace with the Papacy, many of its members rising to eminence as prelates, soldiers and statesmen in the service of the Church as well as of other powers, notably Spain.

THE FARNESE

The Farnese, long prominent in Rome, ruled the Parma duchies from 1545 to 1731. The family was descended from one of the most celebrated *condottieri* of the fifteenth century, Rannuccio il Vecchio Farnese, who commanded the Florentines against Milan in 1424, and was later appointed captain against the Colonna by Pope Eugenius IV. In the fifteenth century, owing to an adroit matrimonial policy, the Farnese greatly increased their powers.

One of Ranuccio's sons married Isabella Orsini, another (Pier Luigi) Giovanella Caetani. Of this latter union was born Alessandro (1468-1549) later Pope Paul III, whose illustrious name and vast culture as well as the love affair of his sister Julia with Pope Alexander VI, ensured his rapid rise at the Roman court. A cardinal at twenty-five, he was elected Pope in 1534 and at the consistory of the 19th August, 1545, in the prevailing spirit of nepotism, detached Parma and Piacenza from the Papal domains and erected them into duchies for his family. Pier Luigi (1503-1547), his son by an unknown woman, pursued a vigorous and efficient internal policy in the duchies but drew upon himself the resentment of Charles V by his ambiguous attitude to the Holy Roman Empire. It is probable that Charles V favoured the conspiracy of the nobles who assassinated Pier Luigi at Piacenza in 1547.

Pier Luigi's grandson, Alessandro (1545-1592), was one of the most prominent of the later Farnese. He fought at the battle of Lepanto (1571) and eventually became Spanish governor of the Netherlands.

PIETRO BEMBO

Pietro Bembo was born at Venice on the 20th of May, 1470. A brilliant scholar of the Italian Renaissance, his writings evoke, more completely than those of his contemporaries, the spirit of the age.

His works, entirely characteristic of the early Renaissance, include a history of Venice from 1487 to 1514, dialogues, essays, poems and the famous *Gli Asolani* (1505) in praise of Platonic love and dedicated to Lucrezia Borgia who was his patron at Ferrara. The history of Venice (later in life he was official historian of the city state) and his *Prose della volgar lingua* (1525) are worthy of particular note. The latter was a major effort to impose classical norms on the developing Tuscan or Florentine tongue, and greatly contributed to the development of the Italian language.

Principally educated by his father, Bernado Bembo, and introduced by him to the higher ranks of Florentine society under Lorenzo the Magnificent, Pietro accompanied Giulio de' Medici to Rome, and in 1513 became secretary there to Pope Leo X. On the death of the Pope he retired to Padua, becoming historian of Venice in 1529 and librarian of St. Marks shortly afterwards. In 1539 he returned to Rome to don a cardinal's hat, where his devotion to classical history and to theology earned him the bishoprics of Bergamo and Gubbio. He was a candidate for the Papacy at the time of his death in 1547.

PINTURICCHIO (1454-1513)

Bernardino di Betto, a painter of the Perugian school, was nicknamed "Pinturicchio" (Little Painter) because of his small stature, but actually he excelled in large-scale decoration. He travelled to Rome with Perugino and received a first major assignment collaborating on the Sistine Chapel frescoes, painting among others the well-known *Circumcision of Moses*. Other outstanding works of his include the decoration of the Borgia apartments in the Vatican, and the frescoes of the life of San Bernadino in S. Maria Aracoeli. The patronage of the della Rovere family made him fashionable in Rome, and in 1492-1495 he worked for the Borgias, introducing their portraits (Lucrezia as St. Catherine and Alexander VI in adoration) into biblical scenes, curiously interwoven with figures from Egyptian mythology and heraldic symbols.

In 1501 he was working in Spello, where his frescoes can still be seen, and shortly afterwards began the series of scenes from the life of Pius II in the library of Siena cathedral. His painting was characterized by bold, flat patterns, glowing colours, a superb arrangement of figures, and a mastery of space composition and landscape – qualities which are also in Perugino and other Umbrian painters, and which strongly influenced the style of Raphael. Pinturicchio's work is marked by a lack of interest in perspective as compared with that of many of his great contemporaries.

318

ARIOSTO (1474-1533)

Lodovico Ariosto was born at Reggio in Modena and served the Este family of Ferrara for most of his life. His poems, satires and learned plays were both popular and respected in his day, but his masterpiece remains the *Orlando Furioso*, (Mad Roland) a continuation of Boiardo's *Orlando Innamorato* (Roland in love) of 1495. This is a long narrative poem in octave stanzas dealing with the adventures of Roland and the other knights of Charlemagne in wars against the Saracens.

MACHIAVELLI

Statesman and writer, patriot and thinker of genius, whose acute understanding of contemporary politics and insight into human nature produced masterpieces that have too often been misjudged as immoral or cynical, Niccolo Machiavelli was born in Florence in 1469. Early poverty may explain why his education did not suit his ability, for he never embarked on the study of Greek and studied Latin only under inferior masters. At twenty-nine he was nevertheless head of the second chancery in Florence, and secretary to the magistracy which directed foreign affairs. His first important mission was to the French court in 1500.

On his return to Florence he found the republic, owing to the ambitions of Cesare Borgia, on the verge of ruin and was sent on two missions to Cesare. During the second of these (October, 1502 to January, 1503) he witnessed the bloody vengeance taken by Cesare on his mutinous captains at Senigallia, and wrote a famous account of the incident, " On the Manner adopted by the Duke Valentino to Kill Vitellozzo. " Cesare, in fact, caught the imagination of the Florentine statesman – implacable, resolute and cunning, he had conquered a dominion for himself in only a few months, and Machiavelli was to adapt his qualities and methods to his own ideal of the new " Prince, " whom he considered alone able to provide the desperate remedy needed for the desperate ills of Italy. It is evident that this was a case of idealization, for Machiavelli's admiration for the Prince was far greater than

319

his admiration for the man. In 1503 Machiavelli was sent to Rome for the duration of the conclave which elected Pope Julius II, and there witnessed the inglorious decline of his hero with ever-increasing scorn. In the end he rejoiced in Cesare's imprisonment, " which he deserved as a rebel against Christ. "

In Florence Machiavelli became right-hand man to Piero Soderini and took the opportunity to realize in practice some of his prolific military ideas. Impressed both by the enterprise of ancient Rome and by his own observations in France and in the Romagna (where Cesare Borgia had replaced mercenaries with levies from his own territory), Machiavelli ardently promoted the idea of giving the Florentine state a militia of its own, recruited from its citizens. This carefully-built-up force, however, was routed by the Holy League in 1512, and the aftermath saw the end of Machiavelli's hopes and ambitions. Soderini was deposed, Machiavelli deprived of his position, imprisoned and tortured on a charge of implication in the 1513 Boscolli conspiracy, and the Medici returned in triumph as masters of the city.

Unable to gain the good graces of the Medici and hounded by poverty and unhappiness, Machiavelli sought refuge in the little property at Sant' Andrea inherited from his father, where he employed his leisure in writing, between the spring and the autumn of 1513, his two most famous works, *Il Principe*, and a large part of the *Discourses on the First Decade of Livy*. He hoped that the dedication of the *Prince* to Lorenzo, between 1515 and 1516, would obtain from the Medici an office to support him and his family and satisfy his love of action, but it was in vain.

Regarded as the inventor of the " reason of state, " his ideal was nevertheless a society of good and pure men. This is evident even in the *Prince* (where the underlying ideas are similar to those in the *Discourses*), which has won greater favour for its incisive style and imagery and the bluntness of its aphorisms – often taken too literally by contemporaries and posterity alike. A great writer because a great thinker, Machiavelli was also a poet. But his poetry is to be found not so much in his verse as in his prose, which has no equal in Italian literature.

SAVONAROLA

Girolamo Savonarola, reformer and martyr, was the son of the court physician to the Este family, and was born at Ferrara in 1452.

His education, which laid special emphasis on the scriptures and on the works of Thomas Aquinas, was strict and puritanical, more akin in outlook to the thirteenth than to the fourteenth century. The ability and desire to interpret the scriptures in their original purity led Savonarola in later years to his highest achievements, as well as to his downfall. Even his earliest poems and adolescent writings reveal the main characteristics of the later reformer: he looked upon humanistic paganism as a corruption of manners, art, poetry and especially of religion. This is clearly illustrated in his famous poem *De Ruina Mundi,* written before he became a Dominican friar in 1475. After this date he began a militant campaign of purification, directed against the corruption he saw spreading downwards from the highest levels of the Church hierarchy. In 1482 he began lecturing at the convent of San Marco in Florence, and gained a rapidly increasing reputation for learning and asceticism. Absent from Florence from 1487 to 1490, he was recalled by Lorenzo, who tried too late to stem the dangerous flow of eloquence with threats and flattery. " Il Magnifico, " towards the close of his life, had unwittingly opened the gates of his city to the bitterest enemy of Medici rule.

When the French took Florence, Savonarola regarded it as a divine judgement for Medici wickedness, a theme which he carefully developed in his prophetic sermons. Once Medici rule had been overthrown by Charles VIII, his power reached its height – as he predicted it would. Florence then lay at his mercy, and a democratic government was introduced, the best the city had ever had. The results Savonarola obtained were undoubtedly amazing – the splendid but corrupt Tuscan capital was transformed into what seemed to a contemporary a foretaste of paradise.

But his triumph was too great and too sudden not to give rise to much jealousy and suspicion. Alexander VI's alliance with the French brought the Papal wrath down on his head, and Florence began to waver in its support of the reformer, whose denunciation of the higher levels of the Church hierarchy continued unabated. Finally on the 23rd May, 1498, after trial and torture by a Papal commission, Savonarola and two companions, Fra Domenico and Silvestrio, were hanged as heretics and their bodies burnt. Before mounting the scaffold Savonarola piously received the Pope's absolution and plenary indulgence. Catholic and Thomist to the marrow, his quarrel was not with the Roman pontiff, but with the clerical decadence and corruption of which Alexander VI was merely the most scandalous example.

BIBLIOGRAPHY

Archivio Segreto Vaticano. A.A. Arm. IX. VIII. 5020, 5021, 5024, 5027.

Archives, Este State Archives at Modena. *Dispatches of Este Ambassadors to Rome, 1500–1503. Letters of Lucrezia Borgia to Ercole and Alfonso d'Este, 1502–5. Letters of Lucrezia Borgia, Duchess of Bisceglie.* Nepi. 1500.

Ambrosiana Library, Milan. *Autograph letters of Lucrezia Borgia, Duchess of Ferrara, to Pietro Bembo.*

ARIOSTO, L. *Orlando Furioso.*

ACTON, Lord *The Borgias and their latest historian.* London, 1907.

ADY, Cecilia *Pius II Aeneas Sylvius Piccolomini.* London, 1913.

BELLONCI, Maria *Lucrezia Borgia.* Mondadori, Milan, 1939.

BEMBO, Pietro *Gli Asolani*, dedicated to Lucrezia Borgia. Aldine Press, 1505.

BEMBO, Pietro *Lettere giovanile di Messer Pietro Bembo.* Milan, 1558.

BÉRENCE *Lucrèce Borgia.* Paris, 1937.

BLAZE DE BURY 'Les Borgia', *Revue des deux mondes.* 1877.

BRANTÔME *Vie des Hommes illustres*, vol. 15.

BUGGELLI *Lucrezia Borgia.* Milan, 1929.

BURCKHARDT, Jacob *Renaissance in Italy.* Translation, London, 1878, 2 vols.

BURCHARD, Johann *Diarium.* Edition Thuasne, Paris, 1883.

CARTWRIGHT, J. *Isabella D'Este, Marchioness of Mantua*, 2 vols. London, 1903.

CASTIGLIONE, Baldassare *Il Cortegiano*, new edition. Florence, 1919.

CHERRIER *Histoire de Charles VIII*, 11 vols. Paris, 1868.

CLERMONT, Verron *Les Borgia, Alexandre VI, César and Lucrèce Borgia.* Paris, 1882.

CIAN, V. *Un decennio della vita di Pietro Bembo.* Turin, 1885.

CLARK, Sir Kenneth *Leonardo da Vinci.* Cambridge University Press, 1939.

COLLISON, Morley   *The Story of the Borgias.* London, 1932.

COMMINES, Philippe de   *Mémoires,* prefaced by an autobiographical note. New edition, Paris, 1843.

CORVO, Baron Frederick (Rolfe)   *Chronicles of the House of Borgia.* London, 1901.

CROCE, Benedetto   *La Spagna nella vita Italiana durante La Rinascenza.* Bari, 1907.

CRICHTON, M.   *History of the Papacy,* vol. 4 and 5. London, 1907.

D'AUTON, Jean   *Chroniques de Louis XII.* Paris.

DUMAS, Alexandre   *Crimes célèbres,* vol. 3 and 4. 1877.

DELABORDE, H.   *L'expédition de Charles VIII en Italie.* Paris, 1888.

DENNISTOUN, G.   *Memoirs of the Dukes of Urbino.* London, 1851.

FELICANGELI, B.   *Il Matrimonio di Lucrezia Borgia con Giovanni Sforza, Signore di Pesaro.* Turin, 1901.

FERRARA, O.   *The Borgia Pope,* translated by F. J. Sheed. London, 1942.

FUNCK-BRENTANO   *Lucrèze Borgia.* Paris, 1930.

GARNER, J. L.   *Caesar Borgia, A Study of the Renaissance.* London, 1912.

GARDINER   *Dukes and Poets in Ferrara.* London, 1914.

GILBERT, W.   *Lucrezia Borgia, Duchess of Ferrara,* 2 vols. London, 1869.

GIOVIO, Paolo   *La Vita di Alfonso da Este Duca di Ferrara. Tradotta in Lingua.* Toscana da Q. P. Gelli. Venice, 1597.

GIOVIO, Paolo   *Les Vite del Gran Capitan e del Marchese di Pescara.* Bari, 1931.

GIUSTINIAN, Antonio   *Dispacci,* edited by P. Villari, 3 vols. Florence, 1886.

GREGOROVIUS, Ferdinand   *Lucrezia Borgia,* translated by John L. Garner. London, 1908.

GREGOROVIUS, Ferdinand   *History of the City of Rome in the Middle Ages,* translated by Hamilton, vol. 7. 1894, 1902.

GUICCIARDINI, F.   *Storie del Italia,* 5 vols. Bari, 1929.

GUICCIARDINI, F.   *Storie Fiorentine del 1478-1509.* Bari, 1931

HARE, Augustus   *Walks in Rome,* 2 vols. London, 1871.

HÖFLER, G.   *Die Katastrophe des Herzoglichen Hauses der Borjas von Gandia.* Vienna, 1892.

HÖFLER, G.   *Don Rodrigo de Borja und seine Söhne.* 1889.

INFESSURA, Stefano *Diario della Citta di Roma*. Rome, 1890.

LUZIO, Alessandro *Isabella d'Este e i Borgia con nuovi documenti*. Milan, 1916.
LUZIO, Alessandro *Mantova e Urbino*. Turin, 1893.

MARICOURT *Le procès des Borgia*. Paris, 1882.
MACHIAVELLI, Nicolo *Il Principe*.
MACHIAVELLI, Nicolo *Letters to Florence on his Mission to Valentino*.
MATTHEW, A. H. *The Life and Times of Rodrigo Borgia*. London, 1924.
MORSOLIN 'Pietro Bembo e Lucrezi Borgia', *Nuovo Antologia*, vol. 52. 1885.

PASOLINI, Conte *Caterina Sforza*. Rome, 1893.
PASTOR, L. von *The History of the Popes from the Close of the Middle Ages*, edited by Frederick Antrobus, vols. 4, 5 and 6. London, 1898.
PORTIGLIOTTE, G. *The Borgias*, translated by Bernard Miall. 1929.

ROSCOE, W. *Life and Pontificate of Leo X*. London, 1827.

SALATINI *The Life of Cesare Borgia*. London, 1912.
SANUDO, Marino *I diari 1496–1533*. Edition Venice, 1903.
SCHLUMBERGER *Charlotte d'Albret et le Chateau de la Motte-Feuilly*.
SYMONDS, J. Addington *The Renaissance in Italy*, 3 vols. London.

TEDALINI, Sebastiano di Branca *Diario Romano*. May, 1485; June, 1524.
TOMASI, Tomaso *La Vita del Duca Valentino*. 1655.

UGOLINI *Storia dei conti e duchi d'Urbino*, 2 vols. 1859.

VASARI *Lives of the Most Eminent Painters, Sculptors and Architects*. Trans. London, 1913.
VILLARI, Pasquale *The Life and Times of Savonarola*, translated by L. Vellari. London, 1888.
VILLARI, Pasquale *Life and Times of Machiavelli*. 1892.

WIND, Edgar *Bellini's Feast of the Gods* (A Study in Venetian Humanism). Harvard University Press, 1948.

WOODWARD, Harrison *Caesar Borgia, A Biography*. London, 1913.

YRIARTE, Charles *César Borgia, sa vie, sa captivité, sa mort*. Paris, 1889.

YRIARTE, Charles *Autour des Borgia*. Paris, 1891.

ZUCCHETTI, G. *Lucrezia Borgia, Duchessa di Ferrara*. Mantua, 1860.

SOURCES

OF THE ILLUSTRATIONS

Frontispiece: Italian dagger of early 16th century. From Musée d'art et d'histoire, Geneva.

1. Lucrezia Borgia as a young girl. Detail from fresco by Pinturicchio in Borgia Apartments at the Vatican.
2. Ceiling of the Borgia Apartments with frescoes by Pinturicchio. Skira.
3. Pope Alexander VI. Detail from fresco by Pinturicchio, Vatican. Mansell Collection.
4. A Papal procession before the Castle of St. Angelo, Rome. From the *Legend of St. Ursula* by Carpaccio, Academy of Venice. Skira.
5. Portrait of a courtesan by Carpaccio. Borghese Gallery, Rome. (photo Anderson-Giraudon).
6. Portrait of Machiavelli by unknown painter. Uffizi Gallery, Florence.
7. A French political caricature, late fifteenth century. Bibl. Nationale, Paris. (photo Giraudon).
8. Costume of a young girl of the Roman nobility, late fifteenth century or early sixteenth. Bibl. Nationale, Paris.
9. Cover of a collection of Venetian love songs, Venice 1512. Bibl. Nationale, Paris.
10. Portrait of Cesare Borgia by Palmezzano. Correr Museum, Venice.
11. An Italian treatise on swordsmanship, fifteenth century. Bibl. Nationale, Paris.
12. Young courtiers of Ferrara. Detail from a fresco by Francesco del Cossa in the Schiffanoia Palace, Ferrara.
13. Pietro Bembo, from *Galleries des hommes illustres,* by Thevet, 1584. Mansell Collection.
14. A court lady of Ferrara. From an Italian treatise on coiffures, sixteenth century. Bibl. Nationale, Paris.
15. Fresco in the Schiffanoia Palace at Ferrara. (photo Giraudon).
16. Francesco Gonzaga, by Mantegna, 1496. Detail from his *Madonna della Vittoria.* Musée du Louvre, Paris. (photo Giraudon).
17. Alfonso d'Este and his son, Ercole d'Este, mid-sixteenth century. Bibl. Nationale, Paris.
18. Pope Julius II, by unknown Italian artist. (photo Giraudon).
19. Lucrezia in her prime. Engraving by von Balen (seventeenth century?). Bibl. Nationale, Paris. (photo Giraudon).

Page 294. The city of Ferrara. From *Théâtre des villes italiennes,* early seventeenth century. Bibl. de Genève.

INDEX

This book, designed by
André Mistelli
is a production of
Edito-Service S.A., Geneva

Printed in Switzerland

R 4